This is an annual. That is to say,
it is substantially revised each year,
the new edition appearing each November.
Those wishing to submit additions,
corrections, or suggestions for the
2002 edition must *submit them prior*
to February 1, 2001, using the form
provided in the back of this book.
(Forms reaching us after that date will,
unfortunately, have to wait for the
2003 edition.)

What Color Is Your Parachute?

Other Books by Richard N. Bolles

The What Color Is Your Parachute? Workbook

Job-Hunting on the Internet,
  1999 edition, revised and enlarged

The Career Counselor's Handbook
  (with Howard Figler as co-author)

The Three Boxes of Life,
  And How to Get Out of Them

How to Find Your Mission in Life

Job-Hunting Tips for the So-Called Handicapped

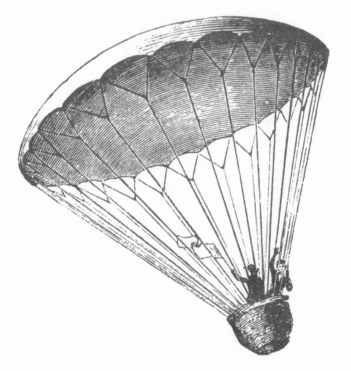

2001 Edition

What Color Is Your Parachute?

A Practical Manual for Job-Hunters & Career-Changers

by

Richard Nelson Bolles

Ten Speed Press
Berkeley   Toronto

PUBLISHER'S NOTE

This publication is designed to provide accurate and authoritative information in regard to the subject matter covered. It is sold with the understanding that the publisher is not engaged in rendering professional career services. If expert assistance is required, the service of the appropriate professional should be sought.

The drawing on page 90–91 is by Steven M. Johnson, author of *What the World Needs Now.*

Distributed in Australia by Simon and Schuster Australia, in Canada by Ten Speed Press Canada, in New Zealand by Southern Publishers Group, in South Africa by Real Books, in Southeast Asia by Berkeley Books, and in the United Kingdom and Europe by Airlift Book Company.

Library of Congress Catalog Card Information on file with the publisher.
ISBN 1-58008-242-4, paper
ISBN 1-58008-241-6, cloth

Published by 1⊜ Ten Speed Press, P.O. Box 7123, Berkeley, California 94707
www.tenspeed.com

Typesetting by Star Type, Berkeley
Cover design by Thomjon Borges
Printed in the United States of America

2   3   4   5   —   2001

Contents

continued

interview. The fear behind employers' questions. How to deal with handicaps. How to end the interview: the six essential questions. The importance of thank-you notes. How and when to negotiate salary. How to win at salary negotiation. Fringe benefits. What to do when interviews never lead to a job. Reasons job-hunters get rejected. Who gets hired the most often.

How To Find Your Mission In Life

An optional epilogue, for those interested in relating their faith to the job-hunt. God and one's vocation. The job-hunt as turning point. Meaning of the word mission. What we need to unlearn. The three stages to learning one's mission in life.

Your Flower Diagram

How to Choose A Career Counselor

If you decide you need one, how to find a good career counselor. Your initial visits to them. How to evaluate them. Bad answers they may give you. Good answers to listen for. What to do if you 'get taken.' A Sampler of career counselors around the world. How to use the Sampler. My own annual International Two-Week Workshop. Who can attend.

To Carol Christen,
The love of my life,
Now and always.

Preface to the 2001 Edition

The Man Behind the Book[1]

**Master Teacher and author of a
colossal best seller, Richard Bolles
has changed the way millions of Americans
view the way they work and live.**

The audience sits in a darkened room, ready to receive secrets. They are career counselors, social workers, ministers, teachers and ordinary citizens bewildered about how to manage their own working lives. Some have been declared superfluous by their employers; others are stuck in jobs they deplore but cannot summon the nerve to leave. And standing down below in the well of the amphitheater in his stocking feet is the man, they think, who will make them whole by delivering the answers.

Brandishing large pieces of fluorescent chalk in the dark, he stabs down ideas that glow in ultraviolet light on his large easel. He lectures softly at first to get things started, leavening his message with cornfed humor. As the plaintive questions come, his answers begin to shape a revolutionary theme. With painful, ministerial patience, he is asserting that the answers are within the questioner and can be teased out with a little thought and work. The responsibility for managing one's career is personal. It is the employee who hires the employer. When a guidance counselor asks a practical question about how he, in turn, is going to teach these notions to others, the teacher says, "We are not going through this for the people you are teaching, we are going through this for you." He delivers his answers through lips that are taut with strain, and another reason for the darkened room is made

---

1. This article was originally written by David Maxey, here revised and updated.

plain. The teacher, the leader, the possessor of secrets is as shy as an adolescent boy.

Back in 1968, Richard Bolles was laid off from his job. He had to scramble to find another job, but eventually did. Once off the beach himself, Bolles noticed immediately that he was not the only one in that decade to have fallen on hard times. In his new supervisory work of a bunch of men in the nine Western-most States, he soon discovered they too were being laid off, one by one, just as he had been. They asked him for help, so he set out to discover the best ways for people to job-hunt or shift careers. He found himself asking two questions wherever he went: "How do you change careers, without necessarily having to go back to school?" *and* "How do you go job-hunting, if resumes, ads, and employment agencies don't turn up a job for you?" He interviewed and researched for more than two years, and at the end of 65,000 miles of travel he wrote up his findings in a little book which he entitled *What Color Is Your Parachute?* -- his favorite rejoinder when people said to him, "Well, I'm gonna have to bail out."

The first publisher of his work was the photocopying machine near Bolles' office, and many a copy was given away rather than sold. Bolles can remember being so broke one Friday in 1971, that he faced the weekend with $5.18 in his pocket. He offered up prayers for a few sales of *Parachute*, and was answered by an order in the afternoon mail and a personal visit at his office from another buyer, and so, made it through the week. In 1972, at the invitation of a publisher named Phil Wood, he turned publication of the book over to Ten Speed Press of Berkeley, California; it was becoming clear that he could no longer handle the the mailing or the orders. Without quite realizing it, Bolles had written a colossal best seller. Since 1972, in a vivid measure of the urgency Americans (and others) have about changing careers, *Parachute* has been through thirty-one annual editions and revisions, and has sold over 6 million copies, at the current rate of 20,000 per month. The book has been on the *New York Times* paperback best-seller list a total of 288 weeks in its lifetime, and haunts other best-seller lists to this day. It has been translated into twelve languages around the world (the latest is Bulgarian). And in 1995, the Library of Congress pronounced it one of 25 books that have shaped people's lives.[2]

---

2. The twenty five books on the list of the Center for the Book at the Library of Congress were: *The Adventures of Huckleberry Finn*, by Mark Twain; *Atlas Shrugged*, by Ayn Rand; *The Autobiography of Benjamin Franklin*; *The Autobiography of Malcolm X*;

Bolles puts the job-seeker in charge, arguing that the best jobs are those that employers are not yet aware of.

What, pray, was all this excitement about? According to Bolles, who is scrupulous about saying so, there are few new ideas in *Parachute*. Works going back to 1901 had proposed similar ideas. Admitting that, we must then shove Bolles' modesty aside to notice that he has assembled a great deal of unusual information about job-hunting, and made it available in a simple, attractive and systematic way. He is a brilliant synthesizer of ideas. With what he calls "my passion for overkill," the book hammers in its principles doggedly and lucidly. Just for starters, the book grinds down the traditional methods of searching for jobs that people assume work beautifully. For example:

- The Internet is claimed to have changed the whole job-hunt process, but in fact it is only an electronic version of the old Neanderthal job-hunting system that has existed for decades in this country (and others). The hype far exceeds the performance: a recent study revealed that only 4% of those who job-hunt on the Internet actually find a job thereby. *(Forrester Research, April, 2000)*

- Our ears do not interpret statistics well. To overcome this, we must learn to think and speak in terms of 'failure rates' rather than 'success rates' for any particular job-hunting method. For example, instead of a 4% 'success rate,' the Internet should be thought of as having a 96% 'failure rate': that is, 96 out of every 100 job-hunters who go job-hunting on the Internet do not find a job thereby.

- Even if you perform splendidly, thinking other companies will see your performance and 'come after you,' you may sit and languish *forever*, unless you are in certain jobs, such as computer hardware engineers, designers, and programmers. They, however, are the exceptions; in the thousands of other industries 'out there,' you may

The Bible; The Catcher in the Rye, by J.D. Salinger; *Charlotte's Web*, by E.B. White; *The Diary of a Young Girl*, by Anne Frank; *Don Quixote*, by Miguel de Cervantes; *Gone with the Wind*, by Margaret Mitchell; *Hiroshima*, by John Hersey; *How to Win Friends and Influence People*, by Dale Carnegie; *I Know Why the Caged Bird Sings*, by Maya Angelou; *Invisible Man*, by Ralph Ellison; *The Little Prince*, by Antoine de Saint-Exupery; *Little Women*, by Louisa May Alcott; *The Lord of the Rings*, by J.R.R. Tolkien; *Roots*, by Alex Haley; *The Secret Garden*, by Frances Hodgson Burnett; *To Kill a Mockingbird*, by Harper Lee; *Treasure Island*, by Robert Louis Stevenson; *Walden*, by Henry David Thoreau; *War and Peace*, by Leo Tolstoy; *What Color Is Your Parachute?* by Richard Nelson Bolles; and *The Wizard of Oz*, by L. Frank Baum.

sit and languish *forever,* waiting for someone to save you from the job-hunt, by noticing how good you are, and hiring or promoting you.

- Ads, whether on the Internet or in newspapers, don't begin to tell you all the jobs available, and many companies don't hire any employees through ads or job postings. Moreover, even the ads which are run are sometimes not to be trusted, as some ads are fakes, hung up by agencies to attract you to their services.

- Resumes amount to "people in the form of paper," writes Bolles, and human resource departments (in those 15% of U.S. companies that have them) are usually designed to screen resumes *out,* not in. He cites one study that reports that in the world of work even in the best of times, there is only one invitation for a job interview extended and accepted, for every 245 resumes received.

- Private employment agencies place only 15 percent of all Americans who are switching jobs, and only 14 percent of those who are beginners in the job market.

In sum, job-hunting is a game, and it is important to know the rules of the game. Otherwise, says Bolles, you may think something is wrong with you, when it's really the game that is defective.

What Bolles finds most seriously wrong with traditional ways of searching for work is the idea of applicant as panhandler or beggar, cowering before the employer in an attempt to wedge him or herself into a particular job description. Bolles strives to put the job-seeker in charge, arguing persuasively that he is out to hire a company, and that the best jobs are those that the employer has not yet created. In Bolles' recipe, before the job-hunt starts the prospective employee marshals the skills he or she likes using most, decides where to use them as to field or interest as well as geography, and figures out what kind of job is described by those skills. Then the research for the appropriate company and the person who has the power to hire (usually not the human resources department) can start.

The Bolles recipe sounds deceptively simple and obvious, and it is -- once you've read the book. What all the paper-and-pencil exercises do -- which amounts to a great gift -- is to give the applicant a means for making his or her thinking formal and explicit. All it takes is paper, pencil, or colored pencils or crayons, and a lot of patience. Not a little, a lot.

One of the typical Bolles workshop exercises - - based on the work of John L. Holland, and outlined in both *What Color Is Your Parachute?* and *The Parachute Workbook* - - begins with the fantasy of a party in which six groups of people are collected in various parts of the room. Each group contains people who have the same or similar interests. In one corner, for example, are those who "have athletic or mechanical ability, prefer to work with objects, machines, tools, plants or animals, or to be outdoors." Over there is the group containing "people who like to observe, learn, investigate, analyze, evaluate or solve problems." The student's task is to pick out the three groups from the six that he or she would be most likely to join, and put these in order of preference. Shyness is not allowed. The selection is an act of self-revelation, since we are likely to buddy up with people whose abilities and preferences are like our own. And that is a first step toward identifying the specific skills or God-given gifts that we most enjoy using. Bolles is big on 'enjoyment.'

With a first rough idea of useful skills nailed down, the student turns author to write detailed reports of the seven most satisfactory achievements or accomplishments he or she can remember. The list could include organizing the ninth-grade spelling bee, designing the Golden Gate Bridge or leading a platoon against some enemy of the U.S. The important part of the exercise is detail, and particularly detail about what specific skills (organizing materials, cutting something out, giving a speech) the person had to employ to make the most satisfying experience come to pass. Then, each autobiographical story, fascinating by definition, is compared to a functional/transferable skills inventory in the book, which Bolles invented, and what pops out are patterns that show oft-used skills employed in highly satisfactory experiences.

Consistent with his emphasis on 'enjoyment,' Bolles next brings into play the question of where the seeker would like to use his skills. San Diego? Cleveland? Bali? The point is to narrow the area of search, as well as to identify those places you wouldn't be found dead in. The winnowing process goes further: special knowledge that the seeker would like to employ (accounting, basket weaving); the kind of people he or she would like to be surrounded by; the attractive or repugnant goals of various organizations; working conditions (inside? outside?); and - - there we come to it - - money. What is the least you would take? What is the most you hope to get?

Nowhere in this blizzard of paper and priorities is there room for a person to say, "I want to be a plumber." Instead, a picture of the job the person is looking for emerges in Bolles' whimsical appeal to the visual sense, as a flower with six petals and a center.

Bolles' vision of the actual job search proceeds from that flower. A central idea is that most jobs that fit the picture may not currently exist, or may be only an idea in somebody's head at particular organizations - - hence are not advertised, and so, won't be found by orthodox methods. He suggests practice interviewing to make the job-seeker comfortable, then information interviewing with companies that interest the job-seeker, to find out what those companies do and how they do it. Two students from the Bolles workshop I attended actually wedged themselves unannounced into the office of the president of the Chicago Bears. Information interviews are not job chats in the usual sense of the word. Since the job-seeker announces himself as looking only for information, the person on the other side of the desk can relax and talk about something compelling - - himself, and what he does and how his company works. From such information, the seeker can find the name of the person within the company who actually has the power to create the job depicted on the flower. After a series of such informational interviews which 'pre-test' a particular job or vocation, then, and only then, does the job-seeker go out as a job applicant in the traditional sense of the word. As best as Bolles can estimate it, eighty-six out of every one hundred who faithfully follow this method (which Bolles is scrupulous to say he didn't invent) wind up with a job, and a job they like.

A superb instructor, he is richly capable of riveting people in their seats in daylong workshops.

It is in his workshops that Bolles shows another signal talent. He is a master teacher, richly capable of riveting people in their seats for hours at a time in sessions that involve, for the most part, lectures, arguments and entertainment by Bolles himself. Standing up there like a big, amiable 6' 5" faun, he exudes whimsy mixed with a sense of compassion and ministerial caring that is patently real. As with most charismatic leaders, there is a confident sense of self to Bolles, but his hurry to confess to that, or to commit almost any other act of self-revelation, is so disarming that cynics are left pecking at this supposed Achilles tendon in vain.

Parachute, revised and updated each year, floats on and on as a best seller, the demand for personal speeches and appearances at workshops by Bolles seems solid, and the truth is that Richard Nelson Bolles does not *have* to do anything any more. But he puts in a full-day most of the year, writing (currently) two new books: *The Song of a Broken Heart* (about the loss of his wife, Carol), and *The Hunger for God* (about the increasing interest in spirituality, at the workplace). He maintains a website (www.jobhuntersbible.com). He also does speaking and consulting all over the world. And, he finds time always, to play. Bolles is all for playing as you go; he is a sensual man, who relishes friends (he has legions), travel, restaurants, movies, theater, classical music and camping out. He has done tent camping in forty of the fifty U.S. states.

Bolles, the author of the most famous and best-selling job-hunting book in the history of the world, is an ordained Episcopal priest. The job he lost in 1968 was that of canon pastor of Grace Cathedral, on Nob Hill in San Francisco. Since then he has served the world, rather than a particular parish.

Bolles, the parish priest, was visible to a relatively small number of people. Bolles, the author, the priest without a parish, is now famous wherever he goes in the world, and his reviews of that fact are mixed: "To be human is to be ambivalent. Sure, there are times when I like it, but I remember that when I was still a deacon, people would praise me for my sermons, on the quality of my pastoral visits. I asked the older priest whom I assisted how I should treat such admiration and he said 'Listen -- but don't inhale.'" Bolles listens and tries not to inhale -- "grateful for the admiration and great gratitude I get from my readers, but also grateful that there isn't any more" -- happy in his role as author, teacher, leader and possessor of secrets -- and still as shy as an adolescent boy.

Footnote from the author:

• *My thanks first of all to my 6,000,000 readers, and most especially to the thousands who send me letters during the course of each year. I rarely can answer them any more, but I do read every one of the letters that come in, and feel that no author could possibly ask for more loving, and appreciative readers -- not in a million years. Thank you so much for writing me, for updating me on new ideas that you have discovered, or for letting me know when and how this book has helped you.*

• *My thanks to my longtime friend and publisher (for 28 years now) Phil Wood, and to all the folks over at Ten Speed Press in Berkeley, who help get this book out, each year: Kirsty Melville, Aaron Wehner, Hal Hershey, Jackie Wan, and Linda Davis, our caring typesetter. My most especial gratitude and appreciation to Bev Anderson, my layout artist for the past 29 years -- a genius if ever there was one.*

• *My thanks also to those intellectual leaders in the field who have been such good friends to me over the years, kind and helpful: John Holland, the late John Crystal, Sidney Fine, Harvey Belitsky, Dick Lathrop, Daniel Porot, Arthur Miller, Tom and Ellie Jackson, Nathan Azrin, and Howard Figler. (Howard and I have recently written, and Ten Speed last year published, a new book entitled,* The Career Counselor's Handbook, *by Figler and Bolles.)*

• *My thanks to my friends who have helped me with this work over these many years, and particularly with my annual two-week workshop each August: Verlyn Barker, Daniel Porot, David Swanson, Jim Kell, Carol Christen, Brian McIvor, Marie-Carmelle Roy, Rose Offner, John Webb, Mary Ann Kaczmarski, Rita Morin, Ellen Wallach, Erica Chambré, Norma Wong, Howard Figler, and a host of others, including the late John Crystal, and the late Bob Wegmann. (Do note, on page 334, that the year 2001 will see the last of these two-week workshops.)*

• *My thanks also to my family, who have given me so much encouragement and love over the years: my four grown children, Stephen, Mark, Gary, Sharon -- and their families; my stepdaughter, Serena; my sister, Ann Johnson; and last but hardly least, my ninety-eight-year-old aunt (as of 2/3/2001), Sister Esther Mary, of the Community of the Transfiguration (Episcopal) in Glendale, Ohio, who has taught me to serve the Lord, from my youth up.*

• *Surely, no litany of thanks would be complete without my thanking The Great Lord God, Father of our Lord Jesus Christ, and source of all grace, wisdom, and compassion, Who has given me this work of helping so many people of different faiths, tongues, and nations, with their job-hunt, and the meaning of their life. I am grateful beyond measure for such a life, such a mission, and such a privilege.*

Dick Bolles
P. O. Box 379,
Walnut Creek
California 94597-0379
8/24/2000

My Annual Grammar & Language Footnote

Throughout this book, I often use the apparently plural pronoun "they," "them," or "their" after *singular* antecedents -- such as, "You must approach *someone* for a job and tell *them* what you can do." This sounds strange and even *wrong* to those who know English well. To be sure, we all know there is another pronoun -- "you" -- that may be either singular or plural, but few of us realize that the pronouns "they," "them," or "their" were also once treated as both plural and singular in the English language. This changed, at a time in English history when agreement in *number* became more important than agreement as to sexual *gender*. Today, however, our priorities have shifted once again. Now, the distinguishing of sexual *gender* is considered by many to be more important than agreement in *number*.

The common artifices used for this new priority, such as "s/he," or "he and she," are -- to my mind -- tortured and inelegant. Casey Miller and Kate Swift, in their classic, *The Handbook of Nonsexist Writing,* agree, and argue that it is time to bring back the earlier usage of "they," "them," and "their" as both singular and plural -- just as "you" is/are. They further argue that this return to the earlier historical usage has already become quite common *out on the street* -- witness a typical sign by the ocean which reads "*Anyone* using this beach after 5 p.m. does so at *their* own risk." I have followed Casey and Kate's wise recommendations in all of this.

As for my commas, they are deliberately used according to my own rules -- rather than according to the rules of historic grammar. My own rules are: I write conversationally, and put in a comma wherever I would normally stop for a breath, were I speaking the same line.

The same conversational rule applies to my use of *italics.* I use *italics* wherever, were I speaking the sentence, I would put *emphasis* on that word or phrase. Rarely, I also use italics where there is a digression of thought, and I want to maintain the main thought and flow of the sentence. All in all, I write as I speak.

P.S. Over the last twenty-eight years, a few critics (very few) have claimed that *Parachute* is too complicated in its vocabulary and grammar for anyone except a college graduate. An index in England that analyzes a book to tell you what grade in school you must have finished in order to understand it, rated my book a 6.1, which means you need only have finished sixth grade in an English school in order to understand it.

Here in the U.S., a college instructor phoned me to tell me that my book was rejected by the authorities as a proposed text for his college course, because the book's language/grammar was not up to college level. "What level was it?" I asked. "Well," he replied, "when they analyzed it, it turned out to be written on an eighth-grade level." Sounds about right to me.

R.N.B.

CHAPTER ONE

A Hunting We Will Go

It's a new day,
For job-hunters,
So they say.
The Internet's here.
Hip, hip, hooray.
Just get online,
Type in the job
You're looking for,
Yessiree, Bob,
And fifteen employers
Will come your way,
You'll hear from them
The very next day,
Pleading with you to take a look
At them;
You can throw away this book,
Won't read it,
Turns out, after all,
Won't need it,
You'll just have a ball
Sifting the offers,
You are King!
The Internet's changed everything!
Oh, don't you wish!
It's not that easy,
No matter what the magazines shout,
You can spend hours on the Web,
Searching, posting,
And still strike out!

What's goin' on?
Why doesn't it work?

Makes you feel
    Like quite a jerk
        To know that everyone else
            But you
                Can find the job they want;
                Boo hoo!
                    "What's wrong with me?"
                You ask yourself
                "Why am I staying
                On the shelf?
                I'm really trying
                To play the game
                The way they said;
                It's such a shame
                Nobody wants me."
            Waitaminute!
            Before you put
        Your whole foot in it!
        Who says that everyone else
        But you
      Has found a job,
    By going online?
  That's hype!
I've got some statistics here
That I think will make you feel just fine.

Four percent.
That's what I said,
Four percent.
 That's what I read,
  Forrester Research gave us the news
   Only four percent,

Of all who used
The Web,
Could find a job thereby;
It's enough to make you
Want to cry!
Why are we told
"The Web's the way"
To job-hunt,
When on any day
Ninety-six of each one hundred
Who try
Find that employers
Just pass them by?
Well, the answer's really not hard
To find,
It's: money, silly!
Keep in mind
That sites where lots of people
Tune in
Are the kind
That make investors grin
Be it greeting cards,
Or giveaways,
Or jobs;
The content doesn't matter
If millions flock,
That's all that counts,
Investors love that pitter-patter.

You will have friends,
Of course,
Of course,

Who boast,
Without a tinge of remorse,
How they used the Web
Successfully,
To find their last five jobs,
For free.
And in the time it took
To consume
A donut and coffee
In their room.
Note well: such people
Were put on earth
To challenge us;
Give them a wide berth
Lest you get depressed.
The figures stand,
Only 4 percent.
Time to take in hand
This book,
Go fish it out of the trash
Where you threw it,
When the Internet
First sang its siren song
In your ears,
Press on:
Your hunt isn't over yet.

There are many other ways
To find
The kind of job
You have in mind,
Or -- if that's the problem --

You really don't know
Just where it is
You next want to go,
There are ways
To figure that out, too.
By discovering a little more
About You.
Sure, it takes some work,
And diligence too,
But it's not that hard,
As you review
The stories of the skills
You used
In past times,
When you were amused
And happy,
Proud,
Even satisfied.

Now that you're about
To take that ride
Into the future
You've always dreamed,
I think you will
Certainly see,
You *can* find
Satisfying work,
And be who you want to be!

R.N.B

8

*Well, yes, you do have
great big teeth; but, never mind
that. You were great to at least
grant me this interview.*

Little Red Riding Hood

CHAPTER TWO

Rejection Shock

Chapter 2

Wild Life by John Kovalic, © 1989 Shetland Productions. Reprinted with permission.

OUR JOB-HUNTING SYSTEM

We begin with a simple fact: our whole job-hunting system is Neanderthal. That's why, in the U.S., there are currently over six million people out of work, even in the best of economic times.

Year after year this so-called system fails one job-hunter after another, condemns man after man, woman after woman, to go down the same path, face the same problems, make the same mistakes, endure the same frustrations, go through the same loneliness, and end up feeling as though there is something wrong with them.

It knows only one goal: to go after *known vacancies*. And it offers only three ways to do this: sending out or posting one's **resume**, answering newspaper **ads** or job postings, and going to employment **agencies**. Strategies which have spectacularly low success rates.

Consequently, year after year this system forces millions of us to remain unemployed after months and months of job-hunting, or -- if we find a job -- to end up *underemployed*, in the wrong field, at the wrong job, doing the wrong tasks, well below the peak of our abilities.

It doesn't matter what you do: you can send your resume out by the bushels, hang it from every tree on the Internet, read every ad, go to every agency, contact every search firm - - only to discover after a lengthy period of time that none of this works for you, and you are still unemployed.

REJECTION SHOCK

When - - and if - - this happens to you, you will find yourself feeling as though you're experiencing some kind of "Rejection Shock." It's a kind of personal psychological Shock, character-ized by a slow or rapid erosion of your self-image, and the con-viction that there is something wrong with you, leading to lower expectations, depression, desperation, and despair. This can assume, consequently, all the proportions of a major crisis in your life, your personal relations and your family, leading to withdrawal (often), estrangement (frequently), where divorce is often a consequence and even suicide is not unthinkable. My first introduction to this was when the front page of our local newspaper described a job-hunter who put a plastic bag over his head, leaving a suicide note that said "Even a genius can't find a job." (He was a member of Mensa.)

It's bad enough not to be able to find a job. But add to that, this feeling of Rejection, and . . . *Yuck!* Most of us *hate* rejection. We dedicate a large part of our lives to avoiding it - - when dat-ing, when proposing new ideas, and so forth. We'll even reject others first, if we think they're about to reject us. We'll do any-thing to avoid rejection, and I mean *anything.* As we grow older, we become pretty good at throwing Rejection out of our lives.

But then, along comes the job-hunt. Eight times in our life-time (usually) we have to go through this painful process. And, except at its very end, it is **nothing but** a process of rejection. My friend Tom Jackson (in his *Guerrilla Tactics in the Job Market*) has aptly captured this, in this depressingly accurate descrip-tion of a typical job-hunt, as you go to employer after employer, asking, "Will you hire me?":

NO NO NO NO NO NO NO NO NO NO NO NO NO NO
NO NO NO NO NO NO NO NO NO NO NO NO NO NO
NO NO NO NO NO NO NO NO NO NO NO NO NO NO
NO NO NO NO NO NO NO NO NO NO NO NO NO NO
NO NO NO NO NO NO NO NO NO NO NO NO NO YES.

Rejection shock, indeed! The job-hunt makes a root canal look like a walk in the park.

When we turn to industry personnel experts or human resources people and say, "Show me a better way," it becomes obvious that many of them in their quiet meditative moments are just as baffled by the job-hunt as we are.

This is never more clear than when they themselves are out of a job - - as increasingly happens in these days of mergers, hostile takeovers, and downsizings - - and they have to join the many who are out 'pounding the pavements.' You would think that they would absolutely be in their element, and know precisely what to do. Yet the average hiring executive who yesterday was interviewing to screen out or hire others, and today is out job-hunting, is often just as much at a loss as anyone else, in knowing how to go about the job-hunt systematically, methodically and successfully.

Very often the best they can suggest for themselves is what they suggested, in the past, to others: 'the numbers game,' they call it. Just a fancy name for our old friends: resumes, ads, and agencies.

THE NUMBERS GAME

You can guess where the term came from. It came from the world of gambling, where if you place sufficient bets on enough different numbers, one of them is bound to pay off, for you.

Ah, I see you have grasped immediately what the analogue of this is, in the job-hunt. Resumes, you say? Ah yes, resumes.

You play them just like a bunch of bets: place enough of them, and one is bound to pay off. According to a study some time back, it pays off on the 1470th bet - - that is to say, there is one job offer tendered and accepted (and only one) for every 1,470 resumes that are floating around out there in the whole world of work. It's as though sending out 1,469 gets job-hunters nowhere. It's the 1,470th that pays off, and gets a job. Hence, "the numbers game."

In its original evolution, someone must have worked it all out, *backwards*. The logic of the numbers in a job-hunt would have gone like this:

For the job-hunter to get a job he or she really likes, they need to have two or three job offers -- in the end -- to choose from.

In order to get those two or three offers, the job-hunter probably would have to interview at six to nine different companies, that have *known vacancies.*

In order to get those six to nine 'high-chance' interviews, the job-hunter must have contacted 'x' number of companies, by sending them some kind of mail -- resumes and/or cover letters -- that will cause those companies to invite the job-hunter in.

And what is 'x'? Well, some experts will tell you it's 100 -- that you must send out 100 resumes to get one job interview. Others will tell you it takes 200 resumes sent out, to get one job interview. And still others will tell you it takes 500, on up to 1200 or more.

Consequently, the consensus is that you should send out between 500 and 1000 resumes, though some experts say there is no limit: send out 10–15 resumes a day, they say, until you get the interviews that result in the three job offers you need.

That's how it all got worked out, *backwards.* (And a backwards system, it remains.)

WHERE
THE NUMBERS GAME
CAN BE FOUND

You like?

Many of the books you can pick up in the job-hunting section of your local bookstore -- or online at such sites as amazon.com -- *will sell you this game,* for twenty bucks or so.

Many of the job-hunting resources listed in your local Yellow Pages directory under 'Career and Vocational Counseling' or 'Resume Service' *will sell you this game,* for a hundred bucks or so.

Many of the executive counseling firms you can go to, the ones with the big fee up-front -- *will sell you this game,* with a little psychological testing and interview-role-playing thrown in, for three thousand bucks or so.

Many of the welfare-to-work programs *sell this game* to their clients, at varying costs to their funding sources.

And the Internet with its thousands of job-posting sites and resume-posting sites *will sell, sell, sell you nothing else but this game,* for just the modest cost of a computer, modem, and Internet Service Provider.

In all of the above, there may be a few clever variations here and there, especially in the vocabulary they use to describe what they are selling, so that you will think they are selling you something entirely new.

But if it all comes down to *known job vacancies,* if it all comes down to resumes, ads/postings, and agencies, I assure you you have happened upon The Little Ol' Game We've All Come to Know and Love So Well: Numbers.

THE INTERNET
NUMBERS

How bad are the numbers? How much are they stacked against us, as we go out job-hunting? For an answer to that question, we turn to the latest darling of 'the Numbers game,' namely, the Internet. Fortunately for us, the Internet *loves* numbers. It counts *everything*.

Let's look at the resume numbers, then. Job-hunters have thronged to the Internet to post their resume, sometimes on a number of sites. What we want to know is: *how many* job-hunters, and (more importantly) *how many* employers, ever meet on these sites?

On the career site of the *Wall Street Journal* (`www.careers.wsj.com`) Peter Weddle put up a fascinating Guide to some of these major resume-posting sites on the Web, giving us a great deal of information about each. With his kind permission, I constructed a chart, summarizing the numbers that Peter gathered *from the sites themselves*. It is on page 16.

They were for the period January 1998 in every case, in order that the statistics might be comparable -- *so don't think this is the current traffic on these sites*. This was just one moment frozen in time, so that we could see what the numbers are . . . typically. Newer information is now hard to come by.

As you will see in the chart, the numbers are depressing.

One site had 59,283 resumes, but only 1,366 employers even *looked* at them during the 90 days previous to this survey; another had 85,000 resumes, but only 850 employers even looked at them over a period of three months; another had 40,000 resumes, but only 400 employers looked at them; another had 26,644 resumes, but only 41 employers looked at them.

Here are the gory details with the number of job *listings* or job *postings* thrown in, gratis -- since, in the absence of the other figure, these *sometimes* indicate the relative employer involvement on that site:

Number of Resumes Here	Charge for Posting Your Resume?	Employers Searching Here in Last 90 Days	Name of the Site and Its URL
275,000	No	(Figure Not Available) Only 25,000 Job Listings	The Monster Board www.monster.com
200,000+	No	(Figure Not Available) Only 10,000 Job Listings	NationJob Network www.nationjob.com
150,000	No	(Figure Not Available) Only 45,000 Job Listings	JobTrak www.jobtrak.com
125,000	No	(Figure Not Available) Only 4,034 Job Listings	CareerSite www.careersite.com
120,989 Technical jobs	No	(Figure Not Available) 100,000 Job Listings	PassportAccess www.passportaccess.com
85,000	No	850 employers 37,502 Job Listings	Net-Temps www.net-temps.com
76,441	No	(Figure Not Available) 109,862 Job Listings	Online Career Center
70,000	No	(Figure Not Available) Only 3,500 Job Listings	Career.Com www.career.com
59,283	No	1,366 employers 24,312 Job Listings	Westech Virtual Job Fair www.VJF.com
56,945	Yes	(Figure Not Available) 121,826 Job Listings	GUARANTEED Job Search Success www.jobLynx.com
55,000	No	(Figure Not Available) 70,000+ Job Listings	CareerMosaic www.careermosaic.com
40,000	No	400 employers Only 1,000 Job Listings	Town Online Working www.townonline.com/working
38,000	No	(Figure Not Available) 12,734 Job Listings	Job Options www.espan.com
30,723	No	(Figure Not Available) Only 3,627 Job Listings	HotJobs www.hotjobs.com
30,000	No	15 employers (new) Only 350 Job Listings	US RESUME www.usresume.com
26,644	No	41 employers 40,000 Job Listings	America's Employers www.americasemployers.com

What depressing numbers! 85,000 job-hunters (in one example) playing 'the Numbers Game' faithfully, by posting their resume on one of these sites, as they have been told to do; and only 850 employers even *look* at those 85,000 resumes, over a three-month period. That's less than 10 employers per day!

The moral of this, for job-hunters building their online resume? *If you build it, they will not come.* In most cases. There are always, of course, the lucky ones.

The latest self-help book for pessimists

EMPLOYERS' FAVORITE WAYS OF HIRING

From this we see that employers and job-hunters search in entirely different ways! You can understand this if you look at a diagram of our job-hunting system in the U.S. and in most of the developed world, on page 19.

What makes our job-hunting system Neanderthal, you ask? Well, let's start with the left-hand (red) arrow in the diagram. This indicates the way a *typical* employer likes to find a new employee. Starting at the bottom of the diagram, and working up, we see that **their preferred method is first of all to hire from within, moving or promoting an employee whose work they already know and like.**

Only if that doesn't work, do they then move on up to their next favorite method: asking their friends and colleagues if there is someone whose work *they* like, that they could recommend for the job that employer is trying to fill. At this point, they're also open to job-hunters who offer proof of what they can do -- via a 'portfolio' in the case of an artist, or anything similar in the case of other professions.

Only if that doesn't work, do they then move on up to their next favorite method: turning to a search firm (in the case of higher-level employees) or an employment agency (in the case of lower-level employees), and asking them to find somebody for them.

Only if none of the above methods work, do they then reluctantly move on up to their least favorite methods: looking at job-hunters' resumes, or posting a 'help-wanted ad' in the newspapers or on the Internet.

Now compare the left-hand (red) arrow to the right-hand (gray) arrow in the diagram. The latter indicates the way a typical job-hunter likes to find a new employer. Starting at the top of the diagram, we see that **a job-hunter's preferred methods are in exactly the reverse order from that of employers.** The methods that employers like the least are the ones which job-hunters like the most! Now, that's Neanderthal!

OUR NEANDERTHAL JOB-HUNTING SYSTEM

The way a typical job-hunter likes to hunt for a job (starts here)

6 "I will place an ad to find someone."

Newspaper Ads

5 Resumes

"I will look at some resumes which come in, unsolicited."

Employment Agency for Lower Level Jobs

4 "I want to hire someone for a lower level job, from a stack of potential candidates that some agency has screened for me."

This is called 'a private employment agency,' or -- if it is within the company -- 'the human resources department,' formerly the 'personnel department.' Incidentally, only 15% of all organizations have such an internal department.

Search Firm for Higher Level Jobs

3 "I want to hire someone for a higher level job, from among outstanding people who are presently working for another organization; and I will pay a recruiter to find this outstanding candidate for me."

The agency, thus hired by an employer, is called 'a search firm' or 'headhunter'; only employers can hire such agencies.

A Job-Hunter Who Offers Proof

2 "I want to hire someone who walks in the door and can show me samples of their previous work."

"I want to hire someone whose work a trusted friend of mine has seen and recommends."

That friend may be: mate, best friend, colleague in the same field, or colleague in a different field.

From Within

1 *Employer's Thoughts:*

"I want to hire someone whose work I have seen." (Promotion from within of a full-time employee, or promotion from within of a part-time employee; hiring a former consultant for a regular position (formerly on a limited contract); hiring a temp for a regular position; hiring a volunteer for a regular position.)

The way a typical employer prefers to fill vacancies (starts here)

We could of course improve the numbers, and the efficiency of the job-hunt, if employers would just adopt the resume as their favorite way of finding applicants. *Then we'd have a match between employers' favorite approach and job-hunters' favorite approach.*

So, why don't they? Well, we begin with:

LIES, DAMN LIES, AND STATISTICS

That's how someone once declined the word "lies." "Lies" and "resumes" got married to each other a while back. In 1992, it was discovered that one-third of all 15 to 30-year-olds believed it was okay to lie on a resume.[1] *Heaven only knows what the statistic is today!* Nor is this trend restricted to the young. People in high places -- executives, superintendents of schools, and the like -- have falsely claimed doctorates, and otherwise lied on their resumes. (And been caught.) Experts now estimate that one-third to one-half of all job-hunters lie on their resumes.[2]

They lie by: inflating their title or responsibilities, omitting their firings or failures, inflating their results, inflating their credentials, hiding jobs where they did terribly, and a lot of other subterfuges.

Now if you were an employer, how much faith would you put in a piece of paper where you know there are lies on one-third to one-half of it? Not much.

MOUNTAINS OF MAIL

Ah, but still they come -- unbidden, unrestrained -- over the Internet and through the mails, mostly because everyone's been told this is the best way to apply for a job. The myth dies hard.

Some companies receive as many as 250,000 resumes a year; even small companies may receive as many as ten to fifteen a week. As experts have noted, companies feel at times as though they're floating on a sea of resumes.

---

1. In a survey of 6,873 high school and college students, done by the Josephson Institute of Ethics, reported in *USA TODAY,* 11/13/92.

2. *The San Francisco Chronicle,* 10/10/92.

> Resume: An ingenious device that turns a human being into an object (an eight and a half by eleven inches piece of paper). This transformation device is then often used to try and convince people we have never met to invest thousands of dollars in us, by hiring us for a job we have not yet specifically identified.
>
> *Michael Bryant*

Consequently, employers' first intent is not *selection*, but *elimination*. (Of course, if you're agriculturally-minded or Biblically-oriented, you may prefer the phrase: *winnowing the crop*.) The Human Resources department, if they have one (only 15% of businesses do), or some hapless secretary or clerk, is given the task of getting the stack down to *manageable size*. "See who you can eliminate."

Whose resume gets selected for this dubious honor? Well, first of all, resumes that don't *feel* good -- rough paper, etc. The first impression a resume gives is to the fingers of the 'Eliminator,' even before their eyes see what's on the paper. So, the fingers vote to eliminate you even before the eyes do. It is to cry. *"I was eliminated by crummy paper."*

Secondly, resumes that the Eliminator's eyes don't like, format-wise, even before they read the content thereof. It is to cry, even more. *"I was eliminated by poor typography."*

And: resumes so poorly written that employers can't tell anything about the person behind them. Or: resumes so slickly written (by a professional service) that employers can't tell anything about the person behind them.

Not to mention, resumes that have a $206-a-week clerk applying for the CEO's job; or a $100,000-a-year executive applying for the mail room. Or people attempting a dramatic career change.

The theme at the receptionist's desk or in the human resources office of a company, is: Elimination. This is why you can send out bushels of resumes, and never once get called in for an interview. This is why millions remain unemployed, in the U.S. alone. It's all about 'numbers.'

RESUMES

Well I know you believe everything I've said so far, but you're going to put together a resume anyway, aren't you? After all, your best friend got their job through a resume, and you know that you can too! Gonna write the thing, gonna hang the thing on the Internet, or mail it out, and see if it will pay off for you too, by golly!

And even if it doesn't, you *love* the thought of having a resume out there on the Internet or sitting on some employer's desk. Right?

"Resumes make sense: there is no way a harried executive or department head can set aside the time to interview every inquiry about employment that is made to his or her organization; there is not enough time."

(Anon.)

Okay. There are lots of instructions *out there*, about how to do that. They are:

• **In print:** There are dozens of books on resumes, available at any large bookstore (Borders, SuperCrown, Barnes & Noble, B. Dalton, and amazon.com, for example), and also at any small bookstore or your local library. Browse. You'll be amazed. My personal favorites are:

Richard Lathrop, *Who's Hiring Who?* Ten Speed Press, Box 7123, Berkeley, CA 94707. Richard describes and recommends "a qualifications brief" -- the idea that in approaching an employer you should offer him or her a written proposal of what you will do in the future, rather than "a resume" or summary of what you did in the past. The most popular 'resume' book, according to our mail.

Yana Parker, *The Damn Good Resume Guide.* 1996. Ten Speed Press, Box 7123, Berkeley, CA 94707. Describes, in ten steps, how to write functional and chronological resumes. Employers' comments upon resumes which actually got people jobs, are especially helpful. The next most popular resume book (according to our mail). Yana's other resume resources, available from Ten Speed Press, Box 7123, Berkeley, CA 94707, are: *The Resume Workbook.* (1998); *The Resume Catalog: 200 Damn Good Examples.* (1996); *Blue Collar & Beyond: Resumes for Skilled Trades and Services.* (1995); *Ready-To-Go Resumes* software. (1995); *Resume Pro: the Professional's Guide.* (1993). For further information about any of these, you can contact her at Damn Good Resume Service, P.O. Box 3289, Berkeley, CA 94703, 510-658-9229, or on her Website (www.damngood.com)

David Swanson, *The Resume Solution; How To Write (and Use) A Resume That Gets Results.* 1991. JIST Works, Inc., 720 North Park Ave., Indianapolis, IN 46202-3431. (Dave was on staff at 19 of my two-week workshops.)

Tom Jackson, and Ellen Jackson, *The New Perfect Resume.* 1996, revised. Anchor Press/Doubleday, Garden City, NY 11530. This is Tom's best-selling book, and with good reason. This edition is completely updated with 100+ resume samples and with some good career advice.

• **On the Internet:** There are many sites giving explicit, detailed instructions on how to write a resume, and how to post it on the Internet. So many, in fact, that you need a list of them all. I think the best list by far, is by Gary Will (www. golden.net/~archeus/reswri.htm#Articles2). He lists the best articles on the Internet, rates them, summarizes them, links to them, and gives you his evaluation of them. My favorite sentence on his dazzling site: "If you plan things just right, you will have a perfect resume by the time you're old enough to retire." *(Amy Lindgren)*

All right, we've spent enough time on resumes; let's look at the rest of the numbers game, and see if any of it *might* be useful to you. It's dicey, the odds are stacked against you -- but no one has the right to tell you not to at least *try* it.

The main parts of this game, as you will recall, are:
  • resumes
  • ads
  • agencies

We've tackled resumes. Now, let's briefly look at the other two, to see what's involved.

ADS OR
JOB POSTINGS

Ads are found in various places, masquerading under various names: "classifieds," "help wanted," "job listings," "job postings," and plain old "ads." Keep in mind the fact that ads (on the Internet or off) do not give you a complete picture of the job-market, by any means. A study conducted in two sample cities -- one large, one smaller -- revealed that "85% of the employers in San Francisco, and 75% in Salt Lake City, did not hire any employees through want ads" in a typical year. Yes, that said *any* employees, during the whole year.

So, what you get with ads are only "descriptions of vacancies that some employers couldn't fill any other way" (see page 19).

These days, there are three places where you can find such ads:

On the Internet. This is where *certain kinds of jobs* -- high tech, financial, healthcare, computer, engineering, government and academic jobs -- are increasingly (and sometimes exclusively) to be found. On the Internet, want ads are called "job-postings" or "job-listings." How to find them, if you have Internet access? Well, there are lots of ways, but the simplest is to go to my site (www.jobhuntersbible.com), and thence to its sub-section called (not surprisingly) "Job Postings." That section has reviews of, and links to, the major job listing sites on the Internet, together with an evaluation of how helpful such sites are, in general.

In Newspapers: This, of course, is where people without Internet access go, to find job ads. Experts advise you, for the sake of thoroughness, to study the job ads in your local daily or weekly newspaper each issue, and to study all of them, from A to Z -- because ads are generally alphabetized by job title, and sometimes the work you're looking for is buried under a title you would never guess. Increasingly, lots of newspapers post their ads on the Web as well; the Parachute site above will take you to these, again under "Job Postings."

In Newsletters, Clearinghouses or Registers: Each occupation, interest or specialty tends to have a newsletter, or association, or clearinghouse, or register of "Jobs Available." I have listed on page 26ff a sampling of the kind of things you can

Newsletters, Registers, Clearinghouses, of Job Listings

Here are some *examples* (only) of the type of thing you can find for almost any profession, interest, or specialty -- either in print, or on-line, or both; I have chosen to list here the kinds of Registers not easy to categorize:

• For Nonprofit Organizations Doing Public or Community Service: ACCESS, Networking in the Public Interest, 1001 Connecticut Ave., N.W., Suite 838, Washington, D.C. 20036. 202-785-4233. Fax: 202-785-4212. Amy Kincaid, Executive Director. Listings of job opportunities in the nonprofit sector, ranging from entry level to Executive positions, are disseminated through a publication called Community Jobs: The National Employment Newspaper For The Nonprofit Sector. ($25 for three monthly issues). (www.communityjobs.org/)

• For Jobs in the Experiential/Adventure (Outdoor) Education Field: Jobs Clearinghouse. Association for Experiential Education, 2305 Canyon Blvd., Suite #100, Boulder, CO 80302-5651. 303-440-8844. Fax: 303-440-9581. Timmy Comstedt, Manager. Monthly listings of full-time, part-time, seasonal jobs and internships, in the U.S. and abroad, in the experiential/adventure education field. (3 months for $24, or one issue for $9). Write, call or fax for details, if you are interested.

• For Jobs Outdoors: Environmental Opportunities, P.O. Box 4379, Arcata CA 95518. 707-826-1909. Fax: 707-826-2495. Sanford Berry publishes a monthly newsletter (called Environmental Opportunities), listing environmental jobs and internships. Each issue contains sixty to one hundred full-time positions in a variety of disciplines.

• For Jobs in Horticulture: Ferrell's JOBS IN HORTICULTURE, 2214 Douglas Drive, Carlisle, PA 17013-1025. 1-800-428-2474. A semi-monthly guide to opportunities. The rate for individuals is $24.95 for six issues (3 months' worth), or $45 for 12 issues (6 months' worth). For students, the rate is only $19.95. (www.hortjobs.com/)

• For Jobs Working with Horses: Equimax U.S.A. Inc., HC 65, Box 271, Alpine, TX 79830. phone: 915-371-2610 or 800-759-9494; fax: 915-271-2612; e-mail: 73051.1264@compuserve.com For singles or couples interested in jobs where they would be working with horses. Founded by Seth Burgess, who discovered his interest in horses after reading Parachute twenty years ago. Offers a List of Jobs and also a List of

Candidates. Job List subscription with 12 automatic updates, weekly, bi-weekly, or monthly (your choice) costs $45. (www.equimax.com)

• For Jobs as Caretakers: The Caretaker Gazette, P.O. Box 5887, Carefree AZ 85377-5887. phone: 602-488-1970; email: caretaker@uswest.net. For those interested in jobs serving as housekeepers or caretakers or extra hands, sometimes with owners on premises, sometimes not. Lists jobs around the world. $27 for 1-year subscription. (www.angel-fire.com/wa/caretaker)

• For the Blind: Job Opportunities for the Blind, 1800 Johnson St., Baltimore, MD 21230. 1-410-659-9314. A listing and referral service for blind workers, together with info about working with the blind. Operated by the National Federation For the Blind, in partnership with the U.S. Department of Labor. (www.blind.net/bons0003.html)

• For Jobs Outside the U.S.: International Employment Hotline, a monthly newsletter which lists international employment opportunities, founded by Will Cantrell, now published by the Carlyle Corporation. International Employment, 1088 Middle River Road, Stanardsville, VA 22973. They also publish International Career Employment Weekly, $4.95 per issue. phone: 1-800-291-4618; e-mail: cc@internationaljobs.org .

• For Jobs in the Christian Church: Intercristo is a national Christian organization that lists over 19,000 jobs, covering hundreds of vocational categories within 1300 or more Christian Service organizations in the U.S. as well as overseas. Their service is called Christian Placement Network. In 1997-1998, 9,000 people used the Network, and one out of every twenty-five of them found a job thereby (which, of course, means that 24 out of 25 didn't). But if those odds don't bother you, or the fact that some readers feel a large number of the listings are in very conservative church settings, then contact them at 19303 Fremont Ave. North, Seattle, WA 98133 (phone their machine at 1-800-426-1342, or a live person at 1-206-546-7330). The cost of being listed there, for three months, is $45.95. If you prefer quicker action, three months on their Website costs $59.95, but you get an instant listing of jobs that match your criteria. From that same Website you can order (for about $75) the self-guided Birkman Career Assessment Tool, which matches you to job-titles in the non-profit sector (only). You must have an IBM-compatible PC in order to use the disk this will come on. Ann Brooks is their Executive Director. (www.jobleads.org)

turn up. To find other lists, if you have Internet access go to my favorite search engine, Metacrawler, and in the search window, type the word "jobs" plus your interest or specialty, and see what it turns up. (`www.metacrawler.com`)

Now, suppose that in one of these places you find an ad that looks interesting to you; what do you do about it?

RULES FOR
ANSWERING ADS

If you see an ad for which you might qualify, even three-quarters, send off your resume, OR your resume and a covering letter, OR just a covering letter.

● **Keep in mind that you may be competing with a vast number of other people, responding to that same ad.** Number of resumes typically received by an employer as a result of their ad: 20 to 1,000. Ads on the Internet may receive a response within the hour. Ads in newspapers receive a response within 24 to 96 hours, with the third day usually being the peak day.

● **Keep in mind that your most likely fate is that you will be screened out.** Typically only 2 to 5 out of every 100 responses make it past the screening process when received. In other words, 95 to 98 out of every 100 responses are screened out.

● **In spite of the overwhelming odds, answering ads does pay off for some job-hunters.** Indeed, some find their perfect job this way. But in view of the high odds *against that*, most experts say if you're going to play this game, there are certain tips to keep in mind as you draft your response (your covering letter):

● **The goal of your response is to get invited in for an interview, nothing more.** Whether you get hired or not is the task of that interview, not the task of your response to their ad.

● **Keep your response brief.** Just quote all of the ad's specifications, then list what experience or qualifications you have that exactly match each of those specifications, and leave it at that. List them as a series of points, with perhaps "bullets" (●) as they are called, in front of each point.

● **If there's some skill you don't have, like *experienced with motorboats* respond at least with *interested in motorboats*.** Of course, that's only if it's true!

● **If the ad doesn't mention salary requirements, don't you either.** Why give another excuse for getting your response screened out? If the ad does request that you state your salary requirements, some experts say ignore the request, because many employers put it in there only to be able to screen you out without ever having to waste time on an interview. If you omit any mention of it, the employer may suppose you accidentally overlooked it. Other experts say, Naw, don't get cute. Answer the request, but do so by stating a range that's at least three to five thousand dollars wide, and add "depending on the nature and scope of duties and responsibilities," or words to that effect. e.g., *"My salary requirements are between twenty and forty thousand dollars, depending upon the amount of responsibility I would have."*

● **Volunteer nothing else.** Period. Every unnecessary point you add to your response may be the very thing that gets you screened out. So, if there is anything else you want to tell them, save it for the interview -- *if* you get invited in.

● **Your final sentence in your letter ought to leave the control in your hands.** Essentially this means putting the initiative in their hands, but reserving for yourself a backup strategy. Not "I hope to hear from you," but "I look forward to hearing from you, and will call your office next week just to be sure you received this." (A woman did this with a friend of mine a week ago; good thing. He hadn't received her letter.) Be sure to include your phone number, fax number, and e-mail address (if you have one), as every employer has their preferred way of getting in touch with you, if you interest them.

Things to Beware Of In Ads or Job Postings

FAKE ADS

(Positions advertised which don't exist) -- usually posted by placement firms or agencies posing as employers, in order to get you to send in your resume (to a box number, usually) in order to fatten their "resume bank" for future clout with employers. Also run by swindlers so they can get your Social Security number and/or the number of your driver's license (these two numbers alone enable them to take you to the cleaners with merchants, etc.). It's often a 900 number they ask you to call.

BLIND ADS

(No company name, just a box number). These, according to most insiders, are particularly unrewarding to the job-hunter's time. But many job-hunters are skilled at answering them with just the information asked for, and they do get a job as a result. However, if by chance you are presently working, there is always the danger that this ad was placed by your own company unbeknownst to you. If that is the case, you can get fired on the spot -- just for answering it. I know of actual cases where this has happened.

PHONE NUMBERS

In ads: most experts say, "Don't use them except to set up an appointment." Period. ("I can't talk right *now*. I'm calling from work.") They counsel that you should beware of saying more, lest you get screened out prematurely over the telephone. Other experts, however, think it is useful to use the phone number if you can talk to the actual person you would be working for (not the human resources department or a receptionist).

If you get such a person, use the call to inquire for more information *about the job* (without talking about yourself or your own qualifications). Ask, "Could I meet with you or at least send you my resume?" If the employer says yes to the appointment, arrange the time there and then. On the other hand, if they prefer your resume, thank them for their time and then ask to be turned over to their secretary, so that from the latter you can get the exact spelling of this employer's name, title, and address. Thence send a covering letter plus resume. In the covering letter you can say something like, "Thank you for our phone conversation, and thank you for encouraging me to send you my resume." In the remainder of the covering letter, then, highlight the parts of the phone talk you want them to recall.

PHRASES
   Which need lots of translating, like:

   "Energetic self-starter wanted" (= You'll be working on commission)

   "Good organizational skills" (= You'll be handling the filing)

   "Make an investment in your future" (= This is a franchise or pyramid scheme)

   "Much client contact" (= You handle the phone, or make 'cold calls' on clients)

   "Planning and coordinating" (= You book the boss's travel arrangements)

   "Opportunity of a lifetime" (= Nowhere else will you find such a low salary and so much work)

   "Management training position" (= You'll be a salesperson with a wide territory)

● **Make certain the spelling in the letter and resume is absolutely errorless.** "Almost perfect" won't do. Spelling errors will often cause your letter and resume to be put at the bottom of their pile of prospects (if they're desperate) or dismissed completely if they're not. So, before sending it, show your letter and resume to at least two friends or workmates or family whom you know to be excellent spellers. If a spelling error is found, *retype* the entire letter (using 'white-out' for a boo-boo is a no-no).

● **Consider sending your answer by FedEx**, if you're not resorting to e-mail -- or even if you are. Until everyone is doing this (and they're not yet), your response will stand out in the mind of the employer, believe me.

● **Beware of 'cute' strategies.** Some magazine articles counsel cute strategies -- such as mailing your resume in a box, or wearing a sign-board outside the offices of the place you're interested in, or putting "Personal and Confidential" on your envelope as if it were from a friend, etc. Trouble is: some employers have seen these strategies a hundred times, and are decidedly irritated when they see them yet again. Other employers aren't. In other words, it's a risk. You decide whether the risk is worth taking.

● **Stay 'on' an ad that you like.** Some job-hunters go on the Internet or read their local newspaper every day specifically noting ads that a) they would like to respond to, but b) they don't have all the credentials, qualifications or experience that the ad calls for. (They may send their resume and a covering letter in immediately, anyway.) But, they don't stop there. They watch to see if that ad stops running, *and then starts running again some days or weeks later.* That's a sign that the employer is having trouble finding a person with the qualifications he or she was asking for. At this point you can contact them (again) and bargain. Here's how one job-hunter reported her success with this strategy: "The particular ad I answered the first time it ran required at least an associate degree, which I did not have. What I did have was almost ten years' experience in that particular field. When the ad reappeared a month later I sent a letter saying they obviously had not found what they were looking for in the way of a degree, so why not give me a chance; they already had my resume. Well, it worked. I got the interview, I made them an offer that was $6,000 less than they were going to pay a degreed person, but still a $6,000 increase for me, over my prior position. I got the job. Needless to say, everyone was happy. I have recommended this same procedure to three of my friends, and it worked for two out of three of them, also."

EMPLOYMENT AGENCIES

From our youth up, we are taught (out on the street) that there are two places to turn to when you're out of work: want ads (on or off the Internet) and employment agencies. We just dealt with the first of these. Now let us look at the second.

Employment agencies seem very attractive when one is "up against it." We all like to think that somewhere out there is someone who knows where all the vacancies are. But, sad to relate, no place in the country has even a clue as to where all the jobs are.

The best that anyone can offer us is clues about where *some* vacancies are. Places having such information are called employment agencies. The Yellow Pages of your phone book will give you their names.

Basically, you will discover there are four kinds of agencies you can turn to: Government/State Employment Agencies; private agencies; temp agencies; and agencies retained by employers.

• **Government/State Employment Agencies**: This is the United States Employment Service, known in different States by different names: "Job Service," "Employment Development Department," the State Unemployment Office, and so on. (`www.doleta.gov/uses/`) There are almost 2,000 such offices nationwide, and your acquaintances will be able to tell you where the nearest one is; it's where people go to file for unemployment benefits. Most offices serve not only entry-level workers, but also professionals. Their services are free. They of course have lists of job vacancies, and some also maintain a list of which jobs are most in demand. Ask if yours does.

Your local office will have access also to **America's Job Bank**, a nationwide electronic database of job openings. (`www.ajb.dni.us/seeker`) On their computer or yours you can access AJB's list of openings in any of 50 states, typically totaling 1,450,000 vacancies daily.

Although USES has seen its staff and budget greatly reduced over the past twenty years, they still offer services beyond job-listings, providing special assistance to youths aged 16 to 22, veterans, people with disabilities, economically disadvantaged people, and older workers. About one-tenth of these offices also offer job-search workshops.

Effectiveness? According to one study, USES placed only 13.7% of those who looked for a job there; that means of course that 86.3% of the job-hunters who went there failed to find a job.

• **Private Agencies**: There are at least 8,000 private employment or placement agencies in the U.S. The exact number is unknown, since new ones are born, and old ones die, every week. You will find them listed in the Yellow Pages, under "Employment Agencies"; *some* few of them are also on the Internet. Many private employment agencies specialize in particular kinds of openings, as your Yellow Pages listings will usually make abundantly clear: e.g., executives, financial, data processing, or other specialties.

A private employment agency has a contract -- it is the application form filled out by the job-hunter!!! Fees are always charged -- the only question is: do they charge you, or the employer? Be sure to ask which is the case. In 80% of executives' cases, it is the employer who pays the fee.

When it is the job-hunter who must pay the fee, many if not most states have laws governing those fees. In New York, for example, a fee cannot exceed 60% of one month's salary, i.e., a $15,000-a-year job will cost you $750. The fee may be paid in weekly installments of 10% (e.g., $75 on a $750 total).

Some agencies ask you to agree that you will let them have 'exclusive handling' of you, usually on the application form. Experts say, don't grant it -- if you do, and then find a job independently of them, you may still have to pay them a fee.

Private employment agencies are usually a volume business, meaning they live by the numbers game: they need to turn over the most clients in the least amount of time. *If you are a career-changer, you will usually be given little attention; you take too much of their time to place you. Possible exception for you to investigate: a new, or suddenly expanding agency, which needs job-hunters badly if it is ever to get employers' business.*

The agency's loyalty in the very nature of things must lie with those who pay the bills (which in most cases is the employer), and those who represent repeat business (again, employers).

Effectiveness? Some time back, a spokesman for the Federal Trade Commission announced that the average placement rate for employment agencies was only 5% of those who walked in the door. That means a 95% failure rate, right?

• **Temp Agencies**: These are simply private employment agencies which specialize in placing people in temporary, or short-contract, jobs. However, with temp agencies the question of fee is simple: it is always the employer who pays -- directly to the agency. The agency pockets part of the money, as their fee, and gives you, the temp worker, the rest. Temp agencies have multiplied like rabbits in the last ten years, and there is an agency for almost any specialty or career you can think of (including doctors, etc.) *Haven't heard of one for ministers, priests and rabbis, yet, though.*

They are listed in your Yellow Pages, under the heading "Employment – Temporary." They are also to be found under the heading "Employment Agencies." Look in both places.

For executives, there is *The Directory of Executive Temporary Placement Firms*, available from Kennedy Information, Kennedy Place, Route 12 South, Fitzwilliam, NH 03447. phone: 800-531-1026; fax: 603-585-9555. It lists 225 such firms and costs $39.95.

Effectiveness? Higher than the typical private employment agency, though in certain geographical areas and with certain specialties and with certain agencies you can list yourself with them, but never get sent out on a job. If you want a fascinating look "inside the belly of the whale," use your Internet access (if you have it) to go to "The Red Guide to Temp Agencies." Though it's only for New York City, it's where temp workers report their experience with some 65 different agencies, "the morning after." (`www.panix.com/~grvsmth/redguide/`)

• **Agencies Hired by Employers**:

These are called Executive Recruiters or Executive Search Firms; sometimes also "Headhunters." (In the old days, these firms searched only for executives, hence their now-somewhat-outdated title; though, currently, 64% of executive positions are still filled through recruiters.)

These recruiting agencies are retained by employers. *The very existence of this thriving industry testifies to the fact that employers are as baffled by our country's Neanderthal job-hunting 'system' as we are. As I emphasize throughout this book, employers don't know how to find decent employees, any more than job-hunters know how to find decent employers.*

So, what do employers want executive recruiting agencies or firms to do? They want these firms to search for and find executives, financial officers, computer engineers, salespeople, technicians, or whatever, *who are already employed somewhere else, and have a good track record.* Then they want these agencies to lure those people away from where they are working, and get them to come work for the employer who hired them.

For the average job-hunter, this is the old *good news and bad news* dilemma. The good news is, these places are aware of, and are trying to fill, actual vacancies. The bad news is, their primary targets are people who are already employed.

Experts are totally divided as to whether or not the unemployed should waste any time contacting these executive recruiters.

Those who recommend you do, point out that the term "executive recruiter" has become very loosely used, these days. Yesterday's employment agency is often today's executive recruiter. (Employment agencies typically have to operate under more stringent state or federal regulations, hence the migration of some employment agencies to this different, less supervised, genre known as Executive Search.) Whatever they call themselves, these new Recruiters are hungry for the names of job-hunters, before they turn to offer their services to employers -- and in many cases will interview a job-hunter who approaches them politely, and with respect for how busy they are. I have known so-called Recruiters in some of the smaller firms who truly extended themselves on behalf of very inexperienced job-hunters (even *gave* them a copy of *Parachute*).

Look in the Yellow Pages under the heading "Executive Search Consultants." Also, Kennedy Information has a famous Directory of Executive Recruiters, available from Kennedy Information, Kennedy Place Route 12 South, Fitzwilliam, NH 03447. phone: 800-531-1026; fax: 603-585-9555. It lists 3,756 search firms at 5,830 office locations in North America. Cost: $49.95. Updated annually. Kennedy also has an online database for North America as well as an International database, searchable on their Web site (`www.kennedyinfo.com`) for a fee.

Effectiveness? As long as you don't put all your eggs or hopes in this one basket, and as long as you remain realistic that, if you're unemployed or looking for a non-executive position, this pursuit of executive recruiters isn't very likely to lead *anywhere*, you really have nothing to lose -- except some stationery and stamps.

HOW WELL DOES IT ALL WORK?

Well, let's face facts. In spite of the numbers being stacked against us,

For many folks, this Numbers Game works *exceedingly well*. They end up with just the job they wanted, and they are ecstatically happy about the whole thing -- especially if they were just wandering aimlessly about before they discovered this plan. This works just beautifully, by contrast -- *for many people.*

For others, this Numbers Game works *passably well.* They end up with a job of sorts, and a salary of sorts, even though in retrospect they realize it is not really the kind of work they had been looking for and hoping for, and the salary is *way* below what they really needed or wanted. But: a job is a job is a job, and better than ending up unemployed. (Parenthetically, the one thing that the job-hunting system/Numbers game does exceedingly well is to scare people, to the point where they are more than willing to lower their expectations and their self-esteem, and settle for a job far below their initial expectations.)

For the rest of the job-hunting folk who use this 'system,' it just doesn't work at all: they remain unemployed. (In the U.S., as I write, that number is 5,702,000 job-hunters -- and this is during supposedly 'wonderful' economic times in the U.S., with low inflation and 'low' unemployment.) *People trying to change careers have particular difficulty with the Numbers game.*

This week, next week, next month, thousands of job-hunters will send out 400, 500, 600, 800, 1000 resumes or more, post their resume on a dozen Internet job sites, answer one hundred newspaper ads or job postings on the Internet, visit twenty employment agencies, and still not get *one single invitation to come in for an interview.* It happens all the time. It has happened to me. It may happen to you.

CONCLUSION

'The Numbers Game' it is. You play the numbers, in this great Neanderthal job-hunting system of ours.

If it works for you, and you get a fine job, great! But if it doesn't, you may be interested in the other plan -- you know, the one they had saved up for you, in case all of this didn't work?

Small problem: with most of the personnel experts in our country, there is no other plan.

And that

is

that.

*It ain't what you don't know
that gets you in trouble;
it's what you know for sure
that ain't so.*

Mark Twain

You Can
Do It!

Chapter 3

"I DON'T HAVE A PARACHUTE OF ANY COLOR."

From the preceding chapter, two facts have stood out - - like Mount Everest:

(1) The traditional job-hunt is Neanderthal, a matter of playing the numbers and hoping they pay off for you; but, in the end, a big fat gamble.

(2) Most so-called 'experts' - - such as corporations' human resources people - - haven't the foggiest idea how to search for a job except using this system: resumes, ads/job postings, and agencies, as they prove when they themselves are out of a job.

Now, on with our story.

THE CREATIVE MINORITY

Fortunately for all of us, there have always been a creative minority among human resource 'experts' -- starting with John Scott of the Bell Telephone Laboratories, back in 1921 -- who refused to accept the idea that the job-hunt has to be as bad as it is, or as much of an out-and-out gamble, as it is; and sat down to figure out *how it could be done better.*

Even in days before studies were conducted and statistics were gathered, members of the creative minority intuitively grasped three fundamental truths about the job-hunt:

1. There are always jobs (vacancies) out there, waiting to be filled.

2. Whether you can find these jobs or not, depends on what job-search method you are using.

3. If you're job-hunting, and coming up 'empty,' you need to change the method you are using. The jobs (vacancies) are still out there, waiting for you to find them.

What they knew intuitively as far back as 1921, we now know more certainly, because in the interim the job-hunt has been studied *to death!* Particularly in the U.S., though its lessons apply to other developed countries throughout the world.

So let us take a detailed look at these three truths through modern-day glasses.

THE FIRST
FUNDAMENTAL TRUTH
ABOUT THE JOB-HUNT

There are always jobs (vacancies) out there, waiting to be filled.

New jobs are always being created. Each month, in the U.S.,[1] the government tells us exactly how many. It's called the monthly unemployment report, and it's issued on the first Friday of each month.

---

1. People all over the world read and use this book, not only in English but in its many other translations. If you live in another country, I want to make clear that throughout this book, I use the U.S. as but an example of the kind of thing that happens in most countries throughout the world. It is just that most studies of the job-hunt have been done in the U.S., and when we need statistics, it is from the U.S. that they are most available.

As I write, two million new jobs were created in the last twelve months in the U.S. -- jobs that never existed previously.

In addition to these two million new jobs that never existed before, companies and employees were of course also playing musical chairs with the jobs that already existed.

That is to say, among the 132,976,000 jobs that already existed a year ago in the U.S., a number of them fell vacant during the year -- and for the following reasons:

People got promoted -- thus leaving vacant the job they previously held.

People retired -- thus leaving vacant the job they held.

People quit -- thus leaving vacant the job they held.

People decided to move -- thus leaving vacant the job they held.

People got injured or fell sick -- sometimes for a long time, thus leaving vacant for long- or short-term periods, the job they held.

People died -- thus leaving vacant the job they held.

And of course, **people got fired or laid off** -- often due to downsizing, mergers, and hostile takeovers. That should have meant there were less jobs, and that is the case, initially. But studies of such companies reveal they often start hiring again within a very short time (comparatively), as they realize they 'cut too close to the bone,' or need new people with new skills.

For all these reasons, there are always jobs (vacancies) out there.

HOW MANY VACANCIES?

Well, just exactly how many? Since the U.S. keeps statistics on *everything*, we actually know the number. Adding up the new jobs that get created each year, and the old jobs that fall vacant each year, for however brief a time, there were 21,000,000 vacancies waiting to be filled, just in the last six months.

Since you may cordially disbelieve this number, let me tell you how we know it. Since October 1, 1997, every U.S. employer who hires somebody new must report that fact to a designated State agency within twenty days of the date of the hire. Each State then submits its New Hire Reports to the National Directory of New Hires, a component of the Federal Parent Locator Service (FPLS). Adding up all these numbers, the National Directory of New Hires (NDNH) reported 21 million people got newly hired in the U.S. during the six-month period 10/1/97 – 3/31/97.[2] (More current statistics are not available.)

That works out to almost one million vacancies a week - - either due to 'musical chairs' among existing jobs, or the creation of new jobs in the U.S. - - vacancies that have to be filled by *someone*. Believe me, there are always jobs out there, waiting to be filled.

THERE ARE VACANCIES
EVEN DURING RECESSIONS

You may say to yourself, but hey! these are good times in the U.S. - - the best in fifty years. What about other times in the U.S. when things won't be so hotsy-totsy? What about other countries, going through hard times even now? What happens to this claim that there are always jobs out there?

Well, it is perfectly true that *new* jobs don't get created at the same rate in hard times as in good times. But the other factor - - the 'revolving chairs' *among the jobs that already exist* - - holds true even during recessions or 'hard times.' People still get promoted, retire, quit, move, get sick for long stretches, or die - - leaving their job vacant. Even in the hardest of times.

---

2. The NDNH is *online* at
www.acf.dhhs.gov/programs/cse/newhire/employ/employ.htm

For example: in the U.S. there have been nine recessions since World War II. During one of these, the National Federation of Independent Business conducted a survey to discover how many vacancies there were among *small* businesses. They discovered there were one and a half million, at that moment, *even during that recession.* Add to that the number from large businesses, and you have a formidable number of jobs available, even during hard times.

Each year *millions* of people become unemployed, and then successfully find jobs, good jobs, sometimes great jobs, even during hard times.

So, write it on your bathroom mirror when you are job-hunting or trying to change careers: "In good times or in bad, there are *always* jobs out there." *Say it again, Sam.*

THE SECOND FUNDAMENTAL TRUTH ABOUT THE JOB-HUNT

Whether you can find these jobs or not, depends on what job-search method you are using.

We come now to our second fundamental truth about the job-hunt. To illustrate this point, let us step outside the world of work for a moment, and take an example from everyday life.

Suppose you moved to a big city, and found a really nice apartment to rent, but you decided you didn't want (or need) a telephone. And now let us suppose that some months later someone comes looking for you. They *think* you live in this city, but they're just not sure. However, being resourceful they go and look in the telephone book, because they assume that anyone who lives in the big city *must* have a telephone. But when they look, there is no mention of you. They call information to ask if you have an unlisted number. Nope. All their efforts turn up nothing. Nada. Zip.

So, what do they conclude? Well, you know what they conclude. They conclude you don't live in that city. And why did they reach this conclusion? Because they thought if you were there, you must be in the phone book. And if you weren't listed, you must not live in that city. But of course you are there. **They were just using the wrong search method.**

In exactly the same way, job-hunters turn to want ads, job-postings, or employment agencies, to find those jobs that do exist. But they often come up empty -- **because they're using the wrong search method**.

If you're going to find a job, your success does not depend on a good job-market. Everything depends on what search method you're using, to find those jobs that *are* out there, in good times or bad.

THE FIVE WORST WAYS TO TRY TO FIND A JOB

So, let's review what search methods are available to you, listing them in order, from *worst* success rate to *best* success rate:[3]

1. **Using the Internet**. If you are seeking a technical or computer-related job, or a job in engineering, finances, or health-care, I estimate the success rate to be 10%. For the other 10,000 job titles that are out there: 1%. Overall: 4%.

That is, out of every 100 job-hunters who use the Internet (job-postings and resume-postings) as their search method, exactly one of them will find a job thereby. 99 job-hunters out of

---

3. Where no study or survey was available, I made my own personal estimate, based on thirty years of experience with thousands of job-hunters. But there are plenty of studies, done over the past twenty years. Here are the ones which are particularly helpful:

Steven M. Bortnick and Michelle Harrison Ports, "Job search methods and results: tracking the unemployed, 1991," *Monthly Labor Review,* December 1992. Studied the success of job-seekers who had been looking for a job, over a period of 8 weeks.

John Bishop, John Barron and Kevin Hollenbeck, *Recruiting Workers: How recruitment policies affect the flow of applicants and quality of new workers.* The Ohio State University, The National Center for Research in Vocational Education, Sept. 1983. They discovered that "informal search methods" (such as described here in *Parachute*) are more effective than "formal search methods," such as employment agencies.

Carl Rosenfeld, "Job Search of the Unemployed, May 1976," *Monthly Labor Review,* November 1977. A Bureau of Labor Statistics study, which -- unlike the first study cited above -- interviewed job-hunters at only one moment in time.

Bureau of the Census, "Use and Effectiveness of Job Search Methods," *Occupational Outlook Quarterly,* Winter, 1976. A study of ten million job-seekers. Incidentally, I don't think the date of the study matters much. Job-hunting is all about human nature, and human nature doesn't change much over the years.

100 will not find the jobs that *are* out there - - if they use only this method to search for them.

2. **Mailing out resumes to employers at random**. This search method has a 7% success rate.

That is, out of every 100 job-hunters who use this search method, 7 will find a job thereby. 93 job-hunters out of 100 will not find the jobs that *are* out there - - if they use only this method to search for them.

(I'm being generous here with my percentages. One study revealed there is actually only one job-offer made and accepted, for every 1470 resumes floating around out there in the world of work. Another study puts the figure even higher: one job offer for every 1700 resumes floating around out there. If this sounds like good odds to you, thou shouldest clear the cobwebs out of thy brain. Would you take an airplane, if you knew only one out of 1700 got through, to its destination?)

3. **Answering ads in professional or trade journals**, appropriate to your field. This search method also has a 7% success rate.

That is, out of every 100 job-hunters who use this search method, 7 will find a job thereby. 93 job-hunters out of 100 will not find the jobs that *are* out there - - if they use only this method to search for them.

4. **Answering local newspaper ads**. This search method has a 5–24% success rate.

That is, out of every 100 job-hunters who use this search method, between 5 and 24 will find a job thereby. 76–95 job-hunters out of 100 will not find the jobs that *are* out there - - if they use only this method to search for them.

(The fluctuation between 5% and 24% is due to the level of salary that is being sought; the higher the salary being sought, the fewer job-hunters who are able to find a job using this search method).

5. Going to private employment agencies or search firms for help. This method has a 5–24% success rate, again, depending on the level of salary that is being sought.

Which is to say, out of every 100 job-hunters who use this method, between 5 and 24 will find a job thereby. 76–95 job-hunters out of 100 will not find the jobs that are out there - - if they use only this method to search for them.

(It should be noted that the success rate of this method has risen slightly in recent years, *in the case of women* but not of men: in a recent study, 27.8% of female job-hunters found a job within two months, by going to private employment agencies.)

THE THIRD
FUNDAMENTAL TRUTH
ABOUT THE JOB-HUNT

If you're job-hunting, and coming up 'empty,' you need to change the search method you have been using.

I'm sure you noticed that our old friends from the Numbers game - - resumes, ads, and agencies - - all appear on the *Five Worst* List. Ouch![4]

Therefore: if you've just been using resumes, ads, and agencies to find a job - - on or off the Internet - - and this has turned up *nothing*, it's time to change your search method.

---

4. Incidentally, there are at least four other search methods for trying to find the jobs that are out there, that technically fall into the "Least Effective" category. These are:

a. Going to **places where employers pick out workers**. This has an 8% success rate - - that is, out of every 100 people who use this method, 8 will find a job thereby. 92 will not. (15% of U.S. workers are union members, and it is claimed that those among them who have access to a union hiring hall, have a 22% success rate - - that is, 22 out of every 100 find a job using this method. What is not stated, however, is how long it takes to get a job at the hall, and how long a job typically lasts - - in the trades, that may be for just a few days.)

b. Taking **a Civil Service examination**. This has a 12% success rate - - that is, out of every 100 people who use this method, 12 will find a job thereby. 88 will not.

c. Asking **a former teacher or professor** for job-leads. This also has a 12% success rate - - that is, out of every 100 people who use this method, 12 will find a job thereby. 88 will not.

d. Going to **the state/Federal employment service office**. This has a 14% success rate - - that is, out of every 100 people who use this method, 14 will find a job thereby. 86 will not.

THE FIVE BEST WAYS
TO TRY TO FIND A JOB

1. **Asking for job-leads from: family members, friends, people in the community, staff at career centers** - - especially at your local community college or the high-school or college where you graduated. You ask them one simple question: do you know of any jobs at the place where you work - - or elsewhere? This search method has a 33% success rate.

That is, out of every 100 people who use this search method, 33 will find a job thereby. 67 job-hunters out of 100 will not find the jobs that *are* out there - - if they use only this method to search for them.

2. **Knocking on the door of any employer, factory, or office that interests you, whether they are known to have a vacancy or not.** This search method has a 47% success rate.

That is, out of every 100 people who use this search method, 47 will find a job thereby. 53 job-hunters out of 100 will not find the jobs that *are* out there - - if they use only this method to search for them.

3. **By yourself, using the phone book's Yellow Pages** to identify subjects or fields of interest to you in the town or city where you are, and then calling up the employers listed in that field, to ask if they are hiring for the type of position you can do, and do well. This method has a 69% success rate.

That is, out of every 100 job-hunters or career-changers who use this search method, 69 will find a job thereby. 31 job-hunters out of 100 will not find the jobs that *are* out there - - if they use only this method to search for them.

4. **In a group with other job-hunters, using the phone book's Yellow Pages to identify subjects or fields of interest to you in the town or city where you are, and then calling up the employers listed in that field, to ask if they are hiring for the type of position you can do, and do well.** This method has an 84% success rate.

That is, out of every 100 people who use this method, 84 will find a job thereby. 16 job-hunters out of 100 will not find the jobs that *are* out there - - if they use only this method to search for them.

5. **The Creative Approach to Job-Hunting or Career-Change.** This method has an 86% success rate.

That is, out of every 100 job-hunters or career-changers who use this search method, 86 will find a job or new career thereby. 14 job-hunters out of 100 will not find the jobs that *are* out there - - if they use only this method to search for them.

WHAT IS
'THE CREATIVE APPROACH'
TO JOB-HUNTING
OR CAREER-CHANGE?

Since the Creative Approach has the very best success rate, of all the job-search methods available to you, let us see how it got invented and what it involves.

The creative minority began by asking themselves what makes our present job-hunting system so Neanderthal. There were, it seemed to them, three fatal assumptions:

Fatal Assumption No. 1: *"The job-hunter should remain somewhat loose (i.e., vague) about what he or she wants to do, so they will be able to take advantage of whatever vacancies may become available."* Good grief, said the creative minority, this is why we have such a great percentage of people in this country who are *underemployed.* If you don't state just exactly what you want to do, first of all to yourself, and then to the employers you meet, you are - - in effect - - handing over that decision to others. And others, vested with such awesome responsibility for your life, will either duck the responsibility, or define you as only capable of doing such and such level of work (a safe, no risk diagnosis).

Fatal Assumption No. 2: *"The job-hunter should spend his or her time only on those organizations which have already indicated they have a vacancy."* Nonsense, said the creative minority. The job-market isn't like some high-school prom, where the job-hunters have to sit on the edge of the dance-floor, like shy wallflowers, while the employers are whirling around out in the center of the floor, enjoying all the initiative. In many cases, the dancing employers (if we may pursue the metaphor) are stuck with partners who are stepping on their toes, constantly. So, often-times the employer is *praying* someone will pay no attention to the silly ritual, and come to his or her rescue by cutting in. And (to pursue the metaphor further), people who cut in are usually pretty good dancers.

Fatal Assumption No. 3: *"Employers only see people who can write well."* That's pretty ridiculous, when it's put that way. But, say the creative minority, isn't that exactly the assumption that our present job-hunting system is based on? To get hired, you must get an interview. To get an interview, under this system, you must first let them look at your resume -- either by mail, or by posting it on the Internet. But the resume is only as good as your writing ability makes it. If the resume is poorly written, it will of course behave like a Fun House mirror, which distorts dramatically what you are really like. But, *no allowance is made for this possibility by the companies that see your resume, except one time out of a thousand.* Your resume is assumed to be an accurate mirror of who you are. You could be Einstein, but if you don't write well, you will not get an interview. Employers only see people who can write well. Ridiculous? You bet it is. But that's why I say our present job-hunting system is Neanderthal.

THE THREE SECRETS
OF SUCCESSFUL JOB-HUNTING

Once the fatal assumptions of the Numbers Game were brought into the bright light of day, it was of course easy for the creative minority to design a new job-hunting approach -- and one that worked. The prescription almost wrote itself, since it was just the opposite of the three fatal assumptions.

Success Secret #1: **You must decide just exactly what you have, to offer to the world.** This involves identifying, for yourself and others, what your favorite (transferable) skills are -- *in order of priority or importance to you.*

Success Secret #2: **You must decide just exactly where you want to use your skills.** This involves identifying your favorite subjects or fields of interest, as well as your geographical preferences, which you then explore through *research* (in books or on the Internet), and personal *informational interviewing.*

Success Secret #3: **You must go after the organizations that interest you the most, whether or not they are known to have a vacancy.** 'Going after them' means using your contacts -- anybody you know -- to get an appointment there; specifically, to get an appointment with the one individual there who actually has the power to hire you for the job that you most want to do. (Of course, you must have done a little research on them first, to find out just exactly who that is.)

(Incidentally, the word "organizations" is used very broadly throughout this book, to mean small businesses, large corporations, associations, foundations, agencies, the government and any other place that offers employment to people.)

For any job-hunter who is having trouble finding a job by the usual route -- resumes, ads, and agencies -- this prescription of the creative minority is *a lifesaver.*

For any job-hunter who wants more than 'just-a-job' this prescription of the creative minority is *crucial.*

But, for the job-hunter who is trying to strike out in a new direction, or who of necessity must seek a different line of work than they have done in the past, this prescription of the creative minority is *a matter of life and death.*

YOU CAN DO IT!

When you are looking for work, you will get advice from every side, and what it usually adds up to is: *you don't stand a chance. Give up . . . now! That isn't a kind world waiting for you out there, anymore. There isn't a single job out there for you to find . . . trust us, we've looked. And even if there is, it will be at a vastly reduced income for you. Take our advice, and just retreat to your bed, pull the covers over your head, and turn the electric blanket up to nine.*

All in all, a sort of *music to get depressed by.*

You must pay no attention to this advice, of course.

And you must not give up hope.

Even if you already began your job-search -- have sent out resumes or curricula vitae by the bushel, searched want ads by the hour, visited federal/state, and private employment agencies from A to Z, hung out on the Internet, looking at all those job-posting and resume sites for days or weeks -- all without turning up a single thing.

This says nothing about whether or not you can find a job.

There *is* a way. You *can* find a job, and a job which you love. You *can* flourish. The prescription of the creative minority is the key: What, Where, and How.

1. What: **You must decide just exactly what you want to do.**

2. Where: **You must decide just exactly where you want to do it.**

3. How: **You must go after the organizations that interest you the most, whether or not they are known to have a vacancy.**

Successful job-hunting is a learned skill. You have to study it. You have to practice it. You have to master it, just like any new skill. And master it thoroughly, because you'll need it all the rest of your life.

CONCLUSION

Okay, so where are we?

You're job-hunting or trying to change careers.

You've tried 'the system' everyone says is the way to do it: resumes, ads, and agencies, only to discover it is no system at all. It's just 'a Numbers Game.' It's pathetic. It's Neanderthal.

You're intrigued by the Creative Minority's alternative prescription of What, Where, and How.

You want to try it. Even if it takes work, because you know that it has a success rate that is twelve times that of resumes, in turning up jobs.

You're ready. But you want some guidance.

Good.

That's what the remainder of this book is about.

Concerning the creative job-hunting method, a reader (a student graduating from the University of Texas at Austin) wrote recently: "I can't begin to tell you how grateful I am that you wrote this book. I will be graduating this May and will be gainfully employed by an employer of my choice thereafter. I have the job I want, in the field I love (aviation) while my friends are still sending out resumes! To this day, I have never written nor used such a useless piece of paper! I think I'll put all of my friends out of their misery by telling them to quit wasting time on resumes, and buy them all a copy of your book!"

*F*orget *"what's available out there."*
Go after the job you really want the most.

—David Maister

CHAPTER FOUR

The Creative Approach To
Job-Search
and Career-Change

What

DO YOU HAVE,
TO OFFER TO THE WORLD?

You Must Figure Out Which of Your Skills
You Most Delight to Use

Chapter 4

Wild Life by John Kovalic, © 1989 Shetland Productions. Reprinted with permission.

"I CAN'T FIND A JOB"

When a job-hunter tells me: *"I can't find a job"*, that tells me nothing, until they tell me *how* they have been looking for it. The search method one uses, is everything! Everything!

The best job-search method, by far, has turned out to be the so-called **creative job-hunting approach**, as we saw in the previous chapter. This method leads to a job for 86 out of every 100 job-hunters who *faithfully* follow it. Such an effectiveness-rate -- 86% -- is astronomically higher than all other individual job-hunting methods.[1] That's why when nothing else is working for you, this is the method that you will thank your lucky stars for.

This is also the method you must turn to, if you've decided you would like to find a new career -- and you'd prefer not to have to take years out of your life to go back to school and get retrained with a new degree, etc., etc. (Or, even if you do want to go back to school, and need to know what to study or major in.)

---

1. I emphasize that this is for individual job-hunters or career-changers, working by themselves. Group strategies, such as Nathan Azrin's 'job-club' concept, Chuck Hoffman's Self-Directed Job-Search, Dean Curtis's Group Job Search program, etc., where you work essentially as a very well-disciplined class, have also achieved success-rates in the 85-90% range, usually by using telephone approaches to employers, with endless group feedback and coaching.

As I mentioned in the previous chapter this method does take time and effort. Most people like to avoid *effort*. I overheard a conversation in New York City's Central Park between two college students. We'll call them Jim and Fred. In half a minute they perfectly illustrated the amount of effort that altogether-too-many people put into their life-planning:

Jim: Hey, what are you majoring in?

Fred: Physics.

Jim: Physics? Man, you shouldn't major in physics. Computer science is the thing these days.

Fred: Naw, I like physics.

Jim: Man, physics doesn't pay much.

Fred: Really? What does?

Jim: Computer science. You should switch to computer science.

Fred: Okay, I'll look into it tomorrow.

Many career choices (and career-changes) in our culture are made in this fashion -- on impulse and whim, in a moment, in the twinkling of an eye. A casual conversation with someone. A decision to just follow in our parents' footsteps. An article on a news broadcast. An invitation from our father or a friend to come work where they do. Letting 'the job-market' rather than your heart dictate what you should go into.

> When you choose a career, you have got to know what it is **you** want to do, or else someone is going to sell you a bill of goods somewhere along the line that can do irreparable damage to your self-esteem, your sense of worth, and your stewardship of the talents that God gave you.

No, no! If you are going to follow the prescription of the Creative Minority, you must come to this task with your sleeves rolled up, prepared to do The Exercises thoroughly. Just remember: the benefits far outweigh the pain. Here are a couple of comments from readers (courtesy of amazon.com):

"It changed my life. The exercises take some time and thought, but they really led me to a rewarding and fun career I would never have considered without them."

"The exercises took quite a bit of effort, yet the results have permanently shaped the way I think about what I want to do with my life, no matter what my job at the time happens to be. I find myself returning to the insights gained from "Parachute" every few years and am amazed that the essential qualities I identified through the book remain consistent, no matter where I'm working or what I'm doing."

TRAVELS WITH FARLEY by Phil Frank © 1982. Field Enterprises, Inc. Courtesy of Field Newspaper Syndicate.

TREATING EACH JOB-HUNT AS THOUGH IT WERE A CAREER-CHANGE

I didn't invent this method. The Creative Minority did. But let me tell you what I especially like about it (besides the fact that it works so well).

I like the fact that it treats every job-hunt as though *it might be* a career-change.

Traditionally, we have been taught that if you want just a plain-old job-hunt, there is one method for *that*. But if you want to change careers, that's another kettle of fish, entirely.

Not so, with the Creative Minority! They say: **if you want to do a successful job-hunt, you must go through the same process you would if you wanted to change careers.**

Why do I like this philosophy? Because, first of all, **it makes sense to me**. Career-change seems to me to be the more radical process -- therefore more complicated, and time-consuming than just job-hunting. Now if the Creative Minority appear and tell me they've found a more effective method of job-hunting, I would expect it to be more complicated, and time-consuming than the traditional job-hunt -- or about as complicated and time-consuming as a career-change is. The two are of equal complexity; it is not surprising the two processes are virtually the same. This makes vast sense to me.

I like it secondly, because **it leaves open the door of possibilities.** Suppose you're halfway through your job-hunt and you suddenly realize you don't want the same old same old, that you had before. You suddenly realize you want to change careers. With the Creative Minority's process, no problem! You don't have to go back and redo everything. They were treating your job-hunt as though it were a career-change, from the beginning.

Experts say that we should count on having anywhere between three and six careers during our lifetime. The job-hunt is a time when many of us[2] suddenly decide "the time is now" -- for any of the following reasons:

• **We got fired,** and we can't find our old work any more. In this changing life, and changing world, jobs do vanish. You must not necessarily expect that you will be able to find exactly the same kind of work that you did in the past.

• **We are not earning enough,** and we need a new career that pays us more money -- more of what we're worth.

---

2. How many? Well, the U.S. keeps the best statistics; they may be *indicative*, at least, of what happens in other countries.

In the U.S., a survey found that 45% of all U.S. workers said they would change their careers if they could.

And each year about 10% of all U.S. workers actually do. In the most recent year surveyed, that equated to 10 million workers who changed careers that year. Of these: 5.3 million changed careers *voluntarily*, and in 7 out of 10 cases their income went up; 1.3 million changed careers *involuntarily*, because of what happened to them in the economy, and in 7 out of 10 cases, their income went down; and 3.4 million changed careers for a *mixture* of voluntary and involuntary reasons, such as needing to go from part-time to full-time work, etc. (There is no record of what happened to *their* income.)

- **We've been asked to do the work of three,** and we feel stressed out, angry, exhausted, burnt out, and grumpy; we want a job or career that is a little easier on us, so we'll have time to smell the flowers.

- **We had been hardly stretched at all** by our previous work, and we'd like something that offers a real challenge and 'stretches' us.

- **We've been doing this work for ten, fifteen years, but it was a bad choice from the beginning,** and now we've decided to set it right.

- **We had a dream job, but our much-beloved boss moved on,** we now find ourselves working for 'a jerk,' and the dream job has turned into 'the job from hell.' We not only want a new employer, we've decided to go for a new career.

- **We've reached mid-life, and are ready for the famous 'mid-life change.'** [3]

- **We're looking more and more for 'our mission in life,'** and while we don't yet know what that is, we do know for sure that what we're presently doing *isn't it.* (Indeed, most of us are engaged in a life-long search for, and journey toward, *meaning* - - a process in which career-change plays an important part.)

For any or all of these reasons, we may decide to change careers. The job-hunt is often the time that we make that change.

How nice, then, that the Creative Minority came up with a process that treats every job-hunt as though it is to be a career-change.

We're ready for the process. The process is ready for us.

ARLO & JANIS reprinted by permission of NEA Inc.

WHAT IS
CAREER-CHANGE?

It's important to begin by understanding exactly what a career-change is. This is murky territory, because the word 'career' is used in so many different ways in everyday language.

(1) It is used, first of all, to mean *work* in contrast to *learning* or *leisure*. Thus when clothing ads speak of "a career outfit," they are referring to clothes which are worn primarily at work, rather than during learning-activities or leisure-activities.

(2) It is used, secondly, to sum up *a person's whole life in the world of work*. Thus when people say of someone at the end of their life, "He or she had a brilliant career," they are referring to *all* the occupations this person ever held, and all the work this person ever did.

(3) Thirdly, in its most common sense -- the one used here -- it is used as a synonym for the word *'field'* or *'job,'* as in the phrase 'a career-change,' where what is actually meant is a 'job/field change.'[4]

Okay, so much for the word 'career.' Now when we make a 'career-change,' what exactly is it that we're changing? Well, let's take a look-see.

CAREER =

As you see here, **basically a career is made up of two parts: (the name of) an occupation, and a field.** To explain this, let's momentarily 'freeze' the name of the occupation, and say it is: 'secretary.' *(I choose this because more than once in the past, I worked as a secretary myself).*

---

3. Despite the *myth* that career-change is primarily a mid-life phenomenon, in point of fact people can and do change careers at *all* ages. In the study referred to in footnote 2, only one out of ten career-changers was actually in mid-life.

4. Incidentally, 'career' comes from the Latin *carrus*, referring to a racetrack where horses wildly *careen* while competing in a race. We might observe that the wild way in which people often *careen* into a new career today, accidentally preserves the original meaning of the word.

Now, suppose you were just starting out in this occupation of 'secretary.' The next question you would have to ask yourself would be: where you would like to work as 'secretary'? Do you want to be a secretary with . . . a law firm? . . . a gardening store? . . . an airline? . . . a church? . . . a photographic laboratory? . . . a bank? . . . a chemical plant? . . . the Federal government? . . . or what?

All these places are *fields.* Law, Gardening, Air travel, Religion, Photography, Banking, Chemistry, Government -- they are all *fields.* What field you choose makes a big difference.

Let's take another example. Let's 'freeze' the name of the occupation as 'management consultant.'

Suppose you were just going into this career: where would you like to be a management consultant? With . . . a computer firm? . . . an automobile company? . . . a grocery store chain? . . . a leisure company? . . . an HMO? . . . or what? Again, these are all *fields.* Management, Computers, Automobiles, Food, Leisure, Healthcare. The field makes a big difference. *(You will realize that all these fields can be studied in college, or other schools where they are called "Majors," "Subjects," or just plain "Fields." Many can also be picked up, on the job -- through apprenticeship, experience, and finding a mentor there.)*

Memorize this equation, please; it will help you a lot, down the line: **a career = occupation + field**. You must define both, for your job-hunt to succeed.

Failure to do this can cause much damage to your job-hunt or career-change plans. For example, if you have defined your career goal as that of being a management consultant -- but nothing is turning up, you know what your problem is. You have only defined your **occupation**, and that by itself isn't enough.

You must also define what **field** you want to be a management consultant in, if your job-hunt is to be successful. *Until* you've decided what field you want to do management consulting in, your job-hunt has too broad a target. That's why you can't find a job.

The Creative Minority's process enables you to decide both **occupation** and **field** (or the building-blocks thereof), because it treats every job-hunt as though it were a career-change.

As I said, that's what I like about it.

THE THREE STEPS
TO JOB-HUNTING SUCCESS

But now that I have told you what I like about it, let us get on with it.

I am going to use my rich skills at overkill, to not simply *walk you through* the steps of creative job-hunting/career-change, but to gently *drum this process into your head*, until you can hear the steps in your sleep.

I want to do this, because it is essential that you *master* this approach, and master it *for life*. You are in all likelihood going to be out job-hunting again, you are in all likelihood going to be changing careers again. Job-hunting/career-change is a repetitive activity in our lives these days. You never know when you'll need it again. "Sometime. Come soon."

So, to recapitulate from our previous chapter, the creative approach to job-hunting/career-change has three parts to it. And these parts are easiest to remember as *What, Where* and *How:*

---

1. What: **You must decide just exactly what you have to offer to the world.** This involves identifying your gifts, or talents -- which is to say, your favorite skills, *in order of priority or importance to you.* Experts call these **your transferable skills**, because they are transferable to any field/career that you choose, regardless of where you first picked them up, or how long you've used them in some other field.

Once you know your skills, you have the building-blocks of your occupation; with these building-blocks, you can define an occupation that you love to do.

---

2. Where: **You must decide just exactly where you want to use your skills.** This involves identifying your *favorite subjects* or fields of interest, as well as your geographical preferences, which you then explore through *research* (in books or on the Internet), and personal *informational interviewing*. *Where* is primarily a matter of the **fields of knowledge** *you have already acquired,* which you most enjoy using. But it also has to do with your preferred working conditions, what kinds of data or people or things you enjoy working with, where you'd most like to live, etc.

Once you know your favorite subjects, you have the building blocks of your field; with these building-blocks, you can define a field that you would love to do your occupation in. Also, you can now put occupation and field together, to define a career that you would love to do.

3. How: **You must go after the organizations that interest you the most, whether or not they are known to have a vacancy.** 'Going after them' means using your contacts -- anybody you know -- to get an appointment there; specifically, to get an appointment with the one individual there who actually has the power to hire you for the job that you most want to do. (Of course, you must have done a little research on them first, to find out just exactly who that is, not to mention other valuable information about the organization's goals, etc.)

Once you have mastered these techniques, you know how to get into your new career that you love.

THE CRUCIAL IMPORTANCE OF 'WHAT'

Now, faced with this three-fold prescription from the Creative Minority, our immediate instinct is to leap over *What* and *Where*, and go directly to *How* -- *how* do we find vacancies, *how* do we do our resume, *how* do we conduct a job-interview?

There are, indeed, thousands of job-hunting books and job-hunting workshops devoted solely to How: how to do resumes, interviews, salary negotiation - - thereby encouraging job-hunters to think this is all there is, to successful job-hunting.

This is a *huge* mistake.

Your Favorite Transferable Skills Are the Key to Job-Hunting Success

Search for work you only half-care about, and you'll search for it with only half your being; but search for work you are desperately anxious to find, and you'll hunt for it with all of your being.

The more you are searching for the thing that you most love to do, the more you will transform not only your job-hunt, but also your life. This begins with identifying skills you are passionate about using!

'. . . and give me good abstract-reasoning ability, interpersonal skills, cultural perspective, linguistic comprehension, and a high sociodynamic potential.'

THAT BOGEY-WORD: SKILLS

Now, many people just "freeze" when they hear the word 'skills.' It begins with high school job-hunters: "I haven't really got any skills," they say.

It continues with college students: "I've spent four years in college, and still I haven't picked up any skills."

And through our first years in the world of work. "I'm an unskilled worker."

And through the middle years, especially when a person is thinking of changing his or her career: "I just know I'll have to go back to college, and get retrained, because I don't have any skills in this new field, except maybe at entry level."

'Skills' is one of the most misunderstood concepts in the English language -- a misunderstanding that is shared, I might add, by altogether too many employers, personnel or human resources departments, and other so-called 'vocational experts.'

Their misunderstanding is revealed in their use of the terms "skilled and unskilled." To be blunt about it, **there is no such thing as 'unskilled.'** Everyone has skills, and has used them since childhood. They are enshrined in the reputation we get among our friends and family: "A whiz at remembering things," "Great with his hands," "Very outgoing with people," "Can fix anything that's broken," "A wonderful eye for color," and that sort of thing.

But there is such a thing as being deeply unaware of our skills. I know a woman who could walk into a room, look at twenty people there, walk out of the room and from memory perfectly describe every person she had seen in those fifteen seconds, down to the articles of jewelry they were wearing. Ironically, she said she was 'unskilled' -- she thought everyone could do that.

Many of us have skills we are unaware of. By inventorying your skills -- both those you are aware of and those you aren't, you will automatically put yourself way ahead in the job-hunt. Such inventory will also facilitate any career-change you care to make -- without your buying into the folly called 'I can only change careers if I go back to school.'

Maybe in order to change careers you will need some retraining, but very often it is possible to make a dramatic career-change without any retraining. It all depends. And you won't really *know* if you need further training, until you have inventoried your favorite skills and fields of knowledge *that you already possess.*

DEFINING 'TRAITS'

The skills you need to inventory are *your transferable skills.*

Now, many people think transferable skills are such things as: *has lots of energy, gives attention to details, gets along well with people, shows determination, works well under pressure, is sympathetic, intuitive, persistent, dynamic, dependable,* etc. But no matter how widespread this misconception, these are not functional/transferable skills, but the *style* with which you do your transferable skills.

To illustrate, let's take *"gives attention to details."* Suppose one of your transferable skills is "researching"; in such a case, *"gives attention to details"* describes the manner or style with which you do 'researching.'

So these things many job-hunters mistake for transferable skills -- *has lots of energy, gives attention to details, gets along well with people, shows determination, works well under pressure, is sympathetic, intuitive, persistent, dynamic, dependable* -- are actually your **traits.** (They may also be called your 'self-management skills,' 'temperaments,' or 'type.' Popular tests such as the *Myers-Briggs* measure this sort of thing.[5])

---

5. The Myers-Briggs Type Indicator, or 'MBTI,' measures what is called *psychological type.* For further reading about this, see:

Paul D. Tieger & Barbara Barron-Tieger, *Do What You Are: Discover the Perfect Career for You Through the Secrets of Personality Type.* 1992. Little, Brown & Company, Inc., division of Time Warner Inc., 34 Beacon St., Boston MA 02108. For those who cannot obtain the MBTI, this book includes a method for readers to identify their personality types. This is a very popular book.

David Keirsey and Marilyn Bates, *Please Understand Me: Character & Temperament Types.* 1978. Includes the Keirsey Temperament Sorter -- again, for those who cannot obtain the MBTI® (Myers-Briggs Type Indicator) -- registered trademarks of Consulting Psychologists Press.

A publication list of other readings about psychological type can be obtained from the Center for Application of Psychological Type, 2720 N.W. 6th St., Gainesville, FL 32609.

DEFINING
'TRANSFERABLE SKILLS'

All right, then, if what we often mistake as transferable skills are actually 'traits,' then what exactly are transferable skills? Here is a brief crash course on the subject, setting forth the seven principles of transferable skills:

1. Transferable skills are the secret of job-hunting success, because they are the most basic unit -- the atoms -- of whatever career, occupation, or job you choose.

You can see this from this diagram:

Skills as the Basic Unit of Work

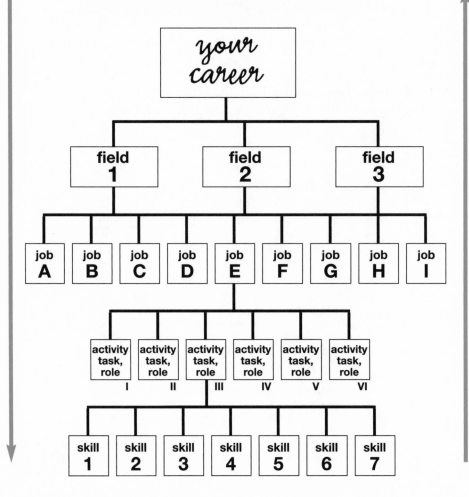

2. Transferable skills are the secret of changing careers without necessarily going back to school, because they allow you to build a picture of a new career from the ground up.

Look at the previous diagram. The creative approach to career-change essentially starts at the top on the left, works down to the bottom, then goes back up the other side to the top.

That is, you take your present or previous career, and you break it down *(through field and tasks -- whether you liked them or not)* to its most basic atomic level: skills.

Then you construct a new career, beginning with the basic level, your favorite skills, and going on up through your favorite tasks to your favorite field.

Down one side of the diagram, up the other side. Voila! a new career. Your favorite transferable skills are the foundation on which all else rests.

3. Transferable skills are almost always verbs.

Specifically, they are action verbs, in the gerund form (ending with -ing), and they may be thought of as 'focussed energies' that act upon some object.

4. Transferable skills divide into three basic families.

Transferable skills are customarily divided into three *families,* according to what kind of object they act upon -- whether it be some kind of **Data** (Information), or **People** or **Things.**

Within each of these three families there are *simple* skills, and there are higher, or *more complex* skills. The families can be diagrammed as three inverted pyramids, with the simpler skills at the bottom in each, and the more complex or higher skills above them, in order:

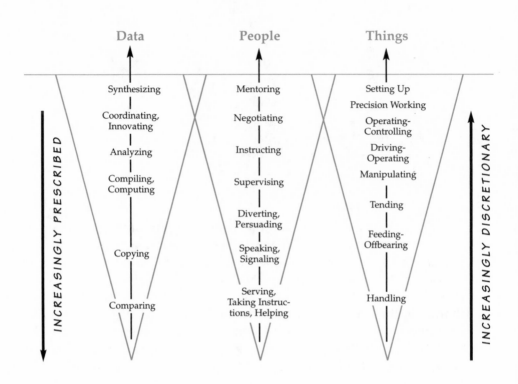

5. When you inventory your transferable skills, you should always claim the *highest* skills you legitimately can on the basis of your past performance.

On *each* transferable skills pyramid, you want to claim the highest skill you legitimately can, based on what you have in the past proven you can do.[6]

As a general rule -- to which there are exceptions -- each skill that is higher on a triangle depends upon your being able to do all the skills listed below it on that triangle. So you probably can claim the skills below the highest skill you claim, on each inverted pyramid. Always check to see if this is so.

---

6. If you desire a more detailed official explanation of what each of these skills is, I refer you to the *U.S. Dictionary of Occupational Titles*, 1991 revised fourth edition, pp. 1005–1006 in vol. II, available in any public library in the U.S.

6. The higher your transferable skills, the more freedom you will have on the job.

Simpler skills can be, and usually are, heavily *prescribed* by the employer, so if you claim *only* the simpler skills, you will have to *'fit in'* - - following the instructions of your supervisor, and doing exactly what you are told. The *higher* the skills you can legitimately claim, the more you will be given freedom to carve out the job the way you want to - - so that it truly fits *you*.

7. The higher your transferable skills, the less competition you will face, because jobs which use such skills are rarely found through the search-methods the average job-hunter or career-changer uses.

Not for you the way of classified ads, resumes, and agencies. No, if you claim higher skills, then to find jobs which use them you *must* follow the creative job-hunting method described in the next two chapters.

The essence of this creative approach to job-hunting or career-change is that you may approach *any organization that interests you, whether or not they have a known vacancy* - - using your contacts to get in, there. Naturally, at whatever places you visit - - and particularly those which have not advertised any vacancy - - you will find far fewer job-hunters that you have to compete with, than would be the case if you were just answering ads or job postings.

In fact, if the employers you visit happen to like you well enough, they may even create for you a job that does not presently exist. *In which case, you will be competing with no one, since you will be the sole applicant for that newly created job.* While this doesn't happen most of the time, it is astounding how many times it *does* happen.

The reason it does is that the employers often have been *thinking* about creating a new job within their organization, for quite some time - - but with this and that, they just have never gotten around to *doing* it. Until you walk in, with a clear idea of exactly what skills you have. Then they decide they don't want to let you get away, since *good employees are as hard to find as are good employers.*

At this point, they suddenly remember the job they have been thinking about creating for many weeks or months, now.

So, they dust off their *intention*, create the job on the spot, and offer it to you! And if that new job is not only what *they* need, but is exactly what *you* were looking for, then you have: Match-match. Win-win.

From our country's perspective, it is interesting to note that by this job-hunting initiative of yours, you have helped *accelerate* the creation of more jobs in your country. How nice to help your country, as well as yourself!

And so, the paradoxical moral of all this: The less you try to 'stay loose' and open to *anything*, the more you define in detail your skills with *Data/Information* and/or *People* and/or *Things*, and at the highest level you legitimately can, **the more likely you are to find a job.** *Just the opposite of what the typical job-hunter or career-changer starts out believing.*

SOME QUICK STRATEGIES
FOR IDENTIFYING YOUR
TRANSFERABLE SKILLS

Ten Tips For The Impatient Job-Hunter

1

✳ Take the job-label off yourself *("I am an auto-worker," etc.)* and define yourself instead as *"I am a person who can . . ."* Then think of how you would finish that sentence. What tasks? What skills can you do? Make a list.

2

✳ Think of some other line (or lines) of work that you could do, can do, and would enjoy doing. Perhaps it's something you've already done, in a very small way, in your spare time *(like: make dresses, repair sailboats, etc.)* Then: what skills does it take to do that? Add these to your list.

3

✳ Ask yourself: "What am I good at? What does everyone tell me?" What skills does it take, etc., etc. Add these to your list.

4

✳ What turns you on? If a thing turns you on, you'll be good at it; if it doesn't, you won't. What energizes you? List the work, and tasks, that energize you, that give you your power in life. What skills are you using at such times? On the list you're keeping, put them down, and put a plus in front of them. Then: what exhausts you with very little effort and for very little reason? What skills are you using at such a time? List them, too, but this time put a minus sign in front of them. Skills that exhaust you usually do so for a reason: you don't like to use them. Avoid them.

5

✳ Ask yourself: "What have I done in the past that I really loved doing?" What are your hobbies? Astronomy? Aerospace? Airplanes? Bicycling? Birding? Boating or kayaking? Books? Cars? Caves? Collecting coins, or stamps, or dolls, or anything else? Cooking? Crafts? Dance? Electronics? Fishing? Flowers or gardening? Genealogy? Horses? Hunting? Juggling? Magic? Martial arts or other physical stuff? Minerals or rocks? Models? Motorcycles? The outdoors? Pets? Photography? Puppetry? Trains? Travel? Woodworking? Or what? Ask yourself, "What *did* I like about these things? What do I *still* like doing?" See what kinds of skills any of these might point to, for you. Add them to your list.

6

✳ Ask yourself: do I primarily like to use my skills with People, or my skills with Things, or my skills with Information? And, which ones? Add them to your list.

7

✳ What natural sensitivities do you have, that you don't think everyone else necessarily has? This could be things your eyes pick up (e.g., colors, facial expressions, bodies showing injury); *or* things your ears pick up (e.g., birdsongs); *or* things your nose picks up (e.g., faint odors in the air); *or* things your mouth picks up (e.g., peculiar tastes); *or* things your body picks up (e.g., air currents, temperature changes); *or* things your brain picks up (e.g., connections, disharmony, remembering details), etc., etc. Add them to your list.

8

✳ What skills, when you even hear their name, do you instinctively feel you possess? Here is a list to choose from. Put a check mark in front of each skill that you believe you possess. Put a star in front of each skill that you enjoy doing. And put a circle in front of each skill that you believe you do well.

The ones, at the end, that have a check mark *and* a star *and* a circle are the ones you should pay particular attention to. Add them to your list.

A List of 246 Skills as Verbs

achieving	acting	adapting	addressing	administering
advising	analyzing	anticipating	arbitrating	arranging
ascertaining	assembling	assessing	attaining	auditing
budgeting	building	calculating	charting	checking
classifying	coaching	collecting	communicating	compiling
completing	composing	computing	conceptualizing	conducting
conserving	consolidating	constructing	controlling	coordinating
coping	counseling	creating	deciding	defining
delivering	designing	detailing	detecting	determining
developing	devising	diagnosing	digging	directing
discovering	dispensing	displaying	disproving	dissecting
distributing	diverting	dramatizing	drawing	driving
editing	eliminating	empathizing	enforcing	establishing
estimating	evaluating	examining	expanding	experimenting
explaining	expressing	extracting	filing	financing
fixing	following	formulating	founding	gathering
generating	getting	giving	guiding	handling
having responsibility	heading	helping	hypothesizing	identifying
illustrating	imagining	implementing	improving	improvising
increasing	influencing	informing	initiating	innovating
inspecting	inspiring	installing	instituting	instructing
integrating	interpreting	interviewing	intuiting	inventing
inventorying	investigating	judging	keeping	leading
learning	lecturing	lifting	listening	logging
maintaining	making	managing	manipulating	mediating
meeting	memorizing	mentoring	modeling	monitoring
motivating	navigating	negotiating	observing	obtaining
offering	operating	ordering	organizing	originating
overseeing	painting	perceiving	performing	persuading
photographing	piloting	planning	playing	predicting
preparing	prescribing	presenting	printing	problem solving
processing	producing	programming	projecting	promoting
proof-reading	protecting	providing	publicizing	purchasing
questioning	raising	reading	realizing	reasoning
receiving	recommending	reconciling	recording	recruiting
reducing	referring	rehabilitating	relating	remembering
rendering	repairing	reporting	representing	researching
resolving	responding	restoring	retrieving	reviewing
risking	scheduling	selecting	selling	sensing
separating	serving	setting	setting-up	sewing
shaping	sharing	showing	singing	sketching
solving	sorting	speaking	studying	summarizing
supervising	supplying	symbolizing	synergizing	synthesizing
systematizing	taking instructions	talking	teaching	team-building
telling	tending	testing & proving	training	transcribing
translating	traveling	treating	trouble-shooting	tutoring
typing	umpiring	understanding	understudying	undertaking
unifying	uniting	upgrading	using	utilizing
verbalizing	washing	weighing	winning	working
writing				

9

＊ Weigh what problems your skills in the past have helped solve for an employer. For example, did your skills help that employer with: making customers want to return, the quality of service, the quality of the merchandise, the timeliness of deliveries, bringing costs down, inventing new products, *or what*? If so, which skills enabled you to do this? Add these to your skills list.

10

＊ Ask yourself: "Among all the people I've met, or know, or have read about, whose job would I most love to have?" Then: what skills does it take to do that? Do you have them? Add them to your list.

HOW TO IDENTIFY YOUR TRANSFERABLE SKILLS IN GREATER DETAIL

If none of this works for you, or if it represents a good beginning, but you want to go deeper, then turn to The Exercises on p. 267, and do the skills analysis described there.

It involves writing seven stories from your life -- times when you were really enjoying yourself -- and then seeing what skills you used there.

Here is a specific example of such a story, so you can see how it is done:

"I wanted to be able to take a summer trip with my wife and four children. I had a very limited budget, and could not afford to put my family up, in motels. I decided to rig our station wagon as a camper.

"First I went to the library to get some books on campers. I read those books. Next I designed a plan of what I had to build, so that I could outfit the inside of the station wagon, as well as topside. Then I went and purchased the necessary wood. On weekends, over a period of six weeks, I first constructed, in my driveway, the shell for the 'second story' on my station wagon. Then I cut doors, windows, and placed a six-drawer bureau within that shell. I mounted it on top of

the wagon, and pinioned it in place by driving two-by-fours under the station wagon's rack on top. I then outfitted the inside of the station wagon, back in the wheelwell, with a table and a bench on either side, that I made.

"The result was a complete homemade camper, which I put together when we were about to start our trip, and then disassembled after we got back home. When we went on our summer trip, we were able to be on the road for four weeks, yet stayed within our budget, since we didn't have to stay at motels.

"I estimate I saved $1900 on motel bills, during that summer's vacation."

Ideally, each story you write should have the following parts, as illustrated above:

I.) Your goal: what you wanted to accomplish: "I wanted to be able to take a summer trip with my marriage partner and four children."

II.) Some kind of hurdle, obstacle, or constraint that you faced (self-imposed or otherwise): "I had a very limited budget, and could not afford to put my family up, in motels."

III.) A description of what you did, step by step (how you set about to ultimately achieve your goal, above, in spite of this hurdle or constraint): *"I decided to rig our station wagon as a camper. First I went to the library to get some books on campers. I read those books. Next I designed a plan of what I had to build, so that I could outfit the inside of the station wagon, as well as topside. Then I went and purchased the necessary wood. On weekends, over a period of six weeks, I . . ." etc., etc.*

IV.) A description of the outcome or result: *"When we went on our summer trip, we were able to be on the road for four weeks, yet stayed within our budget, since we didn't have to stay at motels."*

V.) Any measurable/quantifiable statement of that outcome, that you can think of: *"I estimate I saved $1900 on motel bills, during that summer's vacation."*

The Exercises on page 267ff will take you through this whole process of analyzing seven stories, identifying your transferable skills, and prioritizing them, as below.

PRIORITIZING YOUR FAVORITE SKILLS

There are three steps to skill-identification. You may think of them as: *Inventory, Prioritize, Flesh Them Out.*

Once you have inventoried the transferable skills that you possess, it is *crucial* for you to move on to the second step (Prioritize), by deciding which ones are your favorites. And you must then put your top six most favorite skills -- whether with **Data** or **People** or **Things** -- in exact order of priority, on the following diagram:

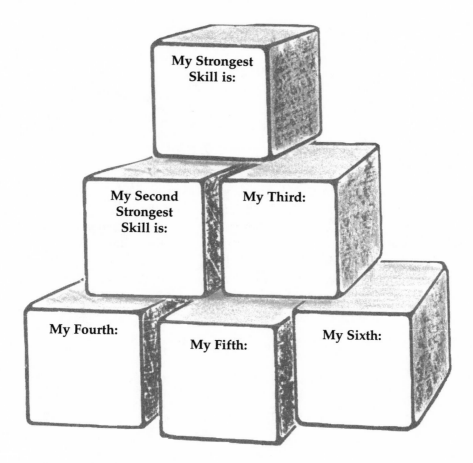

'FLESHING OUT' ONE-WORD DEFINITIONS OF SKILLS

Once you have identified your favorite transferable skills, and put them in order of priority for you as to which ones you enjoy the most, it is time to move on to the third step in skill-identification: *fleshing out* your description of your six favorites, with more than just one word.

Suppose you've listed:

That's a fine start at defining your skill, but unfortunately it doesn't yet tell us much. Organizing what? *People,* as at a party? *Nuts and bolts,* as on a workbench? Or *lots of information,* as on a computer? These are three entirely different skills. The one word *organizing* doesn't tell us which one is *yours.* So, you must *flesh out* each of your favorite transferable verbs with some object -- some kind of **Data/Information,** or some kind of **People,** or some kind of **Thing** -- such as:

"I'm good at organizing information."

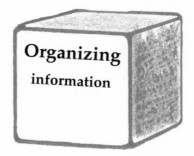

Finally, if you can, add some adverb or adjective phrase. Why? Well,

"I'm good at organizing information *painstakingly and logically*"
and
"I'm good at organizing information *in a flash, by intuition,*"

are two *entirely different* skills. The difference between them is spelled out not in the verb, and not in the object, but in the adjectival or adverbial phrase there at the end.

So, now, what do we end up with? Something like this, in the case of each of your six favorite skills:

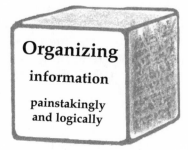

Organizing

information

painstakingly
and logically

Now, that's a good skill-identification -- because it makes you stand out, from 19 other 'organizers'!

When you are face-to-face with a person-who-has-the-power-to-hire-you, you want to be able to explain what makes you different from nineteen other people who can basically do the same thing that you can do. It is often the **adjective** or **adverb** that will save your life, during that explanation.

CONCLUSION

When you have done this with all six of your favorite transferable skills, Voila! You are finished defining WHAT.

In case you've read this whole section, but haven't yet actually gone and done The Exercises, and you feel "Oh, I just can't do all those stories," you may be interested in how a woman job-hunter in England, avoided writing the stories, but found another way (the PIE method she refers to, is fully described in the next chapter):

"I have a Ph.D. in Chemistry, but the last thing I wanted to do on graduating was to work in a laboratory or a research group. I read your book, and tried -- but failed -- to write the stories; it required too much soul-searching! Consequently, it took me nine months before I decided on a new career path. It was Daniel Porot's PIE method that got me there -- Practice Interviewing, Informational Interviewing, Employment Interviewing. It helped build my confidence enormously, and I felt I had the power -- rather than being the victim of the employment market. I followed your ideas and advice, and have just been offered my first permanent position. I am overjoyed, because I chose this new career looking at my interests and skills, rather than my qualifications. Now I am a Clinical Research Scientist in a hospital. I feel now at long last, at 27 years of age, I am finally on the right track to finding my mission in life."

"WHILE YOU'RE WAITING FOR YOUR SHIP TO COME IN, WHY DON'T YOU DO SOME MAINTENANCE WORK ON THE PIER ?"

A Friendly Word to Procrastinators

If two weeks have gone by, and you haven't even *started* doing the inventory described in this chapter and in the Exercises, then -- I hate to tell you this -- you're going to have to get someone to help you.

Your life in the world of work will consume 80,000 hours of your time on this earth. Yet, most of us spend more time planning next summer's vacation, which will consume only 224 hours of our time on this earth, than we do in trying to figure out what we want to do with those 80,000 hours.

So, don't procrastinate any longer! Choose a helper for your job-hunt -- a friend rather than family, if possible. A tough friend -- you know, *taskmaster*. Ask them if they're willing to help you. Assuming they say yes, put down in *both* your appointment books a regular *weekly* date when you will guarantee to meet with them, and they will guarantee to meet with you, check you out on what you've done already, and be very stern with you if you've done little or nothing since last week's meeting.

If you have no friend who will help you, then you're probably going to want to think about professional help. (See pages 305–335, in Appendix B.) Go talk to several career-counselors. Choose the one you like best, and *get on with it.*

You've only one life to live, my friend. The time to make sure it is the life you really most want, is now.

I have learned this
At least, by my experiment:
If one advances confidently
In the direction of his dreams,
And endeavors to live
The life he has imagined,
He will meet with a success
Unexpected in common hours.

—Henry David Thoreau

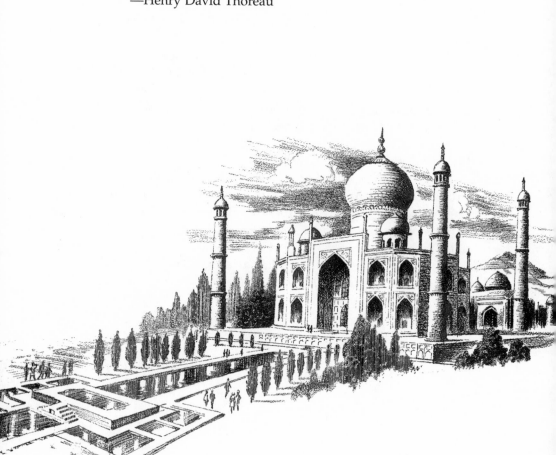

CHAPTER FIVE

The Systematic Approach To
Career-Change
And Job-Hunting

Where

DO YOU MOST WANT TO
USE THOSE SKILLS?

You Must Figure Out
Just Exactly What Field
and What Kinds of Places
You Would Most Delight to Work In

Chapter 5

YOU'LL LIKE THIS JOB, EXCEPT EVERY NOW AND THEN, WHEN THEY DUMP A LOT OF PAPER WORK ON YOU.

THE THREE STEPS TO JOB-HUNTING (AND CAREER-CHANGING) SUCCESS: WHAT, WHERE AND HOW

We come now to the second part of the creative approach to job-hunting and career-change. In case two weeks (or two months!) have passed since you last looked at the previous chapter, let me briefly summarize.

In the previous chapter we dealt with the first part of the creative approach, What, viz:

1. What: You must decide just exactly what you have to offer to the world. This involves identifying your gifts, or talents -- which is to say, your favorite skills, *in order of priority or importance to you.*

In this chapter, the one you are presently reading, we come to the second question:

2. Where: **You must decide just exactly where you want to use your skills.** This involves identifying your *favorite subjects* or fields of interest, as well as your geographical preferences, which you then explore through *research* (in books or on the Internet), and personal *informational interviewing.* **Where** is primarily a matter of the **fields of knowledge** *you have already acquired*, which you most enjoy using.

But it also has to do with your preferred working conditions, what kinds of data or people or things you enjoy working with, where you'd most like to live, etc.

Once you know your favorite subjects, you have the building blocks of your field; with these building-blocks, you can define a field that you would love to do your occupation in.

Also, you can now put occupation and field together, to define a career that you would love to do.

So: in the previous chapter, you did the homework on your favorite **skills** -- *or at least saw how it is done.*

But, as we have seen, it is not sufficient to simply say *I love using my skills.* You must define for yourself Where you want to use those skills, that is, in what field. And the building blocks of your field are your favorite knowledges.

THE FIVE
STEPS TO
'WHERE'

You approach Where through a series of five steps, each taken in turn. They are:

• STEP #1

What are the names of my favorite subjects or interests?

• STEP #2

What field do these interests point me toward?

• STEP #3

What occupation in this field do I especially like?

• STEP #4

What **career** would give me a chance to do this occupation in this field -- combining my most enjoyable skills with my greatest interests?

• STEP #5

What are the names of organizations that hire people who choose this career, and match my particular values?

Now let us see how you find the answers to these questions, step by step (all five of them).

Where

Step One:

Your
Favorite Subjects
or
Interests

The thing we are looking for here -- 'Favorite **knowledges**' -- has two other names. They are sometimes called 'favorite **subjects**.' And they are sometimes called "your **interests**."

All three terms are pretty interchangeable, and refer to the fact that each of us knows a little bit about a lot of things. Among all the things we know something about, we naturally have preferences. Some subjects interest us; some don't.

Take my case. I know a little bit about accounting, but I'm basically not interested in the subject.

I know a lot about fundraising, but again, I'm basically not interested in the subject.

On the other hand, I know a lot about job-hunting, and I am interested in the subject. Very.

You see the point, I'm sure. One of my interests (there are others) is: job-hunting. Another way of saying it, is: job-hunting is one of my favorite subjects.

Now, turning from my life to yours, the question at hand is: What subjects or bodies of knowledge are *you* interested in? Even better, which subjects *turn you on?*

SOME QUICK STRATEGIES FOR IDENTIFYING YOUR FAVORITE SUBJECTS OR INTERESTS

Ten Tips For The Impatient Job-Hunter or Career-Changer[1]

1

❋ What are your favorite hobbies or interests *(Computers? Gardening? Spanish? Law? Physics? Department stores? Hospitals? etc., etc.)*? Start a list.

2

❋ What do you love to talk about? Ask yourself: if you were stuck on a desert island with a person who only had the capacity to speak on a few subjects, what would you pray those subjects were?

If you were at a get-together, talking with someone who was covering two of your favorite subjects at once, which way would you hope the conversation would go? Toward which subject?

If you could talk about *something* with some world expert, all day long, day after day, what would that subject or field of interest be? Add any ideas that these questions spark in you, to your list.

3

❋ What magazine articles do you love to read? I mean, what subjects? You get really interested when you see a magazine article that deals with. . . . *what subject?* Add any ideas to your list.

4

❋ What newspaper articles do you love to read? You get really interested when you see a newspaper special report that deals with. . . . *what subject?* Add any ideas, here, to your list.

---

1. I am indebted to Daniel Porot of Geneva, Switzerland, for many of these suggestions.

5

⁕ If you're browsing in a bookstore, what sections of the bookstore do you tend to gravitate towards? What subjects there do you find really fascinating? Add any ideas, here, to your list.

6

⁕ What sites on the Internet (if you have Internet access) do you tend to gravitate towards? What subjects do these sites deal with? Do any of these really fascinate you? Add any ideas, here, to your list.

7

⁕ If you watch TV, and it's a 'game show,' which categories would you pick? If it's an educational program, what kinds of subjects do you stop and watch? Add them to your list.

8

⁕ When you look at a catalog of courses that you could take in your town or city (or on TV), which subjects really interest you? Add any ideas, here, to your list.

9

⁕ If you could write a book, and it wasn't about your own life or somebody else's, what *would* be the subject of the book? Add it to your list.

10

⁕ There are moments, in most of our lives, when we are so engrossed in a task, that we lose all track of time. *(Someone has to remind us that it's time for supper, or whatever.)* If this ever happens to you, what task, what subject, so absorbs your attention that you lose all track of time? Add it to your list.

DON'T DECIDE
YOUR FUTURE
BEFORE YOU'VE FIRST
INVENTORIED
YOUR PAST

The quick exercises above may yield a very satisfying list of your favorite subjects, or interests. That's if your knowledge of yourself is very very clear.

But in most cases our self-knowledge could use a little more work. A weekend would do.

In a weekend, you can cast a wider net, and inventory *all* the fields you know anything about - - whether or not they are your favorites. *(You can, of course, stretch the inventory over a longer period of time, if you prefer. It's up to you as to just how you do it.)*

On the following page, fill out each column. *You can copy this chart on to a larger piece of paper (or to a spreadsheet on your computer) if you need more room.*

Here are three points to keep in mind, as you fill this out.

1. **Every column/category on the chart is worth thinking about.**

2. **It is only necessary that you love talking about a subject, and know *something* about it - - it is not necessary that you have a *mastery* of it.** Your degree of *mastery* is irrelevant - - unless you want to work at a level in the subject or field that demands and requires mastery.

3. **It doesn't matter *how* you picked up the knowledge.** As John Crystal used to say, it doesn't matter whether you learned it in college, or sitting at the end of a log. It can be a subject that you just picked up a lot of knowledge about as you went along the way in life - - say, *antiques,* or *cars,* or *interior decorating,* or *music* or *movies* or *psychology,* or *the kind of subjects that come up on television 'game shows.'* Let's take *antiques* as an example. Suppose it's one of your favorite subjects, yet you never studied it in school. You picked up your knowledge of antiques by going around to antique stores, and asking lots of questions. And you supplemented this by reading a few books on the subject, and you subscribe to an antiques magazine. You've also bought a few antiques, yourself. That's enough, for you to put antiques on your list of subjects or interests.

Subjects I Know Something About

Which column you decide to put a subject in, below, doesn't matter at all. The columns are only a series of pegs, to hang your memories on. Which peg, is of no concern. Jot down a subject anywhere you like.

Column 1	Column 2	Column 3	Column 4	Column 5
Studied in High School or College or Graduate School	Learned on the Job	Learned from Conferences, Workshops, Training, Seminars	Learned at Home: Reading, TV, Tape Programs, Study Courses	Learned in My Leisure Time: Volunteer Work, Hobbies, etc.
Examples: Spanish, Typing, Accounting, Computer Literacy, Psychology, Geography	*Examples: Publishing, Computer graphics, How an organization works, How to operate various machines*	*Examples: Welfare rules, Job-hunting, Painting, How to Use the Internet*	*Examples: Art Appreciation, History, Speed Reading, A Language*	*Examples: Landscaping, How to sew, Antiques, Camping, Stamps*

PRIORITIZING YOUR FAVORITE KNOWLEDGES OR INTERESTS

Once you have made an inventory of the subjects you *know something about*, the next step is to pick out your favorites from among them all. You must not skip over this step.

The quickest way to pick out your favorites is to look at the chart and your other lists, and simply let your instinct or intuition tell you which is your favorite subject -- or your *three* favorites.

The Game of Paper and Bowl

Sometimes playing a game will help your intuition.

(1) Go to your chart, and copy each subject by itself on a little slip of paper.

(2) Then get a bowl (of any size), and play this pretend game: you have to give away all those subjects to others, except for three that you may keep for yourself.

(3) One by one drop into the bowl any piece of paper that has a subject written on it that you are willing to give to someone else.

(4) If you come to a piece of paper that has a subject on it you aren't sure you want to let go of, hold on to it.

(5) Keep going, until you are left with only the subjects you just can't bear to give away; they may be one to twenty en toto.

(6) At this point, empty the bowl, and now from those subjects that remain in your hand, drop into the empty bowl the subject you are *least reluctant* to let go of. Repeat, with the pieces of paper that remain in your hand. Keep going, until you are down to just three pieces of paper in your hand. All the subjects in the bowl (now) are worth jotting down on a piece of paper. But the ones that remain in your hand are the subjects or interests you care the most about.

If you'd prefer a more step-by-step left-brain approach, then from the chart and other list(s), randomly pick out what you think are your top ten favorites (in no particular order), and then turn to the Prioritizing Grid on page 279. Using that Grid and comparing those ten just two at a time, you will be able to put them in exact order of your own personal preference: "this is my favorite," "this is my next favorite," and so on, and so forth.

Put your top three on the following diagram:

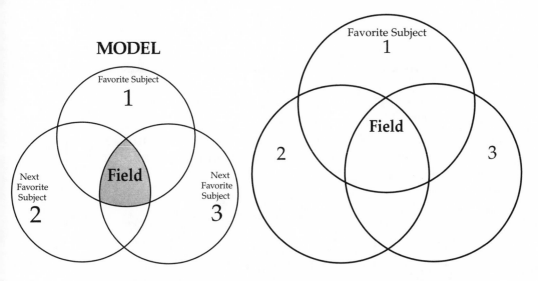

As I said earlier, your favorite Subjects form the building blocks for defining your favorite Field. Since you now know your three favorite Subjects, you are ready to define your "Field."

Where

Step Two:

Your Favorite Field

THE JOB-MARKET VS. YOUR HEART

The way in which most people choose a field is from a list of what **the job-market** wants. Magazines, newspapers and the Internet just *love* lists like these:

The Top Ten Fields In Terms of Percentage-Growth Between Now And The Year 2006

Computer and data processing services (experts think this field will have grown 108% between 1996 and 2006), Health services (68%), Management and public relations (60%), Miscellaneous transportation services (60%), Residential care (59%), Personnel supply services (53%), Water and sanitation (51%), Individual and miscellaneous social services (50%), Offices of health practitioners (47%), Amusement and recreation services (41%).[2]

The Top Ten Fields In Terms of Pay (Median Earnings)

Engineering, mathematics, computer and information sciences, pharmacy, architecture/environmental design, physics, accounting, economics, health/medical technologies, and physical therapy.[3]

We are brainwashed, from our youth up, to thus let the job-market determine what field we should go into. Unfortunately, choosing a field in this manner often puts us into a field we learn to cordially hate as we grow older. It's like putting on a suit that's three sizes too small for us. The 'fit' is terrible!

The Creative Minority's prescription for how you choose a field starts at the opposite end: it begins, not with the job-market, but with you!

You! What are your passions? What is your mission on earth? What are your dreams? Talk to yourself! Tell yourself what your interests are. And *then* choose a field that honors and uses those interests.

You should be the guiding light in how you choose a field -- not the job-market, with its alleged needs.

If you choose a field you love, will there be jobs you can do, in that field? Of course -- but we can figure those out later!

If you choose a field you love, will there be vacancies in that field? Of course -- but we can scout those out later!

For now, choose a field you love! Choose a field that fits you, by identifying your interests -- the subjects to which your heart is drawn -- as you have just done; and then letting the top three point to a field that uses them all.

Begin with your heart! Find a field you love, and you will hunt for a job in it with every fibre of your being. **Passion is the key to perseverance, and perseverance is the key to finding a job.**

That's the prescription for finding work you can love. That's the prescription for finding your mission in life. That's the prescription for job-hunting success. So say the Creative Minority, with their 86% success rate!

2. http://stats.bls.gov/news.release/ecopro.table4.htm

3. Source: "Earnings of college graduates, 1993: Fields of study is a major determinant of the wide variations in earnings." *Monthly Labor Review,* December 1995.

COMBINING
INTERESTS
TO FORM
A FIELD

How do we put three interests of yours together to form or define a field? Let's take an example of an actual job-hunter/career-changer, whom we'll call Larry.

After doing the exercises above, Larry discovered that his three favorite interests or favorite subjects were: psychiatry, plants, and carpentry.

So far, so good. Now, how did he define a field, from these? The same way you will. There are seven steps to be followed:

1. **You're going to have to go talk with people.** Printed resources usually won't 'cut it' for this part of the process. You're going to have to talk with people, either face-to-face, or on the phone, or through an Internet newsgroup.

2. **Choose an expert in each of your favorite three knowledges.** How did Larry choose who to talk to? He took his favorite knowledges or interests, above -- psychiatry, plants, and carpentry -- and tried to think of an expert in each subject.

For psychiatry, the expert was obviously a psychiatrist, or a professor of psychiatry at a nearby university.

For plants, the expert was obviously a gardener or landscape artist.

And for carpentry, the expert was obviously a carpenter.

3. **Get names for each of those 'expert' categories.** Having chosen the *occupational categories*, Larry had to then go find names of actual psychiatrists, gardeners, and carpenters. How did he do that? Combination of the telephone company's Yellow Pages, and anyone from among the people he already knew, who was either a psychiatrist, or gardener, or carpenter.

4. **Plan to go talk to them**. Face-to-face is best, but you can use the phone or Internet mailing lists, of course.

5. **Decide to visit first the expert with the largest overview.** This is often, but not always, the same as asking: who took the longest to get their training? The particular answer here, from among psychiatrists, gardeners and carpenters: *the psychiatrists.*

6. **Visit two or three of these experts, in each category. Don't take just one person's word for anything.** Larry went to see three psychiatrists -- the head of the psychiatry department at

the nearest university, plus two in active practice,[4] and (showing them his three-circles diagram, below) he asked them:

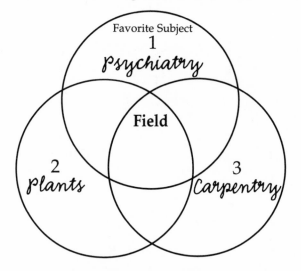

Do you have any idea how to put these three interests of mine -- carpentry, plants, and psychiatry -- together into one field or career? He knows it may be a career that already exists, *or* it may be he will have to create this career for himself.

7. **If the experts don't know, ask them for a referral.** Experts are good for two things: the actual information you're looking for; or the suggestion of the name of another expert -- who might know what they don't.

In Larry's case, he kept going until he found how you can put all three of his interests together in one field. A psychiatrist eventually told him:

"There is a branch of psychiatry that uses plants to help heal people, particularly those who have been catatonic.

"That would combine your interest in plants and psychiatry. As for your carpentry interests, I suppose you could use that to build the planters for your plants."

Voila! Larry had found his field, even though it didn't have a *precise* name in his mind, as yet:

---

4. If there were no psychiatrists at any academic institution near him, then he would do all his research with psychiatrists in private practice -- getting their names from the phone book -- and asking them for, and paying for, *a half session.* This, if there is no other way.

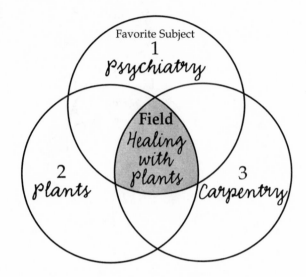

And so can you, if you just follow these seven steps.

When you know the name of a field that uses your three favorite subjects or three greatest interests, put the name of that Field in the center of your three-circles diagram here (or on page 264).

Put Your Three Favorite Subjects
and the Field They Point To
Here:

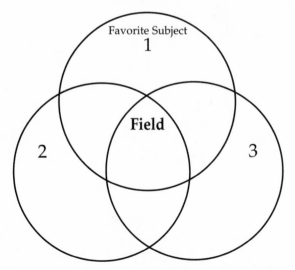

A Sampler of Internet Resources about Fields

Once you've identified a field, you want to find out more about it. There is the Internet, of course. Go to my Web site, if you have Internet access (www.jobhuntersbible.com), and then to the subdivision of my Net-Guide called "Research." There, under the subheading, "Research Sites: Career Fields," you will find a list of sites that may help you find information about the field you have chosen.

A Sampler of Print Resources about Fields

There are also resources in print that you can turn to, in your local libraries. They include:

Occupational Outlook Handbook. Department of Labor, NTC Publishing Group, 225 W. Touhy Ave., Lincolnwood, IL 60646.

Occupational Outlook Handbook for College Graduates. Superintendent of Documents, U.S. Government.

Dictionary of Holland Occupational Codes.

Dictionary of Occupational Titles.

Encyclopedia of Associations, Vol. 1, National Organizations of the U.S.; Vol. 2, Geographic and Executive Indexes; Vol. 3, New Associations and Projects. Gale Research, Inc., 835 Penobscott Bldg. Detroit, MI 48226-4094. Lists 25,000 organizations, associations, clubs and other nonprofit membership groups that are in the business of giving out information. There is a companion series of books: *Regional, State and Local Organizations,* a five-volume set, which lists over 50,000 similar organizations on a regional, state or local level. There is another companion volume, also: *International Organizations.* This lists 4,000 international organizations, concerned with various subjects.

Newsletters in Print. Gale Research, Inc., 835 Penobscott Bldg. Detroit, MI 48226-4094. Detailed entry on 10,000 newsletters in various subject fields, or categories. It includes newsletters that are available only online, through a computer and modem.

Standard and Poor's Industry Surveys. Good basic introduction, history, and overview of any industry you may be interested in.

Standard Industrial Classification Manual. 1991. Reprint of material originally published by the U.S. Government Printing Office. Available from: Gordon Press, P.O. Box 459, Bowling Green Station, New York, NY 10003. Gives the Standard Industrial Classification code number for any field or industry -- (often called the SIC code) which is the number used by most business references in their indices. Soon to be replaced.

U.S. Industrial Outlook. Reprinted from material published by the U.S. Department of Commerce. Available from JIST Works, 720 N. Park Ave., Indianapolis, IN 46202. Covers 350 manufacturing and service industries. Gives the trends and outlooks for each industry that you may be interested in. Updated annually.

Information Industry Directory. Gale Research, Inc., 835 Penobscott Bldg. Detroit, MI 48226-4094. Lists 30,000 computer-based information systems and services, here and abroad. Their companion volume, *Gale Directory of Databases.* Gale Research, Inc., 835 Penobscott Bldg. Detroit, MI 48226-4094, lists trade shows, conventions, users' groups, associations, consultants, etc., worldwide.

Professional's Job Finder, by Daniel Lauber. Planning/Communications, 7215 Oak Ave., River Forest, IL 60305. Lists over 3,003 associations, directories, journals, trade magazines, newsletters, computerized job-listings, online services, job-matching services, salary surveys, etc. -- *categorized* very helpfully by fields, industries and occupations -- where contacts may be found, or job-leads advertised. Very thorough.

Non-Profits' and Education Job Finder, by Daniel Lauber. Planning/Communications, 7215 Oak Ave., River Forest, IL 60305. Lists over 2,222 associations, directories, journals, trade magazines, newsletters, computerized job-listings, online services, job-matching services, foundations, grants, and salary surveys, etc. -- dealing with education and all of the non-profit sector -- where contacts may be found, or job-leads advertised.

Government Job Finder, by Daniel Lauber. Planning/Communications, 7215 Oak Ave., River Forest, IL 60305. Lists over 2,002 associations, directories, journals, trade magazines, newsletters, computerized job-listings, online services, job-matching services, salary surveys, etc. -- dealing with local, state or federal government work in the U.S. and abroad -- where contacts may be found, or job-leads advertised. Very thorough. Also, free updates are available online for all three of these books at:
`http://jobfindersonline.com`

National Recreational Sporting and Hobby Organizations of the U.S. Columbia Books, Inc., 777 14th St. NW, Washington, DC 20005.

Research Center Directory. Gale Research, Inc., 835 Penobscott Bldg. Detroit, MI 48226-4094. Also: *Research Services Directory.* The two volumes together cover some 13,000 services, facilities, and companies that do research into various subjects, such as feasibility studies, private and public policy, social studies and studies of various cultures, etc.

Where

Step Three:

Your Favorite Occupation

WHAT CAN YOU DO
IN YOUR CHOSEN FIELD?

Look at your circle diagram. Think about the field you've written there. Enjoy the thought of working in it.

Now, what you may well be thinking next is: "Well, I see what field it is that I would love to work in, but I know there is no job in that field that *I* would be able to do."

An understandable fear! But, dear friend, let me say it gently: you don't know any such thing. **There is some place for your skills, in any field you choose.**

A field is like a meadow, a large meadow. No matter what field you choose, lots of people are out standing in it.

Let us take Movies, Cinema, or the Film Industry as our example.

Suppose you love Movies, and want to choose this field for your next career. Your first instinct will be to think that this means if you don't have skills as an actor or actress, or a screen writer, or a director, or movie critic, there's nothing for you in this field.

Not true. There are many other skills needed in this field called Movies. The closing credits at the end of any movie will show you what those skills are -- and their occupational name:

Researchers *(especially for movies set in another time)*, Travel experts *(to scout locations)*, Interior designers *(to design sets)*, Carpenters *(to build them)*, Painters *(for backdrops, etc.)*, Artists, computer graphics designers *(for special effects)*, Costume designers, Make-up artists, Hair stylists, Photographers *(camera operators)*, Lighting technicians, Sound mixers and sound editors, Composers *(for soundtrack)*, Conductors, Musicians, Singers, Stunt people, Animal trainers, Caterers, Drivers, First aid people, Personal assistants, Secretaries, Publicists, Accountants, etc., etc.

And so it is with any field.

No matter what your transferable skills are, they can be used in any meadow or field that you choose.

PUTTING A NAME
TO YOUR SKILLS

Now, and only now, that you have identified a field where you could happily use your favorite skills, is it time to put an occupational name to those skills you identified (*in the previous chapter*) as your favorite transferable skills.

Here's how you go about doing that.

1. **On one piece of paper, write down your six favorite transferable skills, plus your chosen field.** Put the skills on the top half of the paper, the field that you just identified, on the bottom half. Under the name of the field, add your three favorite interests. Thus, in Larry's case, the bottom half of his paper would read:

Healing with Plants
  (Psychiatry)
  (Plants)
  (Carpentry)

Every field gives you a broad choice between jobs with *people*, jobs with *data*, or jobs with *things*. Let's take the field of agriculture as an example. Within agriculture:

You could be driving tractors and other farm machinery -- and thus be working primarily with **things**; or

You could be gathering statistics about crop growth for some state agency -- and thus be working primarily with **information**/data/ideas; or

You could be supervising a crew on a farm, and thus be working primarily with **people**.

Many jobs combine two or more of these factors, as for example teaching in an agricultural college -- thus working with both **information** and **people**.

You have to decide, after looking at your favorite transferable skills, which of these three would be your priority in your chosen field. Write it at the top of the paper.

2. **At the very top of the paper, now write down whether -- broadly speaking -- you want to work primarily with people, or primarily with information/data/ideas, or primarily with things.**

3. **Choose at least ten friends, family, or professionals whom you know, to show this paper to.** These people should be from as many different backgrounds, education, and occupations, as possible. Try to include, when you can, people from the field that interests you.

4. **Show this piece of paper to them.** Tell them you are looking for names of occupations that would use these skills. Ask each one of them to look at the paper, to look at the skills in particular, and tell you what job or jobs these suggest to them.

5. **Jot down** *everything* **these ten people tell you.**

6. **If none of it looks valuable, choose five additional people you know in the business world and non-profit sector or your (new) chosen field.** Go show them your paper; ask them the same questions, as before.

7. **Once you've got some worthwhile ideas, go home, and study what they have said.**

SOME QUICK STRATEGIES FOR IDENTIFYING YOUR OCCUPATION

Seven Tips For The Impatient Job-Hunter or Career-Changer

If you're just too shy or too busy (I did not say, 'lazy') to do the above research, here are some quick strategies that may -- or may not -- be helpful, in putting a name to an occupation that you would love -- precisely because it would use your favorite transferable skills.

1

❊ After looking over your list of favorite transferable skills, ask yourself: which occupational family sounds as though it might match your favorite transferable skills. There are traditionally twenty such families, as follows:

OCCUPATION FAMILIES

1. Executive, Administrative, and Managerial Occupations
2. Engineers, Surveyors, and Architects
3. Natural Scientists and Mathematicians
4. Social Scientists, Social Workers, Religious Workers, and Lawyers
5. Teachers, Counselors, Librarians, and Archivists
6. Health Diagnosing and Treating Practitioners
7. Registered Nurses, Pharmacists, Dieticians, Therapists, and Physician Assistants
8. Health Technologists and Technicians
9. Writers, Artists, and Entertainers
10. Technologists and Technicians, Except Health
11. Marketing and Sales Occupations
12. Administrative Support Occupations, Including Clerical
13. Service Occupations
14. Agricultural, Forestry, and Fishing Occupations
15. Mechanics and Repairers
16. Construction and Extractive Occupations
17. Production Occupations
18. Transportation and Material Moving Occupations
19. Handlers, Equipment Cleaners, Helpers, and Laborers
20. Other

2

✳ If you want a longer list, we begin with the fact that experts can name at least 12,741 different occupations out there, with 8,000 alternative names, adding up to a grand total of more than 20,000.[5] Twenty thousand occupations to choose from! Most of us would find it impossible to choose between 20,000 of *anything*. In fact, we have trouble choosing between 20 items on a restaurant menu!

So of course, experts have produced shorter lists of occupations for you to look at. Some U.S. experts have hacked the 20,000 down to just 1,222 options, because (they say) you can find 95% of the 133 million workers in the U.S. in a mere 1,222 of those 20,000 occupations. (The other 18,778 job titles are filled by just 5% of the workforce.)[6]

And 50% of the 131 million workers in the U.S. are to be found in just 50 occupations (they say). See if any of these sound as though they might match your favorite transferable skills:

The Top Fifty Most Common Occupations

Automobile mechanics, carpenters, electricians, light- or heavy-truck drivers, construction laborers, welders & cutters, groundskeepers & gardeners, electrical and electronic engineers, freight, stock, and material movers or handlers, guards and police, production occupations, supervisors, farmers, commodities sales representatives, laborers, lawyers, farm workers, stockhandlers & baggers, insurance sales, janitors & cleaners, managers & administrators, supervisors & proprietors, machine operators, teachers -- university, college, secondary and elementary school, stock & inventory clerks, accountants & auditors, underwriters and other financial officers, secretaries, receptionists, childcare workers, registered nurses, typists, bookkeepers, textile sewing machine operators, nursing aides, orderlies & attendants, hairdressers & cosmetologists, waiters & waitresses, maids and housemen, cashiers, general office clerks, administrative support occupations, sales workers, computer operators, miscellaneous food preparation occupations, production inspectors, checkers & examiners, cooks, real estate salespeople, and assemblers. *You will note that many of these do not require extensive training or schooling.*

3

✳ If you want to be sure that your occupation is one that is in great demand, here are the Top Ten Occupations In Terms of Number of New Workers Needed By The Year 2006. See if any of these sound as though they might match your favorite transferable skills: Cashiers, Systems analysts, General managers and top executives, Registered nurses, Salespersons in retail, Truck drivers (light and heavy), Home health aides, Teacher aides and educational assistants, Nursing aides, orderlies and attendants, Receptionists and information clerks.[7] *You will note that many of these do not require extensive training or schooling.*

---

5. A description of 20,000 job-titles in the U.S. can be found in any U.S. library, in a volume known as the U.S. *Dictionary of Occupational Titles.* It is known more familiarly as the *D.O.T.,* and is published by the Bureau of Labor Statistics. Some other countries, notably Canada, have similar volumes.

While vocational experts always recommend using this directory, our readers have found it a *terribly unhelpful* book for the beginning of the twenty-first century. As one reader, a chemist, wrote: "While it claims to be updated to 1991, I found that *every* description I looked up was last updated in 1977! [That's over twenty years ago!] I read the description of my present occupation and it sounds quite good. I only wish I was doing what it described. That may have been what a chemist did 20 years ago but with most companies de-emphasizing research it is hardly what they do today." If you want to dabble in the D.O.T. despite this warning, be sure to supplement what you learn there by talking to people actually doing what you'd like to do. They'll tell you what the job or career is really like.

Incidentally, the D.O.T. is currently being updated and supplanted by O*NET (see the next footnote) The Occupational Information Network. For details, if you have Internet access, go to http://www.doleta.gov/almis/onetnew1.htm

6. This is the strategy of the U.S. Department of Labor, with O*NET. This O*NET system will eventually replace the D.O.T.'s 12,741 job-titles, with just 1,222 of its own.

7. http://stats.bls.gov/news.release/ecopro.table7.htm

4

﹡ If you feel, like Rodney Dangerfield, that you get no respect, and you're looking for an occupation that would give that to you, you might like to know what are The Top Ten Occupations In Terms of Prestige. See if any of these sound as though they might match your favorite transferable skills: Physician (Prestige Score: 82), College professor (78), Judge (76), Attorney (76), Astronomer (74), Dentist (74), Bank officer (72), Engineer (71), Architect (71), and Clergy (70).[8] *You will note that most of these require extensive training or schooling.*

5

﹡ If you've got bills and debts on your mind, here are the Top Ten Occupations In Terms of Pay. See if any of these sound as though they might match your favorite transferable skills: Physicians (Median salary: $148,000), Dentists ($93,000), Lobbyists ($91,000), Veterinarians ($63,069), Management consultants ($61,900), Lawyers ($60,500), Electrical engineers ($59,100), School principals ($57,300), Aeronautical engineers ($56,700), Airline pilots ($56,500), and Civil engineers ($55,800).[9] *You will again note that most of these require extensive training or schooling.*

6

﹡ And, finally, if you like to be 'on the cutting edge,' here is someone's idea of 'The Ten Hottest Occupations.' (No criteria were given, for what makes them the 'hottest.') See if any of these sound as though they might match your favorite transferable skills:

Computer animator, On-line content producer, *Mutual fund manager,* Industrial environmentalist, *Family doctor,* Management consultant, *Intellectual property lawyer,* Priest, rabbi, minister, *Interactive ad executive,* and Physical therapist.[10] *In some cases, extensive training or schooling is first required.*

---

8. Source: The National Opinion Research Center.

9. Source: *Money* Magazine, and *The Bureau of Labor Statistics*

10. Or so *P.O.V. Magazine* says (quoted in *USA Today,* April 11, 1996).

7

❋ Remember, one person's *best career* is another person's *poison*. Before you pick an occupation from a list, you have to first define for yourself what kind of work would make a good 'occupational-fit' for you -- in terms of skills used, tasks undertaken, field of interest worked with, preferred people environment, and so forth. You have to define all that, and until you do, you don't know whether you will thrive in those occupational waters, or sink like a stone.

If these tips give you some useful clues, great! But if not, you know what you must do: go back and do the research suggested prior to the tips here. And do it thoroughly, until you find the name of an occupation that *sounds* as though it matches your favorite transferable skills.

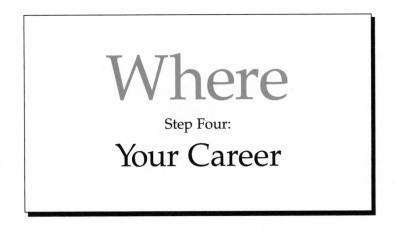

Where

Step Four:

Your Career

PUTTING OCCUPATION
AND FIELD TOGETHER

When you've found the name of an occupation that sounds interesting to you (*you may call your occupation by any name you please -- though one-word or two-word titles are preferred*) you're ready at last to define a career for yourself. Or two. Or three.

Our definition of a career, as you recall, is this equation: **a career = occupation + field**.

In Step Three, just completed, you got some idea of your favorite **occupation** -- based on your skills.

In Step Two, before that, you got some idea of your favorite **field - -** based on your interests and special knowledges.

Voila! You are now ready to put them together: **a career = occupation + field**.

Occupation: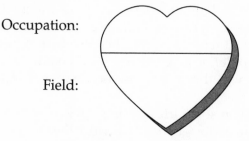

Field:

Once you have a heart, look at both occupation and field, and see if there's some immediately-obvious way you can put them together. For example, if you love to work with numbers, and your favorite field is health, you would obviously want to think about working in the accounting department of a hospital.

WHAT'S
IN A NAME?

All you know at the moment about this occupation or career you have tentatively chosen, is how it *sounds*. What you need to find out, now, is what the job is really like, beneath the high-sounding title.

Where do you begin such exploration? Everyone will tell you: go to the Internet, go to libraries, go to directories. Ah, the wisdom of this world - - if only it were accurate!

The bad news, unfortunately, is that the most dependable and up-to-date information on jobs and careers is *not* found in any of these three ways. It's found by going and talking to *people*.

The reason for this is that last week's absolutely true certifiably guaranteed 100% accurate information (*on the Internet or in printed resources*) about jobs and careers is, today, completely outdated.

Things are just moving too fast. Books can't keep up. They're outdated before they're in print. Even the Internet can't keep up, except on a very few sites.[11] So, if you want to find out if this new career or job *fits* you, **you must go talk to people actually doing the work that interests you.**

And if *talking to people face-to-face* is a problem for you, because you're shy, I have a word to say at the end of this chapter,
about how to deal with shyness.

TALKING TO WORKERS,
'TRYING ON' JOBS

When you go talk to people, you are hoping they will give
you some idea of what the work feels like, from the inside.

You want to get beneath the career title -- say, *psychiatrist
working with plants* -- and get some feel for what the day-to-day
work is like.

---

11. Examples of what I wish there were more of, are to be found at:
http://www.temp24-7.com/ and at http://www.ivillage.com/work/

For this purpose you must, as I said, go talk to people actually doing the work that interests you. In the particular example here, you must go talk to actual *psychiatrists who use plants, in their healing work.*

What are you doing, with such research? Well, in effect, you are mentally *trying on jobs* to see if they fit you.

It is exactly analogous to your going to a clothing store and trying on different suits (or dresses) that you see in their window.

Why do you try them on? Well, the suits or dresses that look *terrific* in the window don't always look so hotsy-totsy when you see them on *you.* Lots of pins were used, on the backside of the figurine in the window. On you, without the pins, the clothes may not hang quite right, etc., etc.

Likewise, careers that look terrific in the window of books or your imagination don't always look so great when you see them up close and personal, in all their living glory, and imagine yourself in that career, day after day, month after month, year after year.

You want to find a career that looks terrific in the window, *and* on you. Toward that end, you are trying to find out what *this* career feels like. Here is how you go about it.

- **Get the names of people who actually do the work you are interested in (defined on page 118, on your heart diagram). Use the Yellow Pages, ask your friends.**
- **Make an appointment with them. Ask for only 10 minutes of their time (and keep to it).** If they are very busy, or a professional, offer to pay them for their time. ("How much would you charge for me to take ten minutes of your time, to learn about the work you do?") When you are face to face with them, here are some questions you should ask:
  - **How did you get into this work?**
  - **What do you like the most about it?**
  - **What do you like the least about it?**
  - **Where else could I find people who do this kind of work?**

(You should always ask them for more than one name, so that if you run into a dead end at any point, you can easily visit the other people they suggested.)

If it becomes apparent to you, during the course of this ten-minute visit, that this career, occupation, or job definitely *doesn't* fit you, then the last question (above) gets turned into a slightly different query:

- **Do you have any ideas as to who else I could go talk to, about my skills and interests (favorite subjects), so I can find out what other careers or work these might point to?** If they can't think of anyone, ask them if they know who *might* know. And so on. And so forth. Then go visit the people whose names they give you.

"THEY SAY
I HAVE TO GO BACK TO SCHOOL,
BUT I HAVEN'T THE TIME
OR THE MONEY"

If you decide you do like this career you've just been exploring with these people, be sure to add the following question, before you leave their presence: "What kind of training do you have to have, before getting into this line of work?"

Many times, unfortunately, you will hear *bad news*. They will tell you something like: "In order to be hired for this occupation, you have to have a master's degree and ten years' experience." If you're willing to do that, if you have the time, and the money, fine! But what if you don't?

Then, this is what you do: you search for *the exception:*

- **Yes, but do you know of anyone in this field who got into it without that master's degree, and ten years' experience?**
- **And where might I find him or her?**
- **And if you don't know of any such person, who might know some names?**

You will need to check and cross-check any information that people tell you or that you read in books (even this one).

Keep clearly in mind that there are people *out there* who will tell you something that absolutely *isn't* so, with every conviction in their being -- because they *think* it's true. Sincerity they have, one hundred percent. Accuracy is something else again.

Therefore, no matter how many people tell you that such-and-so are the rules about getting into a particular occupation, and there are no exceptions -- believe me, there *are* exceptions *(except where a profession has rigid entrance examinations, as in, say, medicine or law.)*

Rules are rules. But somewhere in this vast world, *somebody* found a way to get into this career you dream of, without going through all the hoops that everyone else is telling you are *absolutely essential.*

You want to find out who these people are, and go talk to them, to find out *how they did it.*

Okay, but suppose you are determined to go into a career that everyone says takes *years* to prepare for; and you can't find *anyone* who took a shortcut? What then?

Even here, you can get *close* to the profession *without* such long preparation. Every professional speciality has one or more paraprofessional positions, which require much less training. For example, instead of becoming a doctor, you can go into paramedical work; instead of becoming a lawyer, you can go into paralegal work, etc., etc.

Keep up this information gathering until you find the names of at least *two* careers, or jobs, that really fit you.

Never, ever, put all your eggs in one basket. The secret of surviving out there in the jungle is *having alternatives.*

Be careful. Be thorough. Be persistent. This is your life you're working on, and your future. Make it glorious. Whatever it takes, find out the name of your ideal career, your ideal occupation, your ideal job -- *or jobs.*

INFORMATIONAL
INTERVIEWING

There is a name for this process I have just described: of testing a career by going to talk to people who are actually doing the work you would like to do.

It is called Informational Interviewing.[12] But it is sometimes, incorrectly, confused with other names. Some even think this

---

12. I invented the term many years ago (over the strong protests, I might add, of my mentor at that time, John Crystal, who wanted the word 'interviewing' reserved only for 'the hiring interview'). But the *idea* goes way back in the history of the creative minority. The first one to propose it, at least in embryonic form, was Alphonso William Rahn, an engineer at Western Electric Company. In 1936 he published a book (now out of print) called, *Your Work Abilities.* In it he suggested each job-hunter write a paper describing what functions he knew how to perform; and then show it to everyone. ("Will you take three minutes to read these specifications of what I can do, in case my services might be helpful to you or your associates, either now or later?")

gathering of information is the same as 'Networking.' But it is not.

To avoid this confusion, I have summarized in the chart on the next pages just exactly what Informational Interviewing is, and how it differs from the other ways in which *people* can help and support you during your job-hunt or career-change.

Those other ways are: Networking, Support Groups, and Contacts. I have also thrown in, at no extra charge, a first column in that chart, dealing with an aspect of the job-hunt that never gets talked about: namely, the importance *before your job-hunt ever begins,* of nurturing the friendships you have let slip, over time -- by calling them or visiting them and re-establishing relationships *before* you ever need anything from them, as you most certainly may, later on in your job-hunt.

The Job-Hunter's or Career-Changer's

The Process ⬇	1. Valuing Your *Community* Before the Job-Hunt	2. Networking
What Is Its Purpose?	To make sure that people whom you may someday need to do you a favor, or lend you a hand, know long beforehand that you value and prize them *for themselves*.	To gather a list of contacts *now* who might be able to help you with your career, or with your job-hunting, at some future date. And to go out of your way to *regularly* add to that list. *Networking is a term often reserved only for the business of adding to your list; but, obviously, this presupposes you first listed everyone you already know.*
Who Is It Done With?	Those who live with you, plus your family, relatives, friends, and acquaintances, however near (geographically) or far.	People in your present field, or in a field of future interest that you yourself meet; also, people whose names are given to you by others.
When You're Doing This Right How Do You Go About It? (Typical Activities)	You make time for them in your busy schedule, long before you find yourself job-hunting. You do this by: (1) Spending 'quality time' with those you live with, letting them know you really appreciate who they are, and what kind of person they are, (2) Maintaining contact (phone, lunch, a thank-you note) with those who live nearby, (3) Writing friendly notes, regularly, to those who live at a distance -- *thus letting them all know that you appreciate them* for themselves.	You deliberately attend, for this purpose, meetings or conventions in your present field, or the field/ career you are thinking of switching to, someday. You talk to people at meetings and at 'socials,' exchanging calling cards after a brief conversation. Occasionally, someone may suggest a name to you as you are about to set off for some distant city or place, recommending that while you are there, you contact them. A phone call may be your best bet, with follow-up letter after you return home, unless *they* invite *you* to lunch during the phone call. Asking *them* to lunch sometimes 'bombs.' (See below.)
When You've Really Botched This Up, What Are The Signs?	You're out of work, and you find yourself having to contact people that you haven't written or phoned in ages, suddenly asking them out of the blue for their help with your job-hunt. *The message inevitably read from this is that you don't really care about them at all, except when you can use them. Further, you get perceived as one who sees others only in terms of what they can do for you, rather than in a relationship that is 'a two-way street.'*	It's usually when you have approached a very busy individual and asked them to have lunch with you. If it is an aimless lunch, with no particular agenda -- they ask during lunch what you need to talk about, and you lamely say, "Well, uh, I don't know, So-and-So just thought we should get to know each other" -- you will not be practicing *Networking*. You will be practicing *antagonizing*. Try to restrict your *Networking* to the telephone.

3. Developing A Support Group	4. Informational Interviewing	5. Using Contacts
To enlist some of your family or close friends specifically to help you with your emotional, social, and spiritual needs, when you are going through a difficult transition period, such as a job-hunt or career-change -- so that you do not have to face this time all by yourself.	To screen careers *before* you change to them. To screen jobs *before* you take them, rather than afterward. To screen places *before* you decide you want to seek employment there. To find answers to *very specific questions* that occur to you during your job-hunt.	It takes, let us say, 77 pairs of eyes and ears to find a new job or career. Here you recruit those 76 other people (don't take me literally -- it can be any number you choose) to be your eyes and ears -- once you know what kind of work, what kind of place, what kind of job you are looking for, *and not before.*
You try to enlist people with one or more of the following qualifications: you feel comfortable talking to them; they will take initiative in calling you, on a regular basis; they are wiser than you are; and they can be a hard taskmaster, when you need one.	Workers, workers, workers. You *only* do informational interviewing with people actually doing the work that interests you as a potential new job or career for yourself.	Anyone and everyone who is on your 'networking list.' (See column 2.) It includes family, friends, relatives, high school alumni, college alumni, former co-workers, church/synagogue members, places where you shop, etc.
There should be three of them, at least. They may meet with you regularly, once a week, as a group, for an hour or two, to check on how you are doing. One or more of them should also be available to you on an "as needed" basis: the Listener, when you are feeling 'down,' and need to talk; the Initiator, when you are tempted to hide; the Wise One, when you are puzzled as to what to do next; and the Taskmaster, when your discipline is falling apart, and you need someone to encourage you to 'get at it.' It helps if there is also a Cheerleader among them, that you can tell your victories to.	You get names of workers from your co-workers, from departments at local community colleges, or career offices. Once you have names, you call them and ask for a chance to talk to them *for twenty minutes.* You make a list, ahead of time, of all the questions you want answers to. If nothing occurs to you, try these: (1) How did you get into this line of work? Into this particular job? (2) What kinds of things do you like the most about this job? (3) What kinds of things do you like the least about this job? (4) Who else, doing this same kind of work, would you recommend I go talk to?	Anytime you're stuck, you ask your contacts for help *with specific information.* For example: When you can't find workers who are doing the work that interests you. When you can't find the names of places which do that kind of work. When you have a place in mind, but can't figure out the name of 'the person-who-has-the-power-to-hire-you.' When you know that name, but can't get in to see that person. At such times, you call every contact you have on your Networking list, if necessary, until someone can tell you the specific answer you need.
You've 'botched it' when you have no support group, no one to turn to, no one to talk to, and you feel that you are in this, all alone. You've 'botched it' when you are waiting for your friends and family to notice how miserable you are, and to prove they love you by taking the initiative in coming after you; rather than, as is necessary with a support group, *your* choosing and recruiting them -- asking them for their help and aid.	You're trying to use this with people-who-have-the-power-to-hire-you, rather than with *workers.* You're claiming you want information when really you have some other hidden agenda, with this person. (P.S. *They usually can smell the hidden agenda, a mile away.*) You've botched it, whenever you're telling a lie to someone. The whole point of informational interviewing is that it is a search for Truth.	Approaching your 'contacts' too early in your job-hunt, and asking them for help only in the most general and vague terms: "John, I'm out of work. If you hear of anything, please let me know." *Any what thing?* You must do all your own homework *before* you approach your contacts. They will not do your homework for you.

WHAT IF I GET OFFERED A JOB ALONG THE WAY, WHILE I'M GATHERING ALL THIS INFORMATION?

You probably won't. Let me remind you that during this information gathering, you are *not* talking primarily to employers. You're talking to workers.

Nonetheless, an occasional employer *may* stray across your path during all this Informational Interviewing. And that employer *may* be so impressed with the carefulness you're showing, in going about your career-change and job-search, that they want to hire you, on the spot. So, it's *possible* that you might get offered a job while you're still doing your information gathering. Not *likely*, but *possible*. And if that happens, what should you say?

Well, if you're desperate, you will of course say *yes*. I remember one wintertime when I had just gone through the knee of my last pair of pants, we were burning old pieces of furniture in our fireplace to stay warm, the legs on our bed had just broken, and we were eating spaghetti until it was coming out our ears. In such a situation, *of course* you say yes.

But if you're not *desperate*, if you have a little time to be more careful, then you respond to the job-offer in a way that will buy you some time. You tell them what you're doing: that the average job-hunter tries to screen a job *after* they take it. But you are doing what you are *sure* this employer would do if they were in your shoes: you are examining careers, fields, industries, jobs, organizations *before* you decide where you can do your best and most effective work.

And you tell them that since your Informational Interviewing isn't finished yet, it would be premature for you to accept their job offer, until you're *sure* that this is the place where you could be most effective, and do your best work.

But, you add: "Of course, I'm tickled pink that you would want me to be working here. And when I've finished my personal survey, I'll be glad to get back to you about this, as my preliminary impression is that this is the kind of place I'd like to work in, and the kind of people I'd like to work for, and the kind of people I'd like to work with." In other words, *if you're not desperate yet*, you don't walk immediately through any opened doors; but neither do you allow them to shut.

GETTING INTO
YOUR NEW CAREER

Once you've found a career that really fits you, your next problem is: how do you move into it, from your previous job or work history?

We're talking about **career-change** here. Everyone knows what that is, in a foggy, general sort of way.

But with our equation in hand -- **a career = occupation + field** -- we can now see in more detail just exactly what is involved.

We can see that **a career-change is a change in either occupation or field -- or both.**

Types of Career Change Visualized

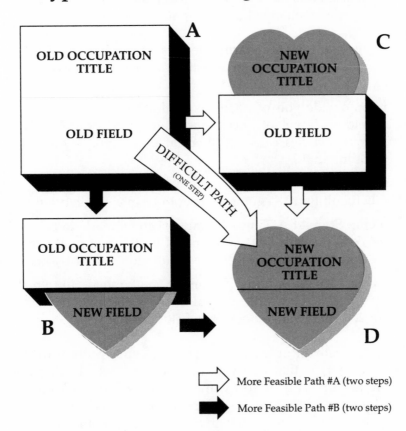

Thus, there are (technically) three kinds of career-change you can choose between:

(1) **You can change just your field** but not your occupation. This is a move from A to B, in the previous diagram. *In spite of its simplicity, this is a career-change. You may become much happier just by moving into a new* field.

(2) **You can change just your occupation**, but not your field. This is a move from A to C, in the diagram. *In spite of its simplicity, this is a career-change. You may become much happier just by changing your* occupation, while you remain in the same field where you are presently working.

(3) **You can change both your occupation and your field.** This is a move from A to D, in the diagram. *This is career-change as people most commonly define it.* You may decide you can only be happy if you change both occupation and field.

HOW TO CHANGE BOTH OCCUPATION AND FIELD

If you decide you want to change both your occupation and your field *(and why not, after all the thought you've put into the earlier exercises in this chapter?)* there are three ways you can go about doing that:

a) **In A Single Bound.** The move can be made all at once (The Difficult Path) -- going from A to D, in a single bound.

b) **One Step At A Time.** The move can be made in two steps (More Feasible Path #A), as indicated by the two white arrows, where you first change only your occupation, but not your field.

c) **One Step At A Time.** The move can be made in two steps (More Feasible Path #B), as indicated by the two red arrows, where you first change only your field, but not your occupation.

To illustrate all of this, let us suppose your present (or most recent career) is that of **an accountant** at a **television** station. You're fed up with it. You want to change careers. You've decided you would like to be **a reporter** who covers the **medical** field. So, your goal is to change both occupation and field.

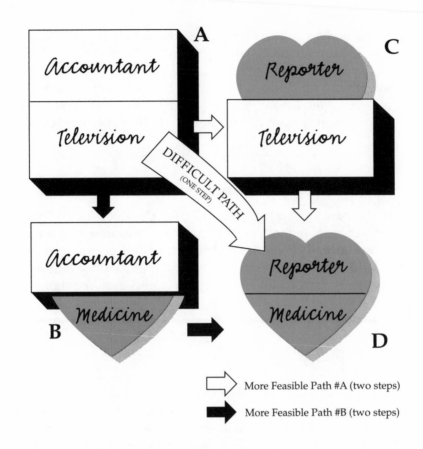

More Feasible Path #A (two steps)

More Feasible Path #B (two steps)

Now of course you could try to make this career-change In A Single Bound -- zowie! Both field and occupation are changed! It's hard, because when asked by your prospective employer what experience you've had in your new career, you may have great difficulty. That's why we call this The Difficult Path.

But there are the other two ways to go, the One-Step-At-A-Time method, that I mentioned above.

Thus, in the diagram above, you can first move from A to C: ask the television station where you already work as an accountant to hire you as a reporter instead, or go to another television station and ask to be hired as a reporter. You'd stay there one year, two, or three; then you'd move from C to D: you'd try to get a job as a reporter at some medical journal, newspaper, or Internet site.

Alternatively, you can first move from A to B: stay an accountant, but get a new job, as an accountant, at some medical journal, newspaper, or Internet site. You'd stay there one year, two, or three; then you'd move from B to D: try to get them to hire you as a reporter where you are, or try to get a different medical journal, newspaper, or Internet site to hire you as a reporter.

"What Experience Do You Have?"

The tremendous advantage of this One-Step-At-A-Time career-change method, is that **each time you make a move, you are already experienced in either the occupation or the field**. This carries much greater weight with would-be employers, than when you have no experience in either.

CHANGING CAREERS
IN A SINGLE BOUND

But suppose you have defined the career of your dreams, and you just can't wait! You want to get there In A Single Bound. You want 'The Difficult Path.' How do you sell yourself to a would-be employer, when you are inexperienced in both occupation *and* field? Good question!

In that case, you must dive beneath occupation and field.

You recall (from the diagram on page 72) that every **occupation** is composed of a series of **tasks** or assignments; and every task or assignment, in turn, requires that you have certain **skills**, to do it well.

Hence, skills must be your preoccupation, rather than titles. Titles are not easily perceived by would-be employers as transferable, but skills are.

You also recall that every **field** is composed of several **interests** or **special knowledges**, such as you inventoried earlier in this chapter.

Hence, your knowledges must be your preoccupation, rather than fields. Fields are not easily perceived by would-be employers as transferable, but special knowledges are.

So, with your focus on skills and on knowledges, how do you prepare for 'The Difficult Path'?

• **You go and chat with three or more people who are already in that job or career.**

• **You ask them:** What tasks or assignments do you have to do, in this job or career? **You follow up on this, immediately, by asking them:** What skills does it take to do such tasks or assignments? *Jot down their answers.*

• **You turn then to your other focus, and ask them:** What do you have to know a lot about, what knowledges are you expected to possess, in order to do this job or career? *Jot down their answers.*

• **Throw in a bonus question (for yourself):** What assets or personal qualities are required, in order to be successful in this job or career? *Jot down their answers.*

After interviewing all three people who are already in the job or career you aspire to,

• **You will end up with three lists: 'Skills Needed'; and, 'Knowledges Needed'**, plus your bonus list of 'Personal Qualities Required for Success in this Field.'

• **Compare these lists with the skills and knowledges that you already possess** (as you found out in this chapter and the previous one). On the 'Skills Needed' list, and the 'Knowledges Needed' list, put a check beside each one that you already possess.

• **Now, when you approach a would-be employer, for this new job or career, you can present yourself as someone who is indeed** *experienced.* Of course you are brand new to both **occupation** and **field**, but you *are* experienced where it really counts -- in the **skills** and special **knowledges** needed to do that job, and succeed in that career. And you can try to show that employer how your skills and knowledges will help the employer get more customers, or make more profits, or accomplish more of their goals. Add in, here, the personal qualities you have, that you know are needed for success in this field. And if it's the right employer, you have a chance, of making a career-change in a single bound.

Where

Step Five:

Organizations

NAMES OF ORGANIZATIONS: TOO MANY OR TOO FEW

You've got your career clearly in mind.

Now is the time to look for places where you can do this kind of work.

Keep in mind that here, as throughout your job-search, you are not looking for names of places that have a vacancy.

You are merely looking for names of places that *interest you*, regardless of whether or not they have a vacancy.

That certainly involves using the Yellow Pages.

It may also involve talking to all your contacts (see page 175).

Or, it may involve picking a pretty street in your town, where you would love to work, and looking at every building up and down both sides of that street, to see what kinds of places are there. (I know job-hunters and career-changers who have actually done this -- and found a great place!)

In any and all ways that may occur to you, you search for names of organizations that interest you.

As you do this search, one of two things will happen:

a) you'll be turning up **too many** names of places where you could conceivably work, or

b) you'll be turning up **too few** names of places which hire people in the career that interests you.

Hence, you either need to cut down the territory, or widen it. Let's look at the first scenario, first.

CUTTING DOWN THE TERRITORY

If you end up with too many names of places that could theoretically hire you in the career that interests you, what should you do? The answer is: **cut the territory down, by narrowing your search** *categories.* [13]

Your Flower Diagram

Your search categories are determined by the information you supply for the petals of a Flower Diagram, that you will find in Appendix A.

You can find directions, beginning on page 263, for filling out that Diagram. To do so, you do some brief, helpful, and interesting exercises, that many readers find to be the most interesting part of this book -- whether they need to cut the territory down, or not.

So, interrupt your journey through this chapter to go to Appendix A, and deal with that Flower.

Once you have the Flower filled out, you are ready to come back here, and proceed with this exercise of cutting the territory down.

---

13. If you resist this idea of *cutting the territory down* -- if you feel you could be happy *anywhere* just as long as you were using your favorite skills -- then almost no organization in the country can be ruled out. In the U.S. alone there are currently over 16 million employers, hence 16 million job-markets, out there. (And a *proportional* number in other countries.) So if you aren't willing to cut the territory down, then you'll have to go visit them all. Good luck! We'll see you in about 43 years.

Let's take an example, to see how you go about cutting the territory down. Suppose you discovered that the career which interests you the most is *metalworking*. You tell yourself you want to be a welder. Well, that's a beginning. You've cut the 16 million U.S. job-markets down to:

I want to work in a place that hires welders.

But the territory is still too large. There might be thousands of places in the country, that use welders. You can't go visit them all. So, you've got to cut the territory down, further. Suppose that on your geography *petal* you said that you really want to live and work in the San Jose area of California. That's helpful: that cuts the territory down further. Now your goal is:

I want to work in a place that hires welders, within the San Jose area.

But, the territory is still too large. There could be 100, 200, 300 organizations which fit that description. So you look at your Flower Diagram for further help, and you notice that under *preferred working conditions* you said you wanted to work for an organization with fifty or less employees. Good, now your goal is:

I want to work in a place that hires welders, within the San Jose area, and has fifty or less employees.

This territory may still be too large. So you look again at your Flower Diagram for further guidance, and you see that on the Things *petal* you said you wanted to work for an organization which works with, or produces, *wheels.* So now your statement of what you're looking for, becomes:

I want to work in a place that hires welders, within the San Jose area, has fifty or less employees, and makes wheels.

Using your Flower Diagram, you can thus keep cutting the territory down, until the *'targets'* of your job-hunt are no more than 20 places. That's a manageable number of places for you to *start with.* You can always expand the list later, if none of these 20 turn out to be very promising or interesting. For the time being, you've succeeded in cutting down the territory.

WIDENING THE TERRITORY

Sometimes your problem will be just the opposite: you can't turn up enough names of places that interest you.

What should you do? The answer is: **widen the territory, by broadening your search** *categories.*

Let's take an example. Suppose in your new career you want to be a teacher.

Where do teachers work? Schools, you say.

And finding that schools in your geographical area have no openings, you might say, *"Well, there are no jobs for people in this career."* But that is not true.

The correct answer to "where do teachers work?" is:

- Schools
- Corporate training and educational departments in organizations
- Organizations whose business it is to run workshops
- Foundations
- Private Research Firms
- Firms which offer educational consultants to other places
- Teachers' associations
- Professional and trade associations or societies
- Military bases
- State and local councils on higher education
- Training academies, such as fire and police

And the list can be further widened. You could work:

- at places that would employ you full-time
- at places that would employ you part-time (maybe you'll end up deciding to hold down two or even three part-time jobs, which altogether would add up to one full-time job, in order to give yourself more variety);
- at places that take temporary workers, on assignment for one project at a time;
- at places that take consultants, one project at a time;
- at places that operate with volunteers, etc.
- at places that are nonprofit;
- at places that are for profit;
- and, don't forget, places which you yourself would start up, should you decide to be your own boss.

All this, for teachers. It is the same with almost any occupation: there are *many* places where you could work. As you talk to people about your job-hunt they will accidentally volunteer information not only about organizations, but also about *kinds* of organizations -- as above. Listen keenly, and keep notes.

Keep widening your territory! And ask for *names* of organizations in each category that you discover.

You may also want to look at directories, that give you names.

If it's smaller organizations that you're looking for, your best directory for names is going to be the Yellow Pages of your local phone book. Look under every related heading that you can think of.

Also, see if the Chamber of Commerce publishes a business directory; often it will list not only small companies but also local divisions of larger companies, with names of department heads; and sometimes will even include the (SIC) industry codes. You won't likely lack for names, believe me -- unless it's a very small town you live in, in which case you'll need to cast your net a little wider, to include other towns or villages that are within commuting distance.

Other directories are listed on page 141ff.

Once you have about 20 names of organizations or businesses that might hire you for the kind of work you are dying to do, take the three that look most interesting to you, and do some research on them, *before* approaching them for a hiring interview.

Every worker in the world takes the measure of their organization, and decides whether or not they would enjoy working there. Trouble is, most job-hunters or career-changers do so, *after* they are hired there.

For example, a U.S. survey found that 57% of those who found jobs through the Federal/State employment service were not working at that job just 30 days later; obviously, many of them found out during those 30 days that they wouldn't enjoy continuing to work there. That's a little late to find that out! You want to be wiser than that.

RESEARCHING PLACES BEFORE YOU APPROACH THEM

Why is it important for you to research a company or organization ahead of time? There are three reasons:

You want to distinguish yourself from all those other job-hunters who walk in on a place and say, "Uh, what exactly do you guys do here?" Using contacts, the Internet, and books -- you want to demonstrate that you cared enough about the place, to learn something about it before you walked in.

You want to know if they need someone with your skills and knowledge. You want to know what kind of work they do there. And what their needs or problems or challenges are. And what kind of goals are they trying to achieve, what obstacles are they running into. Then you will be better able to talk about how your skills and knowledges could help them, once you reach the interview.

You want to know if *you* would enjoy working there. You don't want to ignorantly take a job that you'd soon have to quit

because of something about them, that you didn't know or bother to find out, before you started there.

By doing this research of a place ahead of time, you are choosing a better way, by far. Essentially, you are *screening out* places *before* you commit to them. How sensible! How smart!

Okay, so what do you do to try to find out? Well, just ask yourself **what you wish you had known about previous jobs, before you took them.** In that moment after you quit or were fired, as you looked back, what did you wish you had known before you took that job? This will give you your research topics for a future job. For example, you may have wished you had known:

What the real goals of the place were, instead of the folderol they put in their annual report.

What 'the corporate culture' was like, there: cold and clammy, or warm and appreciative.

What kinds of timelines they conducted their work under, and whether they were flexible or inflexible.

What the job was really like.

Whether the skills you care the most about, in yourself, would really get used. Or was all that talk about 'your skills' just window dressing to lure you there -- and you, with rich people skills, ended up spending your time pushing paper?

More about the boss, and what she or he was like, to work for. Ditto for your immediate supervisor(s).

What your co-workers were like: easy to get along with, or difficult? And who was which?

How close the company or organization was to having to lay off people, or on how tight a budget they were going to ask your department to operate.

So, that's what you want to research before you get a job offer at this new place (if you get a job offer there).

Of course **you can't find all of this out** *before* **the interview. But if you're lucky, you will discover some of it.** The rest of it you must try to find out *during* the interview. So, the above topics are your Research Agenda, and they are also your Interview Agenda -- the things you will try to notice or discover during the hiring interview there, should you succeed in 'getting in.'

There are six ways you can discover this information ahead of time. I list the methods here, starting with the quickest and progressing to those which take more time (in order). Most job-hunters or career-changers will start with the easiest level, and progress to the next level *only if* they didn't find out what they wanted at lower levels.

• **Easiest Research:** Friends and Neighbors. Ask *everybody* you know, if they know anyone who works at the organization that interests you. And, if they do, ask them if they could arrange for you and that person to get together, for lunch, coffee or tea. At that time, tell them why the place interests you, and indicate you'd like to know more about it. *(It helps if your mutual friend is sitting in, with the two of you, so the purpose of this little chit-chat won't be misconstrued.)*

This is the vastly preferred way to find out about a place. However, obviously you need some alternatives up your sleeve, in case you run into a dead end here. So we press on.

• **Research Level #2:** The Internet. Go to my Web site, if you have Internet access (`www.jobhuntersbible.com`), and then to the sub-division of my NetGuide called "Research." There you will find a comprehensive list of sites that can help you find out information about companies. Also, you can go to a search engine (try Metacrawler: `www.metacrawler.com`) and type in the name of the organization you're trying to find out more about. See what it turns up. You will find the Internet is better than printed resources if it's a small company that you're looking for.

• **Research Level #3:** What's In Print. There are three repositories for stuff in print:

1) The organization itself may have stuff in print, about its business, purpose, etc. The CEO or head of the organization may have given talks. The organization may have copies of those talks. In addition, there may be brochures, annual reports, etc., that the organization has put out, about itself. How do you get a hold of these? The person that answers the phone is the person to check with, in small organizations. In larger organizations, the publicity office, or human relations office, are the places to check. Human resources may also have some stuff.

(continued on page 142)

A Sampler of Print Resources

You may find these print resources at your local public library (of course), but don't forget other libraries that may be near you, such as a business library or a local university, college, or community college library.

Many public libraries have very efficient database search capabilities, through their computers, and can dig up, copy and mail to you copies of reports on local companies (for a modest cost). For example, one Pennsylvania job-hunter got the Cleveland (Ohio) Library to send him copies of annual reports on a Cleveland-based company. So, if there's an organization or company that interests you in some other city, you might want to try contacting the nearest large public library to that organization's home base, and see what that librarian can turn up for you. (*Please* write and thank them, afterward.)

In addition to public libraries in other cities, there are special libraries located at various places in the U.S. These are listed in:

• *Directory of Special Libraries and Information Centers.* Gale Research, Inc., 835 Penobscott Bldg. Detroit, MI 48226-4094. It lists 22,000 research facilities, on various subjects, maintained by libraries, research libraries, businesses, nonprofit organizations, governmental agencies, etc. Detailed subject index, using over 3,500 key words.

Some of the following books are inexpensive enough for you to purchase, *if you want to* -- from your local bookstore or via the Internet. Browse them, first, if you can.

Other books or directories are *hideously* expensive, in which case *thank God* for your local library.

Indexes/Indices

There are *(mercifully)* indexes/indices to all these directories:

• Klein's *Guide to American Directories;* and

• *Directories in Print.* Gale Research, Inc., 835 Penobscott Bldg. Detroit, MI 48226-4094. It contains over 15,000 current listings of directories, indexed by title or key word or subject (over 3,500 subject headings).

See also:

• *Encyclopedia of Business Information Sources.* Gale Research, Inc., 835 Penobscott Bldg. Detroit, MI 48226-4094. Identifies electronic, print and live resources dealing with 1,500 business subjects. Their companion volume is entitled *Business Organizations, Agencies and Publications Directory*, listing over 24,000 entries, such as federal government advisory organizations, newsletters, research services, etc.

For Researching Large Companies

• Company/college/association/agency/foundation *Annual Reports*. Get these directly from the personnel department or publicity person at the company, etc., or from the Chamber or your local library.

• *The Almanac of American Employers.* Focuses on the 500 largest, fastest growing, most successful corporate employers; available in most public libraries. Covers companies of 2,500+ employees. Plunkett Research, Ltd., P.O. Drawer 8270, Galveston, TX 77553. 409-765-8530.

2) The public library may have files on the organization -- newspaper clippings, articles, etc. You never know; and it never hurts to ask the librarian.

3) The public library has books and directories that may give you information about the organization. This is more likely to be the case if it is a large organization you are trying to research, and not (for example) "a mom-and-pop store." In the latter case, the Internet is usually a better bet, as I mentioned above. In any event, give both a try.

• **Research Level #4:** Getting Information from People at the Organization. If you just can't find out what you want to know from print resources, the Internet, or your friends, you can always go directly to organizations that interest you and ask questions about the place. This is called "Informational Interviewing," as we saw earlier (p. 122) but in this application of it, I must caution you about several things:

At this point in your job-hunt, be careful how you think of yourself. You are not yet "job-hunter," wanting to be hired there. You are still "job-researcher," trying to learn whether or not there would be a fit between you and that organization.

You must first approach the people at that organization whose business it is to give out information -- receptionists, public relations people, 'the personnel office,' etc., before tackling anybody else in the organization. Gather all the printed material they have, about that place, and leave. You can come back at another time, after you've 'digested' what you picked up, there.

You must then read whatever is in print about that organization. You never want to ask questions of anyone at that organization, until you know what questions they have already answered in print (or on their Web site, if they have one). Read all that stuff, before bothering *them*. You should also have visited the library to see what information about the organization is there.

You must then approach *subordinates* to the boss, with your remaining questions, rather than the top person in the place -- unless the boss is the only one who would know the answer.

This is Informational Interviewing, not a plea to be hired.

(continued on page 144)

• *America's Fastest Growing Employers: The Complete Guide to Finding Jobs with over 275 of America's Hottest Companies*, by Carter Smith with Peter C. Hale. Adams Media, 260 Center St., Holbrook, MA 02343.

• *Corporate and Industry Research Reports*. Published by R.R. Bowker/Martindale-Hubbell, 121 Chanlon Rd., New Providence, NJ 07974. Can be very helpful.

• *Corporate Jobs Outlook!* A newsletter published every 60 days, available in most public libraries. Covers companies of 500 to 2,500 employees. Plunkett Research, Ltd., P.O. Drawer 541737, Houston, TX 77254-1737. 713-932-0000.

• *Corporate Technology Directory*. Lists companies by the products they make or the technologies they use. Corporate Technology Information Services, Inc., 12 Alfred St., Suite 200, Woburn, MA 01801-9998.

• *Directory of American Research and Technology: Organizations Active in Product Development for Business*. R.R. Bowker, 121 Chanlon Rd., New Providence, NJ 07974.

• *Directory of Corporate Affiliations*. National Register Publishing Co., Inc.

• *Dun & Bradstreet's Million Dollar Directory*. Very helpful.

• *Dun & Bradstreet's Million Dollar Directory - Top 50,000 Companies*. Very helpful. An abridged version of Dun's *Million Dollar Directory Series*.

• *Dun & Bradstreet's Reference Book of Corporate Managements*.

• *F & S Indexes* (recent articles on firms).

• *F & S Index of Corporations and Industries*. Lists "published articles" by industry and by company name. Updated weekly.

• Fitch Corporation Manuals.

• *Fortune* Magazine's 500; they also publish interesting articles during the rest of the year, on major corporations, such as *"America's Most Admired Corporations."* Visit your local library, and browse back issues.

• *Hoover's Company Profiles on CD-ROM*. Hoover's, Inc., 1033 La Posada Drive, Suite 250, Austin, TX 78752, 512-374-4500. 2,500 profiles of companies. Includes all the companies in Hoover's books, plus 1,100 more. For Windows or DOS computers.

• *Hoover's Handbook of American Business*. Hoover's, Inc., 1033 La Posada Drive, Suite 250, Austin, TX 78752, 512-374-4500. Profiles of over 500 major U.S. companies. A special section on the companies that have created the most jobs in the last 10 years and those that have eliminated the most jobs. Expensive; see your local library.

• *Hoover's Handbook of World Business*. Hoover's, Inc., 1033 La Posada Drive, Suite 250, Austin, TX 78752, 512-374-4500. 250 profiles of major European, Asian, Latin American, and Canadian companies who employ thousands of Americans both in the U.S. and abroad.

• *How To Read A Financial Report: Wringing Cash Flow and Other Vital Signs Out of the Numbers*, by John A. Tracy, CPA. John Wiley & Sons, Business Law/General Books Division, 605 Third Avenue, New York, NY 10158-0012. Also Chichester, Brisbane, Toronto and Singapore.

• *Macmillan's Directory of Leading Private Companies*.

• *Moody's Industrial Manual* (and other Moody manuals).

• Periodicals worth perusing in your public library, in addition to *Fortune*, mentioned above, are *Business Week, Dun's Review, Forbes*, and the *Wall Street Journal*.

Bothering the boss with some simple questions about the place, when someone else there could have answered your question quite handily, is committing *job-hunting suicide*. Bosses have better things to do with their time, than answering elementary questions from a job-researcher. For detailed instructions on how to do this, see page 125.

If you run into a brick wall at the place that interests you the most, go visit similar organizations -- and use them to find out about 'norms' in that field, which may apply then to the organization you're most interested in.

Job-Hunters Who Are Tricksters

I regret to report that there is no honest, open-hearted job-hunting *technique* that cannot be twisted by those with clever, devious spirits, into some kind of *trick*. This has happened with Informational Interviewing. *Some* job-hunters have thought, "Okay, I know I'm just looking for information at this point in my job-hunt. But wouldn't this be a great *trick* to use to get in to see the hiring person -- asking them for some of their time, claiming you need *information,* and then hitting them up for a job?"

In case *you,* even for a moment, are tempted to follow in their footsteps, let me gently inform you what one New York employer told me he said to such a trickster: "You came to see me to ask for some information. And I gladly gave you my time. But now, it is apparent you really want a job here, and you think you've found a clever 'trick' that would get you in my door. You've essentially lied. Let me tell you something: on the basis of what I have just seen of your style of doing things, I wouldn't hire you if you were the last person on earth."

In this Age of Rudeness, Lies, Manipulation, and Getting Ahead At Any Cost, *you* will want, above all else, to be a beacon of integrity, truth, and kindness throughout your job-hunt or career-change -- including the time you are doing Informational Interviewing. *That's* the kind of employee employers are *dying* to find.

(continued on page 146)

• Registers of manufacturers for your state or area (e.g., *California Manufacturers Register*).
  • *Standard and Poor's Corporation Records.*
  • *Standard and Poor's Industrial Index.*
  • *The Adams Jobs Almanac*, by the Editors of Adams Media. Adams Media, 260 Center St., Holbrook, MA 02343. Gives a sampling of the major companies in thirty-one industries, together with the kinds of positions they are usually looking for -- when they're looking. Has a state-by-state index of the major employers, plus an introductory session on career outlooks and job-hunting. This same publisher has a *JobBank Series* for individual cities, which you can find in your local bookstore.
  • *Thomas' Register.* Thomas Publishing Co. There are 27 volumes in the Thomas register. All the manufacturers there are, for 52,000 products and services, plus catalogs, contacts, and phone numbers.
  • *Walker's Manual of Western Corporations.* Walker Western Research Co., 1452 Tilia Ave., San Mateo, CA 94402.
  • *Ward's Business Directory, 6 vols.* Gale Research, Inc., 835 Penobscott Bldg. Detroit, MI 48226-4094. Updated yearly. Despite the titles, helpful in identifying smaller companies, as well as large.

For Researching Smaller Companies

Hoover's Handbook of Emerging Companies, Hoover's, Inc., 1033 La Posada Drive, Suite 250, Austin, TX 78752, 512-374-4500. Lists and profiles of 250 smaller, emerging companies with high growth rates. A *sampler* for those seeking employment at smaller companies.

Chamber of Commerce data on an organization or field that interests you (visit the Chamber in the appropriate city or town).

Better Business Bureau report on a particular organization that you may be interested in (call the BBB in the city where the organization is located). These reports sometimes only tell you if there are outstanding, unresolved complaints against a company; if the company has scrambled to settle a complaint in the past, their record will now look pretty good. Still, it's a useful thing to know -- if there are or have been such complaints.

People Who Know People

Most of these are consultants within specific fields; often they know companies within their field, and individuals within those companies, by name:

Consultants and Consulting Organizations Directory. Gale Research, Inc., 835 Penobscott Bldg. Detroit, MI 48226-4094. Lists over 15,000 firms, individuals and organizations engaged in consulting work. Consultants are usually experts in their particular field, and hence may be useful to you in your information search about that job or career-change that you are contemplating.

Dun's Consultants Directory.

American Society for Training and Development Directory: Who's Who in Training and Development, 1640 King St., Box 1443, Alexandria, VA 22313-2043.

Contacts Influential: Commerce and Industry Directory. Businesses in particular market area listed by name, type of business, key personnel, etc. Contacts Influential, Market Research and Development Services, 321 Bush St., Suite 203, San Francisco, CA 94104, if your library doesn't have it.

• **Research Level #5:** Temporary Agencies. Many job-hunters and career-changers have found that a useful way to explore organizations is to let yourself be sent out by an agency that places workers for short periods, in short-term jobs - - often called 'temp agencies.'

An amazing number of companies use temp agencies. Whereas temp workers only comprised 10% of some companies' workforce in 1989, temps now represent from 25 to 60% of their total workforce.[14] Hence, you get access through a temp agency to a lot of places, where you can do your research on the spot.

This strategy for exploring places does not appeal to everyone. Some job-hunters and career-changers mentally balk at the very idea of enrolling with a temp agency, because they remember the old days when such agencies were solely for clerical workers and secretarial help. But these days there are temp agencies *(at least in the larger cities)* which send out: accountants, industrial workers, assemblers, drivers, mechanics, construction people, engineering people, software engineers, programmers, computer technicians, production workers, managers and executives, nannies (for young and old), health care/dental/medical people, legal specialists, insurance specialists, sales/marketing people, underwriting professionals, financial services people, as well as the professions temp agencies have always handled - - data processing, secretarial, and office services.

So, check your Yellow Pages, under 'Temporary Agencies,' or 'Employment Agencies,' make some phone calls, and if you discover a temp agency which loans out people with your particular skills and expertise, register with them, and let them send you out. (If they don't ever send you out, go seek another agency.) Hopefully, within the space of just a few weeks, you will get a chance to see a number of organizations from the inside.

It may be the agency won't send you to exactly the place you hoped for; but sometimes by working in parallel organizations, you can develop contacts *over there* in the organization of greatest interest to you.

• **Research Level #6:** Volunteer Work. If you don't wish to research a number of places, because your research turned up

---

14. *San Francisco Chronicle,* 6/30/94.

one place that interests you above all others -- a useful way to research that place is to volunteer your services there, for two or three weeks, at no cost to them, with the proviso that they can terminate you as a volunteer at any time.

Of course, some places will turn your offer down, cold. But others will be interested in your offer. After all, you offer them three sterling advantages: (1) You cost nothing. (2) If you turn out to be a *pain*, they won't have to endure you for long. (3) It will be easy for them to tell you to go.

You also get three advantages: (1) You will learn about the place -- and maybe decide you would never want to actually work there. (2) You give them a chance to see you in action, and if they like you, they *may* want to hire you. I say *may*. Don't be mad if they simply say at the end, "Thanks very much for helping us out." That's what *usually* happens. (3) This is a very good strategy for career-changers, in particular, even if it doesn't lead to a hire. If you are trying to move into a new field, volunteering at this place (in that field) will often get you a very good letter of reference, at the end. So, when you then approach other places, and they say, Have you had any experience in this field?, you can hand them the letter of reference, and say, "Yes, I have."

SEND A THANK-YOU NOTE

After *anyone* has done you a favor, during this Informational Interviewing phase of your job-hunt, you must *be sure* to send them a thank-you note by the very next day, at the latest. Such a note goes to *everyone* who helps you, or who talks with you. That means friends, people at the organization in question, temporary agency people, secretaries, receptionists, librarians, workers, or whoever.

Ask them, at the time you are face to face with them, for their calling card (if they have one), or ask them to write out their name and work-address, on a piece of paper, for you. You *don't* want to misspell their name. It is difficult to figure out how to spell people's names, these days, simply from the sound of it. What sounds like "Laura" may actually be "Lara." What sounds like "Smith" may actually be "Smythe," and so on. Get that name and address, *but get it right*, please. And let me reiterate: write them the thank-you note that same night, or the very next day at the latest. A thank-you note that arrives a week later, completely misses the point.

Ideally it should be handwritten, but if your handwriting is the least bit difficult to read (ranging on up to *indecipherable*), by all means type it. It can be just two or three sentences. Something like: *"I wanted to thank you for talking with me yesterday. It was very helpful to me. I much appreciated your taking the time out of your busy schedule, to do this. Best wishes to you,"* and then your signature. *Do* sign it, particularly if the thank-you note is typed. Typed letters without any signature seem to be multiplying like rabbits in the world of work, these days; the absence of a signature is usually perceived as making your letter *real* impersonal. You don't want to leave that impression.

You care about people. Show it.

Wild Life by John Kovalic, © 1989 Shetland Productions. Reprinted with permission.

STARTING YOUR OWN BUSINESS

We have been talking about how you research an organization, prior to persuading them to hire you.

All of this changes, of course, when there is no employer you need to approach, or persuade, because you have decided you want to be your own boss.

You've studied your skills and interests, and decided they point toward starting your own business. In which case, there's no one you have to persuade. You can just . . . go . . . do . . . it!

It takes a lot of guts to try something new. It's easier, however, if you keep three principles in mind:

1. There is always some risk, in trying something new. Your job is not to avoid risk -- there is no way to do that -- but to make sure ahead of time that the risks are *manageable*.

2. You find this out before you start, by first talking to others who have already done what you are thinking of doing; then you evaluate whether or not you still want to go ahead and try it. *Don't ever overlook this step!!*

3. Have a Plan B, already laid out, *before you start*, as to what you will do if it doesn't work out; i.e., know where you are going to go, next. Don't wait, *puh-leaze!* Write it out, now. *This is what I'm going to do, if this doesn't work out:* ....

The things you want to keep in mind if you're going to be working for yourself are as follows:

Twelve Tips for the Impatient About-to-be-self-employed

1. If you're sharing your life with someone, sit down with that partner or spouse and ask what the implications are *for them* if you try this new thing. Will it require all your joint savings? Will they have to give up things? If so, what? Are they willing to make those sacrifices? And so on.

2. Move slowly, if you can. Experts say that if you have a job, *don't* quit it. Better by far to move *gradually* into self-employment, doing it as a moonlighting activity first of all, while you are still holding down that regular job somewhere else. That way, you can test out your new enterprise, as you would test a floorboard in an old run-down house, stepping on it cautiously without at first putting your full weight on it, to see whether or not it is strong enough to support you.

3. Decide if you want to go into a business you already know. Maybe your new business should be something that you've been doing for years -- albeit in the employ of someone else. Now, you want to strike out on your own, and be *an independent contractor*, or *free-lancer* or someone who *contracts out your services*.[15] Fine.

4. Decide if you'd prefer to start a business you haven't ever done before. Experts say that the underlying theme to 90% of businesses started up these days is they sell goods or services that save people time. Mail order, delivery services (home deliveries of local restaurants' dinners, or home delivery of grocery orders from any downtown supermarket, evening delivery of laundry or dry-cleaning at the office or in the evening at people's homes, etc.), services rendered at the office (daytime or evening office cleaning services), services rendered at the home (such as home repairs -- especially in the evening or on week-

---

15. If you decide to launch yourself on this path, be sure to talk to people who have been free-lancers, until you know the name of every pitfall and obstacle in *free-lancing*. Where do you find such people? Well, free-lancers are *everywhere*. Independent screenwriters, copy writers, artists, songwriters, photographers, illustrators, interior designers, video people, film people, consultants, and therapists, are only *some* examples of the type of people who must free-lance, in the very nature of their job. Talk with enough of them, even if they're not free-lancing in the same business you have in mind, until you learn all the pitfalls of free-lancing.

ends -- of TVs, radios, audio systems, laundries, dishwashers, etc., automobile repair or cleaning, fixing or replacement of screens or storm doors at the home, care for the elderly in their own homes, or childcare, etc.).

Don't like any of these? Then look around your own community, and ask yourself what service or product already offered in that community could stand a lot of *improving?* Make a list. There may be something on that list that *grabs* you. If so, go do it.

5. **Decide if you have some invention that could be the basis for your own business.** If you have come up with something really wonderful, made a mock-up -- it's been sitting in your drawer, or the garage -- but you've never attempted to duplicate or manufacture it before, now might be a good time to try. Think out very carefully just how you are going to get it manufactured, advertised, and marketed, etc. There are firms out there which claim to specialize in promoting inventions such as yours, for a fee. However, according to the Federal Trade Commission, in a study of 30,000 people who paid such promoters, not a single inventor ever made a profit after giving their invention to such firms.[16] You're much better off, *of course,* doing your own research as to how one gets an invention marketed. Through the copyright office, your library, and the Internet, locate other inventors, and ask how they succeeded in marketing their own invention. Of course one of the first things they're going to tell you is to go get your invention copyrighted or trademarked or patented, before you ever give it into the hands of someone else.

6. **Decide if you'd like to be working at home.** Three hundred years ago, of course, nearly everybody worked at home or on their farm. Only when the industrial revolution came, did the idea of working *away from* home become the rule. In recent times, however, the idea of working at home has been finding new life, due to congestion on the highways, and the development of new technologies. If you're thinking about working out of your own home, apartment, or condo, you would be joining the more than 23.8 million home-based workers who already do this in the U.S., plus the estimated 25 million additional workers who are *thinking* about doing it.

---

16. *San Francisco Chronicle,* 1/26/91.

"YES, THE BUSINESS HAS BECOME BIGGER, BUT FRED STILL LIKES TO WORK AT HOME."

The major problems of home businesses are obvious: conflict between your business and personal life, interruptions, and the like. Bring carloads of self-discipline, and perseverance, if you decide to go this route.

7. **Decide if you'd prefer to buy a franchise.** Franchises exist because some people want to *buy in* on an already established business -- and they have money in their savings, or can get a bank loan. Fortunately, there are a lot of such franchises. Your library or bookstore should have books that list many of these, in this country and elsewhere.

You will learn that some *types* of franchises have a failure rate *far* greater than others, while others should be avoided like the plague, because they charge too much for you to *get on board*, and often don't do the advertising or other commitments that they promised they would.

There is hardly a franchising book that doesn't warn you eighteen times to go talk to people who have *already* bought that same franchise, before you ever decide to go with them. And I mean *several* people, not just one. If you don't like what you hear, but want something in that same field, go talk to *other* franchises that are competitors to *this one*. Maybe there's something better, that your research will uncover.

If you don't want to do any of this homework first, *'cause it's just too much trouble,* but decide to just 'sign up,' you will deserve what you get, believe me.

8. **Decide if you'd like to run a business from cyberspace, from your favorite leisure spot.** It is possible to define a business -- given cellular phones, regular or Internet telephony, fax machine, e-mail, and the Internet -- that can be run from a ski resort or wherever your preferred environment in the whole world is. If you can run a business with these tools, you can operate anywhere -- because these tools, like skills, can make your business independent of one particular place.

9. **Decide if you'd like a special place to be the site of your business.** For example, your dream may be: *I want a horse ranch, where I can raise and sell horses.* Or *I want to run a bed-and-breakfast place.* Stuff like that.

10. **No matter what business you want to start, you *must* go talk to people already doing that business.** If you can't find an exact match, break your idea down into its parts, take two at a time, and go research *that.*

For example, let's suppose your dream is -- here we take a ridiculous case -- to use computers to monitor the growth of plants at the South Pole. And suppose you can't find anybody who's ever done such a thing. The way to tackle this seemingly insurmountable problem, is to break the proposed business down into its parts, which in this case are *computers, plants,* and *the South Pole* -- and then combine any two of these parts together, to define a parallel business. In this case, that would mean finding someone who's *used computers with plants here in the States,* or someone who's *used computers at the South Pole* or someone who has *worked with plants at the South Pole,* etc. From those in parallel businesses, you can learn the pitfalls that wait for you, and how to overcome them.

11. The secret of success is learning what is: A − B = C. It is *mindboggling* how many people start a new business, at home or elsewhere, without ever talking to anybody else in the same kind of business.

One job-hunter told me she started a homemade candle business, without ever talking to anyone else who had tried a similar endeavor. Her business went belly-up within a year and a half. She concluded: no one should go into such a business. I concluded: she hadn't done her homework, before she started.

To avoid her fate, you need to go talk to people who started up the same kind of business you are thinking about, and find out from them what skills and knowledges are needed to run this kind of business. Make a list. We'll call that list '**A**.'

Then you need to sit down and figure out which of those skills and knowledges you have, using the inventory you did in this chapter and the previous one. Make a list. We'll call this list '**B**.'

Then subtract **B** from **A**, and this yields **C**: the skills and knowledges needed, that you don't have. You'll have to learn them, or go out and hire them.

Doubtless at this point you would like an example of this whole process. Okay. Our job-hunter is a woman who has been making harps for some employer, but now is thinking about going into business for herself, not only *making* harps at home, but also *designing* harps, with the aid of a computer. After interviewing several homebased harpmakers and harp designers, and finishing her own self-assessment, her chart of A − B = C came out looking like the next page.

A − B = C

Skills and Knowledges Needed to Run This Kind of Business Successfully	Skills and Knowledges Which I Have	Skills and Knowledges Needed, Which I Have to Learn or Get Someone to Volunteer, or I Will Have to Go Out and Hire
Precision-working with tools and instruments	Precision-working with tools and instruments	
Planning and directing an entire project	Planning and directing an entire project	
Programming computers, inventing programs that solve physical problems		Programming computers, inventing programs that solve physical problems
Problem solving: evaluating why a particular design or process isn't working	Problem solving: evaluating why a particular design or process isn't working	
Being self-motivated, resourceful, patient, and persevering, accurate, methodical, and thorough	Being self-motivated, resourceful, patient, and persevering, accurate, methodical and thorough	
Thorough knowledge of: Principles of electronics	*Thorough knowledge of:*	*Thorough knowledge of:* Principles of electronics
Physics of strings	Physics of strings	
Principles of vibration	Principles of vibration	
Properties of woods	Properties of woods	
Computer programming		Computer programming
Accounting		Accounting

From this she learns that if she decides to try her hand at becoming an independent harpmaker and harp designer, she needs to learn or hire someone who knows: *computer programming, knowledge of the principles of electronics, and accounting* if she is to be successful. Her choices here: school, or co-opting a friend, or hiring on a part-time basis.

12. **You must do this research at least twenty-five miles away from where you intend to put your own business.** Why twenty-five miles away? Well, actually, that's a minimum. You want to interview businesses which, if they were in the same town with you, would be your rival. And if they were in the same town with you, wouldn't likely tell you how to get started. After all, they're not going to train you just so you can then take business away from them.

But, when a guy, a gal, or a business is twenty-five miles away -- even better, fifty miles away -- you're not as likely to be perceived as a rival, and therefore they're much more likely to tell you what you want to know about their own experience, and how *they* got started, and where the landmines are hidden.

What's the landmine they're *most* likely to tell you about? Job-hunting. Yes, yes, I know. The whole idea of working for yourself is that you can avoid the job-hunt. *Technically*, that's true. But in another sense, it's not. In many businesses you have to hunt, and hunt, and hunt for new clients or customers (think of them as short-term employers). And you have to do it continuously.

If this is the one aspect of running your own business that you have no stomach for, you should plan to start out by *hiring, co-opting, or getting* someone to do this for you -- someone who, in fact, 'eats it up.' There are such, out there; you will have to find and link up with one of them.

But, by observing **A − B = C**, you can succeed in whatever form of self-employment you choose.

Internet Resources about Self-Employment

Once you've decided you want to be self-employed, go to my Web site, if you have Internet access

(www.jobhuntersbible.com)

and then to the division of my NetGuide called "Research." There, under the sub-heading "Resources for Those Seeking Self-Employment," you will find a list of sites with information about various aspects of self-employment.

A Sampler of Print Resources about Self-Employment

There are also resources in print that you can turn to, in your local libraries or bookstores. Below are the *kind* of books you will find at your local bookstore or public library:

Paul and Sarah Edwards, *Finding Your Perfect Work: The New Career Guide to Making a Living, Creating a Life.* A Jeremy P. Tarcher/Putnam Book, 200 Madison Avenue, New York, NY 10016. 1996. The book features an alphabetical directory of self-employment careers. *Incidentally, they advertise this as "The What Color Is Your Parachute for the Next Decade." For the record, that's the fifth book I've seen, with that claim.*

Paul and Sarah Edwards, *Working from Home: Everything You Need to Know about Living and Working under the Same Roof.* 3rd ed. J.P. Tarcher, Inc., 200 Madison Avenue, New York, NY 10016. Now revised and expanded. 440 pages. Has a long section on computerizing your home business, and on telecommunicating.

Barbara Brabec, *Homemade Money: Your Homebased Business Success Guide:* 4th ed. Betterway Books, 1507 Dana Avenue, Cincinnati, OH 45207. 1992. A very fine book, with an A to Z business section, and a most helpful summary of which states have laws regulating (or prohibiting) certain home-based businesses; it is updated regularly. Barbara also publishes a newsletter, *National Home Business Report.* If you wish more information, you can ask for her catalog, by writing to National Home Business Network, P.O. Box 2137, Naperville, IL 60567.

Arden, Lynie, *The Work-at-Home Sourcebook.* 5th ed. 1994. Live Oak Publications, P.O. Box 2193, 1515 23rd St., Boulder, CO 80306.

Nicholas, Ted, *How To Form Your Own Corporation Without A Lawyer For Under $75.00.* 1996. Upstart Publishing Company, Dearborn Financial Publishing, Inc., 155 N. Wacker Dr., Chicago, IL 60606-1719. For mail orders, write: Nicholas Direct, Inc., 1511 Gulf Blvd., P.O. Box 877, Indian Rocks Beach, FL 34635. This is a classic in the field, with over a million copies sold, through fifteen revisions.

Robert Laurance Perry, *The 50 Best Low-Investment, High-Profit Franchises.* 1990. Prentice-Hall, Order Dept., 200 Old Tappan Road, Old Tappan, NJ 07675. 1-800-223-2348. Since there is a disturbing trend in franchises these days toward higher and higher start-up fees, up in the $150,000 category or higher, Perry attempts to list ones which people can afford; most of them are less than $20,000, some less than $5,000.

PURSUING
YOUR DREAM

Whether you are among the 10% of job-hunters who want to start their own business, or the 90% who are content to work for someone else, hold on to your dreams.

The concept of "a dream job" or "a dream career" has been dying a horrible, rattling death, in today's culture. In many places, both in this country and around the world, people consider themselves lucky if they have any job.

But dream jobs still exist. They are found by luck, or they are found by the kind of persevering research described in this chapter. Just the right tasks, in just the right place -- that match your favorite skills and your interests.

But dream jobs only begin with this. They are sustained and maintained, over time, by the attitude you bring to them.

> "We who lived in concentration camps can remember the men who walked through the huts comforting others, giving away their last piece of bread. They may have been few in number, but they offer sufficient proof that everything can be taken from a man but one thing: the last of the human freedoms -- to choose one's attitude in any given set of circumstances . . ."
>
> Victor Frankl

If you demand that your dream job be one which is permanent, allows you to 'lean on the oars,' in a predictable setting, with raises and promotions as your reward, then your likelihood of being happy in this world of work is not very great.

Attitude is everything! Attitude has to do with the way you act, but -- even more -- with how you think about things.

So, what attitudes help to make a job into 'your dream job'? These four:

- **1. Think of every job you get as** temporary. 90% of the workforce (in the U.S. at least) is not self-employed; so, you are probably going to end up working for someone else. And how long that job lasts will be up to them, and not just you. If they so will it, your job may end at any time, and without warning. This has always been true to some degree, but now it is even more true than ever - - due to the nature of today's job market.

So, when you go job-hunting, you must think to yourself, "I am essentially a 'temp' worker, hunting for a job that is basically a temporary job, whose length I do not know. I'm going to have to be mentally prepared to start job-hunting again, at any time."

At your 'dream job,' you must take one day at a time, and take it with gratitude. It may not last forever, but while it does last, savor it and enjoy it.

- **2. Think of every job you get as** a seminar. Almost every job today is moving and changing so fast, in its very nature, that you must think of this job you are looking for, as one that will inevitably be a learning experience for you. Think of it as enrolling in a seminar.

If you would make it your 'dream job,' you must love to learn new tasks and procedures, and at the hiring, emphasize this to the employer, and emphasize that you are a faster learner (if it's true).

- **3. Think of every job you get as an** adventure. Most of us love adventures. An adventure is a series of unfolding events that are unpredictable. That's today's jobs, all right! Power plays! Ambition! Rumors! Poor decisions! Strange alliances! Betrayals! Rewards! Sudden twists and turns that no one could have predicted ahead of time, will unfold before your very eyes.

If you would make this your 'dream job,' go to meet the unpredictableness of it all with high spirits, and a sense of excitement rather than dread.

- **4. You must think of every job you get as one where the** satisfaction **must lie in the work itself.** Despite your best research during your job-hunt, you may end up in a job where your bosses fail to recognize or acknowledge the fine contribution that you make, leaving you feeling unloved and unappreciated. So if this is to be your 'dream job,' you must choose one that gives you satisfaction in the very doing of it.

PURSUING YOUR DREAM IN STAGES

With these four attitudes, you can not only find but, more importantly maintain, 'your dream job.'

Just remember, sometimes that dream job will be found in *stages*, even as we saw in the section on career-change (p. 128).

One retired man we know, who had been a senior executive with a publishing company, found himself bored to death in retirement, after he turned 65. He contacted a business acquaintance, who said apologetically, "We just don't have anything open that matches or requires your abilities; right now all we need is someone in our mail room." The 65-year-old executive said, "I'll take that job!" He did, and over the ensuing years steadily advanced once again, to just the job he wanted: as a senior executive in that organization, where he utilized all his prized skills, for some time. He retired as senior executive for the second time, at the age of 85.

It is amazing how often people do get their dreams, whether in stages or directly. The more you don't *cut* the dream down, because of what you *think* you know about *the real world*, the more likely you are to find what you are looking for.

Most people don't find their heart's desire, because they decide to pursue just half their dream - - and consequently they hunt for it with only *half a heart*.

If you decide to pursue your whole dream, your best dream, the one you die to do, I guarantee you that you will hunt for it *with all your heart*. It is this *passion* which often is the difference between successful career-changers, and unsuccessful ones.

This letter is from a reader, who pursued her dream, and found it:

"I was a woman who majored in Humanities and then floated around after college in several jobs, which were just jobs. To be honest, I was in my early twenties (which I have nicknamed the decade of terror), and had no idea what I wanted to do. Only, I longed for self-expression and passion in my work. I purchased your book, did some informational interviews, even saw a career counselor, all to no avail.

"Five years later, now, I have come back to your book (the new edition, of course), and identified my values, skills and talents. With my values and skills in mind, I went to the library to research government and non-profit careers, and found myself much interested in the latter. I copied a list of them and began contacting the organizations whose values were closely related to mine: helping people in the community.

"One organization in particular called me back the next day, and asked if I could interview for a professional position with them. I did, explored further to be sure I understood what the job entailed, interviewed a second time, and in less than one month was offered the position of my dreams!

"Thanks to you and your advice on the most successful ways to find employment - - previously, over a period of four months, I had applied for at least fifty jobs from the want ads, with no hits - - I am now happily employed doing the kind of work I like best, and I did so in record time."

A Word to Those Who Are Shy

The late John Crystal[17] had to often counsel the shy. They were *frightened* at the whole idea of going to talk to people for information, never mind for hiring. So John developed a system to help the shy. He suggested that before you even begin doing any Informational Interviewing, you first go out and talk to people about *anything* just to get good at *talking to people*. Thousands of job-hunters and career-changers have followed his advice, over the past twenty-five years, and found it really helps. Indeed, people who have followed John's advice in this regard have had a success rate of 86% in finding a job - -and not just any job, but *the* job or new career that they were looking for.

Daniel Porot, the job-hunting expert in Europe, has taken John's system, and brought some organization to it. He observed that John was really recommending three types of interviews: this interview we are talking about, just for practice. Then Informational Interviewing. And finally, of course, the hiring-interview. Daniel decided to call these three the *'The PIE Method,'* which has helped thousands of job-hunters and career-changers in both the U.S. and in Europe. Porot's "PIE Chart" follows on the next pages:

17. John also was the inventor of WHAT, WHERE, and HOW - - which I have used as the basic framework for Chapters 4, 5, and 6, here.

Initial:	Pleasure **P**	Information **I**	Employment **E**
Kind of Interview	Practice Field Survey	Informational Interviewing or Researching	Employment Interview or Hiring Interview
Purpose	To Get Used to Talking with People to Enjoy It; To "Penetrate" Networks	To Find Out If You'd Like a Job, Before You Go Trying to Get It	To Get Hired for the Work You Have Decided You Would Most Like to Do
How You Go to the Interview	You Can Take Somebody with You	By Yourself or You Can Take Somebody with You	By Yourself
Who You Talk To	Anyone Who Shares Your Enthusiasm About a (for You) Non- Job-Related Subject	A Worker Who Is Doing the Actual Work You Are Thinking About Doing	An Employer Who Has the Power to Hire You for the Job You Have Decided You Would Most Like to Do
How Long a Time You Ask for	10 Minutes (and DON'T run over - - asking to see them at 11:50 may help keep you honest, since most employers have lunch appoint- ments at noon)	Ditto	
What You Ask Them	Any Curiosity You Have About Your Shared Interest or Enthusiasm	Any Questions You Have About This Job or This Kind of Work	You Tell Them What It Is You Like About Their Organization and What Kind of Work You Are Looking For.

Initial:	Pleasure P	Information I	Employment E
What You Ask Them *(continued)*	If Nothing Occurs to You, Ask: 1. How did you start, with this hobby, interest, etc.? 2. What excites or interests you the most about it? 3. What do you find is the thing you like the least about it? 4. Who else do you know of who shares this interest, hobby or enthusiasm, or could tell me more about my curiosity? a. Can I go and see them? b. May I mention that it was you who suggested I see them? c. May I say that you recommended them? *Get their name and address*	If Nothing Occurs to You Ask: 1. How did you get interested in this work and how did you get hired? 2. What excites or interests you the most about it? 3. What do you find is the thing you like the least about it? 4. Who else do you know of who does this kind of work, or similar work but with this difference: _____? 5. What kinds of challenges or problems do you have to deal with in this job? 6. What skills do you need in order to meet those challenges or problems? *Get their name and address*	You tell them the kinds of challenges you like to deal with. What skills you have to deal with those challenges. What experience you have had in dealing with those challenges in the past.
AFTERWARD: That Same Night	SEND A THANK-YOU NOTE	SEND A THANK-YOU NOTE	SEND A THANK-YOU NOTE

Why is it called *'PIE'*? [18]

P is for the *warmup* phase. John Crystal named this warmup 'The Practice Field Survey.'[19] Daniel Porot calls it **P** for *pleasure*.

I is for 'Informational Interviewing.'

E is for the employment interview with the-person-who-has-the-power-to-hire-you.

How do you use this **P** for *practice* to get comfortable about going out and talking to people *one-on-one?*

This is achieved by choosing a topic -- *any* topic, however silly or trivial -- that is a pleasure for you to talk about with your friends, or family. To avoid anxiety, it should not be a topic that is connected to any present or future career that you are considering. Rather, the kinds of topics that work best, for this exercise, are:

• a hobby you *love*, such as skiing, bridge playing, exercise, computers, etc.

• any leisure-time enthusiasm of yours, such as a movie you just saw, that you liked a lot

• a long-time curiosity, such as how do they predict the weather, or what do policemen do

• an aspect of the town or city you live in, such as a new shopping mall that just opened

• an issue you feel strongly about, such as the homeless, AIDS sufferers, ecology, peace, health, etc.

There is only one condition about choosing a topic: it should be something you *love* to talk about with other people: a subject you know nothing about, but you feel a great deal of enthusiasm for it, is far preferable to something you know an awful lot about, but it puts you to sleep.

---

18. Daniel has summarized his system in a new book published here in the U.S.: it is called *The PIE Method for Career Success: A Unique Way to Find Your Ideal Job*, 1996, and is available from its publisher, JIST Works, Inc., 720 North Park Avenue, Indianapolis IN 46202-3431. Phone 317-264-3720. Fax 317-264-3709. It is a fantastic book, and I give it my highest recommendation.

19. If you want further instructions about this whole process, I refer you to "The Practice Field Survey," pp. 187–196 in *Where Do I Go From Here With My Life?* by John Crystal and friend. Ten Speed Press, Box 7123, Berkeley, CA 94707.

> ### Enthusiasm
>
> Throughout the job-hunt and career-change, the key to 'interviewing' is not found in memorizing a dozen rules about what you're supposed to say.
>
> No, the key is just this one thing: now and always, be *sure* you are talking about something you feel *passionate about.*[20]
>
> **Enthusiasm** is the key -- to *enjoying* 'interviewing,' and conducting *effective* interviews, at any level. What this **P** exercise teaches us is that shyness always loses its power and its painful self-consciousness -- *if* and *when* you are talking about something *you love.*
>
> For example, if you love gardens you will forget all about your shyness when you're talking to someone else about gardens and flowers. *"You ever been to Butchart Gardens?"*
>
> If you love movies, you'll forget all about your shyness when you're talking to someone else about movies. *"I just hated that scene where they . . ."*
>
> If you love computers, then you will forget all about your shyness when you're talking to someone else about computers. *"Do you work on a Mac or an MS-DOS machine?"*
>
> That's why it is important that it be your enthusiasms -- here, your hobbies -- later, in Informational Interviewing, your *favorite* skills and your *favorite* subjects -- that you are exploring and pursuing in these conversations with others.

Having identified your enthusiasm, you then need to go talk to someone who is as enthusiastic about this thing, as you are. *For best results with your later job-hunt, this should be someone you don't already know.* Use the Yellow Pages, ask around among your friends and family, *who do you know that* loves *to talk about this?* It's relatively easy to find the kind of person you're looking for.

You love to talk about skiing? *Try a ski-clothes store, or a skiing instructor.* You love to talk about writing? *Try a professor on a nearby college campus, who teaches English.* You love to talk about physical exercise? *Try a trainer, or someone who teaches physical therapy.*

Once you've identified someone you think shares your enthusiasm, you then go talk with them. When you are face-to-face with your *fellow enthusiast,* the first thing you must do is relieve their understandable anxiety. *Everyone* has had someone visit them who has stayed too long, who has worn out their welcome. If your *fellow enthusiast* is worried about you staying too long, they'll be so preoccupied with this that they won't hear a word you are saying.

So, when you first meet them, ask for *ten minutes of their time, only.* Period. Stop. Exclamation point. And watch your wristwatch *like a hawk,* to be sure

20. This is what the late Joseph Campbell used to call 'your bliss.'

you stay no longer. *Never* stay longer, unless they *beg* you to. And I mean, *beg, beg, beg.*[21]

Once they've agreed to give you ten minutes, you tell them why you're there -- that you're trying to get comfortable about talking with people, for information -- and you understand that you two share a mutual interest, which is . . .

Then what? Well, a topic may have its own unique set of questions. For example, I love movies, so if I met someone who shared this interest, my first question would be, "What movies have you seen lately?" And so on. If it's a topic you love, and often talk about, you'll *know* what kinds of questions you begin with. But, if no such questions come to mind, no matter how hard you try, the following ones have proved to be good conversation starters for thousands of job-hunters and career-changers before you, no matter what their topic or interest.

So, look these over, memorize them *(or copy them on a little card that fits in the palm of your hand),* and give them a try:

Questions Shy People Can Practice With

Addressed to the person you're doing the Practice Interviewing with:

- How did you get involved with/become interested in this? (*"This"* is the hobby, curiosity, aspect, issue, or enthusiasm, that you are so interested in.)
- What do you like the most about it?
- What do you like the least about it?
- Who else would you suggest I go talk to that shares this interest?
- Can I use your name?
- May I tell them it was you who recommended that I talk with them?
- *Then, choosing one person off the list of several names they may have given you, you say,* Well, I think I will begin by going to talk to this person. Would you be willing to call ahead for me, so they will know who I am, when I go over there?

---

21. A polite, "Oh do you have to go?" should be understood for what it is: politeness. Your response should be, "Yes, I promised to only take ten minutes of your time, and I want to keep to my word." This will almost always leave a *very* favorable impression behind you.

Incidentally, during *this* Practice Interviewing, it's perfectly okay for you to take someone with you -- preferably someone who is more outgoing than you feel you are. And on the first few interviews, let them take the lead in the conversation, while you watch to see how they do it.

Once it is *your turn* to conduct the interview, it will by that time usually be easy for you to figure out what to talk about.

Alone or with someone, keep at this Practice Interviewing until you feel very much at ease in talking with people and asking them questions about things you are curious about.

In all of this, *fun* is the key. If you're having fun, you're doing it right. If you're not having fun, you need to keep at it, until you are. It may take your seeing four people. It may take ten. Or twenty. You'll know.

Summary of This Chapter

There is no limit to what you can find out about Where you'd like to work -- careers, and places which hire for those careers -- if you go out and talk to people. When you find places that interest you, it is irrelevant whether they happen to have a vacancy, or not. In this dance of life, called the job-hunt, you get to decide first of all, through your research, whether or not *you* want them. Only after you have decided that, is it appropriate to ask -- as in the next chapter -- if they also want you.

You're a bunch of jackasses. You work your rear ends off in a trivial course that no one will ever care about again. You're not willing to spend time researching a company that you're interested in working for. Why don't you decide who you want to work for and go after them?

Professor Albert Shapiro,
The late William H. Davis Professor
of The American Free Enterprise System
at Ohio State University

The Systematic Approach To
Career-Change
And Job-Hunting

How

DO YOU OBTAIN SUCH A JOB?

You Must Identify
The Person Who Has The Power to Hire You,
and Show Them How Your Skills
Can Help Them With Their Goals

Chapter 6

'I'll tell you why I want this job. I thrive on challenges.
I like being stretched to my full capacity. I like solving problems.
Also, my car is about to be repossessed.'

Okay, so you've decided *what* skills you most enjoy using.

And you've decided *where* you would like to use them.

Now you've come to the point of it all: *how* do you find such a job? As we saw in chapter 3, the jobs are always out there *but* finding them can be slow and painstaking work.

You must be mentally (and financially) prepared for your job-search to last a lot longer than you think it will. Even the shortest job-hunt lasts between two and eighteen weeks, depending on a variety of factors -- what kind of job you are looking for, where you are living, how old you are, how high you are aiming, and what the state is of the local economy.

Be mentally prepared for it to take eighteen weeks or longer. Experienced outplacement people have long claimed that your search for one of the jobs that are out there will probably take one month for every $10,000 of salary that you are seeking. This may be pure drivel, but you get the picture, don't you?

You, of course -- the Impatient Job-Hunter -- want to know how to do your job-search *faster*. Okay, here are some tips.

How
To Speed Up Your Search

Tips for the Impatient Job-Hunter

Here are twelve ways to speed up your job-search:

1

❋ **Treat your job-hunt as a full-time job, just like any other -- 'punch in' at 9, and 'punch out' at 5**. Don't buy the world's idea that you are 'unemployed.' As of this minute, you have a full-time job (without pay). Your new job-title is "Job-hunter" (or "Career-changer").

The swiftness with which you complete your job-search is usually directly proportional to time you spend on it.

Studies have revealed the depressing fact that two-thirds of all job-hunters spend only 5 hours a week (or less) hunting for a job.[1]

If you would speed it up, you must spend 35 hours a week working at it from 9 to 5 every weekday (giving yourself one hour off for lunch or 'flake-out' time). That should cut down, dramatically, the number of weeks it takes you to find work.

To illustrate, let us imagine a woman job-hunter who devotes only 5 hours a week to her search; and it turns out, in the end, to take 30 weeks, before she finds a job. That means it took a total of 150 hours.

---

1. According to the U.S. Census Bureau, discussed in "Job Search Assistance Programs: Implications for the School," authored by the late Robert G. Wegmann, and first appearing in *Phi Delta Kappan,* December 1979, pp. 271ff.

Now let us suppose that same job-hunter were to be hurled back in time, but this time she knew it was going to take 150 hours. Therefore she decides to give 35 hours a week to the task, in order to 'eat up' the 150 hours faster. As you can figure out for yourself, her 150 hour job-hunt should then take little more than 4 weeks, before she found work -- other things being equal.[2]

2

* **Find some kind of support group,** so that you don't have to face the job-hunt all by yourself. Ever. You'd be amazed how much the support of others can keep you going and speed up your job-hunt. Here are the kinds of support groups you can choose from:

a. **Your mate or partner, grandparent, brother or sister, or best friend.** A loving 'taskmaster' is what you need. Someone who will make a regular weekly appointment to meet with you, check you out on what you've done that week, and be very stern with you if you've done little or nothing since you last met. You want understanding, sympathy, and discipline. If your mate, brother or sister, or best friend, can offer you all of these, run -- do not walk -- to enlist them immediately.

b. **Job-hunting groups that already exist in your city or town,** such as "Forty Plus" clubs, "Experience Unlimited" groups, job-hunt classes at your local Federal/state employment offices, or at the local Chamber of Commerce, or at your local college or community college, or at your local Adult Education center, or at your local church, synagogue, or place of worship.[3] The likelihood that such help is available in your community increases dramatically for you if you are from cer-

---

2. Of course, there are some factors beyond a job-hunter's control, that may prolong the job-hunt, such as how long it takes an interviewing-committee to schedule the next round of interviews at the place that interests you (you will often be invited back two or three times before they make up their mind about you), etc. Nonetheless, the main point of our illustration still remains.

3. The *National Business Employment Weekly* used to publish a "Calendar of Career Events," for many of these kinds of groups in the U.S. But unfortunately, the NBEW ceased publication November 1st, 1999, so this is no longer available.

tain groups held to be disadvantaged, such as low income, or welfare recipients, or youth, or displaced workers, etc. Ask around.

c. **A local career counselor.** I grant you that career counselors aren't usually thought of as 'a support group.' But many of them do have group sessions; and even by themselves they can be of inestimable support. If you can afford their services, and none of the above suggestions have worked, this is a good fall-back strategy. Before choosing such a counselor, however, *please* read pages 306–315 in the back of this book. It will tell you how to locate such counselors, and how to evaluate them.

d. **A job-hunting group that doesn't currently exist, but that you could help form.** Some enterprising job-hunters, unable to locate any group, have formed their own by running an ad in the local newspaper, near the "help wanted" listings. *"Am currently job-hunting, would like to meet weekly with other job-hunters for mutual support and encouragement. Propose using 'What Color Is Your Parachute?' as our guide."* Enlist your priest, minister, rabbi or religious leader, at your local church, synagogue or religious centre, to help find a place to meet.

3

✷ **Enlist your contacts. Tell them what kind of work you're looking for, and ask for their help in getting leads. It takes about eighty pairs of eyes, and ears, to speed up your job-search. Your contacts *are* those eyes and ears.**

This subject of contacts is widely misunderstood. It is often defined as "business contacts," leading many job-hunters to say, "I don't have any contacts." Oh yes you do.

Every person you know, is a contact.
Every member of your family.
Every friend of yours.
Every person in your address book.
All the people whose e-mail addresses you have.
Every person on your Christmas-card list or its equivalent.
Every person in your church, synagogue, mosque, or religious assembly.
Every co-worker you've ever had.

Every doctor, or medical professional you know.

Every one who does personal work on you: your barber, hairdresser, manicurist, physical trainer, body worker, and the like.

Every person you know at your gym or in your athletic pursuits. Every leisure partner you walk with, play golf or tennis with, etc.

The waiters, waitresses, and manager of your favorite restaurants.

Every merchant you know, every gas station attendant.

The tellers, manager and friends at the place where you bank.

Every person you meet in line at the supermarket or bank.

Every professor, teacher, etc. you once knew or maybe still know how to get a hold of.

Every person who comes to do repairs or maintenance work for you.

Every person you know at any group you belong to.

Every person you met at any party.

Every person you meet, stumble across, or blunder into, during your job-hunt, whose name, address, and phone number you have the grace to ask for. (Always have the grace to ask for it.)

4

✳ **Expand your contacts.** There are five ways to 'grow' your contact list:

(1) **Attend lectures.** Some job-hunters make it a point to join the crowd that gathers 'round a speaker at the end of a talk, and -- with notepad poised -- ask such questions as: "Is there anything special that people with my expertise can do?" And here they mention their *generalized* job-title: computer scientist, health professional, chemist, writer, or whatever. Very useful information has thus been turned up. You can also go up to the speaker afterwards, and ask if you can contact him or her for further information -- "and at what address (e-mail or otherwise)?"

(2) **Attend conventions in your chosen field.** These likewise afford rich opportunities to make contacts. Says one college

graduate: "I snuck into the Cable Advertisers Convention at the Waldorf in N.Y.C. That's how I got my job."

(3) **Leave a message on your answering machine, if you have one.** One job-hunter used the following message: " Hi! This is Sandra. Being recently laid-off, I'm busy right now, out looking for a job in the accounting department of some hospital. Leave me a message after the beep, and if you happen to have any leads or contacts for me, be sure to mention that too, along with your phone number. Thanks a lot."

(4) **Study the *things* that you like to work with, and then write to the manufacturer of that *thing* to ask them for a list of places in your geographical area which use that *thing*.** For example, if you like to work on a particular machine, you would write to the manufacturer of that machine, and ask for names of organizations in your geographical area which use that machine. Or if you like to work in a particular environment, think of the supplies used in that environment. Let's say you love darkrooms. You think of what brand equipment or supplies is usually used in darkrooms, and then you contact the sales manager of the company that makes those supplies, to ask where his (or her) customers are. Some sales managers will not be at all responsive to such an inquiry; but others graciously will, and thus you may gain some very helpful leads.

As you expand your contacts list, you may find it helpful to set up a file with 3×5 cards, putting on each the name of one contact of yours, with address, phone number, and anything you know about where they work or who they know that may be of use at a later date.

Go back over those cards frequently. This is the way you stay in touch with the eighty pairs of eyes and ears that you need to speed up your job-search.

5

✳ **Go after any place that interests you. Pay no attention to whether or not there is a known vacancy at that place.** If you base your job-hunt just on places where there is a known vacancy -- advertised in newspapers or posted on the Internet -- you will prolong your search forever! Vacancies often develop at places long before any notice is put out that that vacancy exists.

Moreover, when bosses or managers are thinking of creating a new position, this intention often lies in their mind for quite some time before they get around to doing anything about it. If you contact them during that opportune quiet period, you come as the answer to their prayers.

Be prepared always to tell them what makes you different from nineteen other people who can do the same thing that you do.

And don't be put off by rejection. If they have nothing to offer you, ask them if they know of anyone else who might be hiring. Thank them kindly for any leads they may give you.

Keep going until you find someone who is hiring at a place that you like.

6

※ **Go after organizations with twenty or less employees.** There is a natural tendency for job-hunters to focus their job-hunt only on large, well-known organizations, and when they can't find a job at any of these places, they assume that no one is hiring. Indeed, some job-hunters just read the newspaper and if they read that large organizations are laying off lots of people through mergers and downsizings, they just assume things are bad everywhere. This is a very common, and very costly, mistake.

The fact is, small companies -- with 100 or less employees -- have been creating two out of every three new positions since 1970, even in the worst of times. For example, while the Fortune 500 companies in the U.S. were cutting 3.7 million jobs from their payrolls during the 1980s, smaller companies created 19 million new jobs.[4] You can therefore speed up your job-search by concentrating on small firms in your field that are within commuting distance, and have one hundred or less employees. (Personally, I would *begin* with firms that have twenty or less employees.) The way to locate these is through the Yellow Pages listings in your field.

---

4. *The San Francisco Chronicle,* 2/1/93.

Look in particular for small businesses that seem to be on their way up -- growing, and expanding.[5] The way to locate these is by reading the business news in your daily newspaper, and talking to everyone you can, including the local Chamber of Commerce, to find out which small businesses are growing and expanding -- companies like Apple Computer which started out in a garage, or ASK Group, of Mountain View, California, which started out in a spare bedroom. Target any place that interests you.

7

✳ **Don't just send a resume to a place that interests you; visit the place**. If you want to speed up your job-search, you should physically go to any place that interests you, which might hire someone with your skills. Studies show that 47.7% of job-hunters who knock on doors find a job thereby, while only .06% of those who send resumes do.

Said one job-hunter: *"The very first real job I got was by knocking door-to-door, asking if they needed a draftsman. I got a favorable response at the fifth, but not the last, place I knocked; interviewed a few days after; and was working within the week. I was incredibly lucky, as were they: their current draftsman had given notice that day I knocked. I worked there two years and then went on to a much better position at the invitation of friends I had made at that first job."*

In their pioneering study of the job-hunt some years ago, *The Job Hunt: Job-Seeking Behavior of Unemployed Workers in a Local Economy,* A. Harvey Belitsky and Harold A. Sheppard discovered that going face-to-face at a workplace, even without any introduction or leads, was *the* most effective job-search method if you were a blue-collar worker. Blue-collar and other workers take note.

---

5. "The lion's share of job creation over time," says Bennett Harrison, author of *Lean and Mean: The Changing Landscape of Corporate Power in the Age of Flexibility,* "is contributed by a tiny fraction of new firms." In 1985 there were 245,000 businesses started up, but just 735 of them accounted for 75% of the employment gains between 1985 and 1988. *Paying attention to the business section of your local newspaper, over time, should help you identify which ones are doing the lion's share of hiring. If you lump all small businesses together, the picture is not so rosy.*

8

∗ **Visit at least 2 employers each weekday, face-to-face.**
Studies have shown that the average U.S. job-hunter only contacts six employers a month. That adds up to little more than one employer per week.[6]

They further learned that if a job-hunter contacted two employers a week, the job-search typically lasted up to a year; if ten employers a week, the search typically ended with a job within six months or less; *and*, at twenty employers a week, the search time typically dropped to 90 days or less.[7]

So, determine to visit two employers per weekday, one in the morning and one in the afternoon (at least). Do this for as many weeks (or months) as your job-hunt may last. Thus you will greatly shorten the length of your job-hunt.

9

∗ **When all other approaches fail, canvass by telephone.** If you've tried all other ways to speed up your job-search, and failed, telephoning is your fall-back strategy.[8]

The strategy experts suggest is: call up, one by one, every single company or organization in the Yellow Pages (in your area) that looks interesting to you, to ask them if they might be hiring, for the kind of work you do. Call as many as 100 or 200 per day! It is almost guaranteed to turn up something, just by the sheer weight of numbers.

---

6. A survey cited by the late Robert G. Wegmann in "Job Search Assistance: A Review," in the *Journal of Employment Counseling,* December 1979, p. 212.

7. Goodrich & Sherwood Co., reported in "How to Succeed in Rotten Times," Oct. 1992.

8. Some experts hold the opposite view: never, never use the telephone, they say, because it only makes it easier for the employer to screen you out over the phone.

Nonetheless, all the *successful* group job-search programs that I have studied over the years, from Nathan Azrin's Job Club to Dean Curtis's Welfare Reform programs, based on the Dave Perschau/Chuck Hoffman model, have attributed their great success rates precisely to their heavy use of the telephone.

Nathan had job-hunters make at least 10 phone calls a day; Chuck had them make 100 phone calls in the morning, and 100 in the afternoon. Both were successful, Chuck's program the more so. The implication is clear: the more phone calls you make, the faster you're likely to find a job.

Personally, I infinitely prefer knocking on their doors to phoning them up. But if you're 'striking out' with every other method, and you're really desperate to speed things up, telephoning does work. Naturally, you first have to get over your distaste for the idea -- most people *hate* doing (not to mention receiving) telephone solicitations. But this is on behalf of your own job-search, rather than selling a product.

Here's how to do it, according to job-search veterans:

Plan how many calls a day you're going to try to make, and stick to that goal. Some experts advise you to make 200 calls a day. Others advise fewer calls, making them only to places that *really* interest you, and only after researching each place, before you call.

Stand up when you make your phone calls; your voice is more forceful that way.

Have a mirror in front of you, on the wall, at eye level, so you can watch yourself in it, to see if you are smiling as you talk.

If you're only making a few calls that day, call before 8 a.m., shortly before noon, or after 5 p.m. If it's managers you're seeking, and if they're hardworking, they're likely to be there at those times -- without an intervening receptionist. Of course if you're trying to make 100, 200 phone calls a day, this rule goes out the window.

When you are connected, ask to speak with 'the manager.' In smaller organizations this is the person who will usually know the hiring plans there.

If someone suggested you call this manager, use their name as a reference when you call. Something like this: "Hi! Your name was given to me by . . . ." Alternatively, try to start the call with any connection there may be between you and the caller. "I just read that you . . . and as it turns out I. . . ." (e.g., "I just read that you grew up in Wisconsin, and as it turns out, so did I." *If you can't find a connection, don't invent one.*)

Try to keep your 'little speech' down to fifteen seconds or less. When the manager comes on the line, address them by name, introduce yourself by name, and then *briefly* (in one sentence) describe your greatest personal strength or top skill, a *brief* description of your experience, and then ask if there is a job opening for someone with your skills and background. For example, *"I am an experienced writer, with three published books, and I wonder if you have any job openings for someone with my experience?"* If *"yes,"* set up an interview time, repeat it, and repeat your name; if *"no,"* ask if they know of anyone else who might be hiring a person with your background.[9]

Write all this out ahead of time. Before you make your call, set down the objective of that call in writing and the key points (above) you want to make during the conversation. *Write out every word.* This is your *script*; don't try to *wing it.* When you're talking to the manager, unabashedly read what you wrote out -- but try not to *sound* like you're reading it. Rehearse it several times until it starts to sound (and feel) natural.

If the conversation goes more than one minute, add other tidbits about yourself: if you've done something in the community, written articles for the local paper, served on a volunteer committee, etc., work that into the conversation.

Know how to deal with an interviewer's turndown or objections. Try responding with:

I understand . . .

I can appreciate your position . . .

I see your point . . .

---

9. I am again indebted to Dean Curtis, for this advice.

Of course! However . . .

Thank the manager before signing off, whether they have a job lead for you, or not.

10

✳ **To speed up your job-search be willing to look at different kinds of jobs**: full-time jobs, part-time jobs, unlimited contract jobs (*formerly called 'permanent jobs'*), short-term contract jobs, temporary jobs, working for others, working for yourself, etc. Short jobs often turn into longer jobs, if they are pleased with the quality of your work.

11

✳ **Zero in on several organizations, not just one.** One place may stand out above all the rest, a boss so wonderful you would die to work for them. To get a job there would be the dream of your life.

Well, maybe you'll get that dream-come-true. But -- *big question* -- what are your plans if you don't? If you would speed up your job-search, you've *got* to have other plans **now** -- not when that first target runs out of gas, three months down the road. You must go after more than one organization. (I recommend five, at least.)

I have studied successful and unsuccessful job-hunters for over a quarter of a century, now, and the single greatest thing I have learned is that *successful* job-hunters *always have alternatives.* Alternative ways of describing what they want to do. Alternative ways of going about the job-hunt (not just resumes, agencies, and ads). Alternative job prospects. Alternative 'target' organizations that they go after. Alternative ways of approaching employers. And so on, and so forth.

So, if you would speed up your search, be sure you have more than one employer that you are pursuing at any one time.

12

✳ **Even if all your attempts to speed up your job-search don't seem to be paying off, don't give up.** One job-hunter out of every three becomes an unsuccessful job-hunter *simply because* they abandon their search prematurely. And if you ask them why they abandoned it, they say, "I didn't think it was going to be this hard; I didn't think it was going to take this long."

In other words, what 'does in' so many job-hunters is some *unspoken* mental quota in our head, which goes something like this: *I expect I'll be able to find a job after about 30 phone calls, 15 calls in person, and three interviews.* We go about our job-hunt, fill or exceed those quotas, and then give up. Don't let this happen to you.

Keep going until you find a job. **Persistence** is the name of the game. *Persistent* means being willing to go back to places that interested you, at least a couple of times in the following months, to see if by any chance their 'no vacancy' situation has changed.

The one thing an individual needs above everything else is hope, and hope is born of persistence.

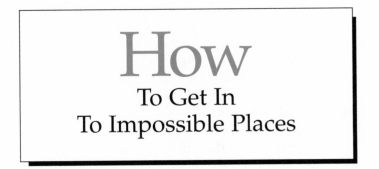

How
To Get In
To Impossible Places

Okay, so you try all these tips for speeding up your job-search, and you're frustrated *because* . . .

You've found a place where you'd *really* like to work. But, the person you'd have to see, in order to get hired there, is in an office castle with fifty-foot walls, with a ring of fire around it, three knights in full-armor guarding it, totally surrounded by a wide moat whose deep waters are filled with hungry alligators.

And you want to know how to get a hiring-interview with this person. Right? Well, it isn't as difficult as it might at first seem . . . if you are determined. Here are the rules:

Find Out How Large The Place Is

Most discussions of job-interviewing proceed from a false assumption: they *assume* you are going to approach a large organization -- you know, the ones where you need a floor-plan of the building, and an alphabetical directory of the staff -- with a large site on the Internet. But, actually many job-hunters don't want to work for a behemoth like that. They want a small organization.

This distinction is important, because the techniques for getting in a small organization vs. a large organization vary greatly.

Getting Into A Small Organization Is 'A Piece of Cake'

We said earlier that a job-hunter is well-advised to concentrate on small organizations. But there is more to be said on the subject.

From a job-hunter's point of view, small organizations have five distinct advantages over large organizations:

1. With a small organization, **you don't need to wait until there's a *known* vacancy, because they rarely advertise vacancies even when there is one.** You just go over there and ask if they need someone with your skills and knowledge.

2. With a small organization, **there is no Personnel or Human Resources Department to screen you out.** Only 15% of all organizations have such a department; small organizations usually belong to the 85% who don't.

3. With a small organization, **there's no problem in identifying the person-who-has-the-power-to-hire-you.** It's *the boss.* Everyone there knows who it is. They can point to his or her office door, easily. It's what we call "The One-Minute Research Project."

4. With a small organization, **you do not need to first approach them through the mail; the boss is much more 'available.'** And if, by chance, he or she is well-protected from intruders, it is relatively easy to figure out how to get around *that.* Contacts are the answer, as we shall see.

5. With a small organization, **there is a greater likelihood that they will be willing to create a new position for you,** *if you quietly convince them that you are too good to let slip out of their grasp.*

Add to these five advantages, the fact that small organizations often are 'job-creating machines' -- representing 80% of all private businesses, employing one-fourth of all workers in the private sector, and creating two-thirds of all new jobs[10] -- and you will see why many job-hunting experts say:

Go after the small organizations -- *especially* if you've been pursuing large organizations previously, and getting nowhere. You can thus overcome a lot of barriers, in one fell swoop.

10. This statistic, first popularized by David Birch of M.I.T., and 'bandied about' for many years, was widely debated during the '90s by economists such as Nobel laureate Milton Friedman, Harvard economist James Medoff, Steven J. Davis, a labor economist at the University of Chicago, John Haltiwanger at the University of Maryland, and Scott Schuh at the Federal Reserve. Critics often concede that small companies do create a lot of jobs in the economy, but then *sniff,* "Small businesses are not the places you see *the best* jobs," as one economist put it. (The emphasis is mine.) 'Best jobs' mean -- to these critics -- jobs with high pay, high benefits, government-mandated health and safety regulations, and union representation. (*San Francisco Chronicle,* 3/29/93). See footnote 5 for more commentary (page 179).

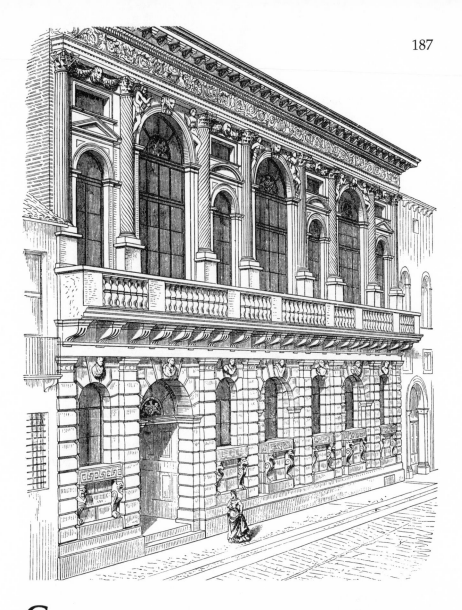

Getting Into A Large Organization Takes A Plan

In getting in to 'impossible places,' it's the large organizations that are the problem -- the ones, as I mentioned above, where you need a floor-plan of the building, and an alphabetical directory of the staff.

There are problems in approaching such giants for a hiring-interview, not the least of which is that many of them are not creating new jobs -- they're playing downsizing, merger and takeover games these days, with thousands laid off as a consequence.

If you approach these places by mail (or resume), you're very likely to be politely dismissed or get no answer at all. And if you go knock on their door, you're very likely to end up in the human resources or personnel department, whose basic job *all too often* is to screen you out. Oops!

Still, there is a way to get in. It begins with three basic truths:

1. You don't want to just get into the building. **You want to see *a particular person* in that building, and only that person**: namely, the person–who–has–the–power–to–hire–you for the job you are interested in. Most job-hunters don't even *try* to find out who that person is, before approaching a large organization.

Rather, they approach each large organization in what can only be described as a haphazard, scatter-shot fashion - - sending the organization their resume or c.v.[11] with some cover letter (or posting same on the Internet) - - and hoping it will haphazardly fall into the hands of 'the right person.'

It usually doesn't. It falls into the hands of 'the screening-out committee,' and it only takes them eight seconds (it's been timed) to scan your resume and reject you.

If you want to get in there, you have to find out ahead of time *who* at that organization has the power to hire you for the position you have in mind.

---

11. C.v. stands for *curriculum vitae,* a term for *resume* that is favored outside the U.S., as well as in academic circles within the U.S.

2. **You want to get an interview with the person–who–has–the–power–to–hire–you** *through personal contacts,* **and not by sending your resume.** Once you have identified *who* at that organization has the power to hire you for the position you have in mind, you then need to discover what mutual friend the two of you might have in common, who could help you get in there, for an appointment. This intermediary is what I earlier called 'a contact' (page 175). Thus, the person–who–has–the–power–to–hire–you will see you because that mutual friend has made the appointment for you, and recommended you.

It is astonishing how often this approach works -- it has, in fact, an 86% effectiveness rate for getting a hiring-interview and, subsequently, a job, even in 'impossible places.'

But let's talk about the 14% of the time when it doesn't work. You will, of course, be furious that you can't get in to see that person, despite the techniques recommended in this section.

But, could I ask you a question: *"Why* do you want to work for such a person? I mean, never mind that you're taking this very personally, with *Rejection, rejection, rejection* flashing on and off in your brain. But, stop and think for a minute: haven't they *(by these actions)* told you something important about *the way they do things?* And having gained that information, isn't it time for you to reassess *whether you really want to work at a place so guarded, so impenetrable, so 'un-user-friendly'?"*

3. **But after you have had an interview with the person–who–has–the–power–to–hire–you, your resume may be useful.** There's an old saying among the creative minority: "A resume is something you never send ahead of you, but always leave behind you."

Which is to say, after you've concluded an interview there, it may be useful to send your resume to the interviewer the next day at the latest. Reason? It helps the employer to remember you. If they had a very busy schedule the day you were there, you may be just a blur in their mind by next morning. Your resume, together with a thank-you note, helps to correct that.

Also it helps your interviewer explain to others in that organization why they are considering you.

Why send the resume the next day; why not just hand it to the interviewer as you leave? Because, when you say truthfully to the interviewer as you leave: "I don't have my resume with me, but I will mail it to you tonight for sure"-- this gives you the chance to go home and edit (and then reprint) your resume so that it is 'individualized' for this particular place, highlighting all the skills or knowledges that the interview revealed they are most interested in.

But do be sure to mail or fax it that night or early the next morning, at the latest! (And since faxes are often blurred, mail them a neat 'hard copy' the same day.)

Incidentally, there is an exception to the rule -- "A resume is something you never send ahead of you, but always leave behind you." You may need to send the resume on ahead when you're contacting some employer who is halfway across the country. Normally, however, this is not the way to try to get in to large organizations.

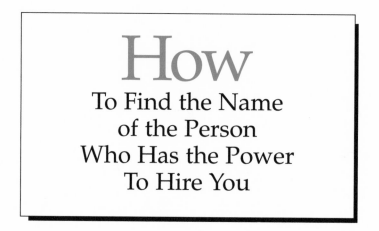

How
To Find the Name
of the Person
Who Has the Power
To Hire You

Okay, let's say the place you're interested in is a large organization called *Mythical Corporation*.

And let's say you know the kind of job you'd like to get there. How do you find out the name of the person–who–has–the–power–to–hire–you there *for that position?*

First Stab at It: You go on the Internet or you go to your local public library, and search the directories there.

On the Internet, go to

`www.jobhuntersbible.com`

and then to the section entitled **Research**, which lists helpful sites such as Hoover's.

If you don't have Internet access, go to the library and ask the friendly librarian for help.

This may give you just the information you want.

But if they don't, there is another way.

One small problem: this takes time, persistence, and lots of determination. It is not a method for everybody, by any means. But, everyone always wants to know, just how do you find information that seems impossible to find. So this is not so much a battle plan, as it is an answer to your curiosity.

Okay, here's how it goes.

Find an insider at your target organization.

You want first of all to find 'an insider' at Mythical Corporation -- not necessarily the person who has the power to hire. Just *someone* who works there.

You go about locating this 'insider' by approaching all the people you know, and asking each of them, "Do you know anyone who works, or used to work, at Mythical Corporation?"

You ask that question again and again of *everyone* you know, or meet, until you find someone who says, *"Yes, I do."*

Bingo! You've found the insider.

Explore how to get in touch with this insider.

When someone has said, "Yes I do know someone there," you then ask them the following questions:

- "What is the name of the person you know who works, or used to work, at Mythical Corporation?"
- "Do you have their phone number and/or address?"
- "Would you be willing to call ahead, to tell them who I am?"

Once you've been connected, you then either phone the insider or make an appointment to go see them ("I won't need more than 10 minutes of your time.") Once you are talking to them, after the usual polite chit-chat you ask them the question you are dying to know.

Ask the insider who in their organization would have the power to hire you -- that is to say, someone with your skills and interests.

Because they are inside the organization that interests you, they are usually able to give you the exact answer to the question that has been puzzling you: "What is the name of the person who would have the power to hire me at Mythical Corporation, for this kind of position (which you then describe)?" If they answer that they do not know, ask who would know.

Keep going until you find out not only that hiring person's name, address, phone, and e-mail address, but also whatever your insider can tell you about that person's job, that person's interests, and their style of interviewing.

Enlist the insider's help in getting an interview with the person–who–has–the–power–to–hire–you.

Once you have the name you want, you explore whether or not this 'insider' could help you get an appointment with the person–who–has–the–power–to–hire–you there. You explore it with this series of questions, asked each in turn:

• "Given my background, and the kind of job I am looking for *(which you here describe)*, would you recommend that I go see them?"

• "Do you know them, personally? If not, could you give me the name of someone who does?"

• "If you know them personally, what can you tell me about him -- or her?"

• "Do you have their phone number and/or address?"

• "May I tell them it was you who recommended that I talk with them?"

• "Would you be willing to call ahead, to tell them who I am, and to help set up an appointment?"

• Before leaving, you can also ask them about the organization, in general.

But suppose the 'insider' you talked to, knows the name of the person who has the power to hire you but doesn't know them well enough to get you an interview, what then?

Well, then you go back to your other contacts outside that organization -- now armed with the name of the person you are trying to get in to see -- and try to find another 'insider.' Approaching as many of your friends as necessary, you ask each of them, "Do you know Ms. or Mr. See, at Mythical Corporation or do you know someone who might?" You keep asking, until you find someone who says, *"Yes, I do."*

Then of course, over the phone or -- better -- in person, you ask this new 'insider' the same familiar questions, above.

Always remember to thank them. Always write them a thank-you note, *that night.*

All of this does take time and work, but when you've gotten an appointment in this fashion, set up by 'a mutual friend,' you will find it is indeed possible to 'get in' to impossible places.

This technique works also, of course, for a small organization. It is based on a universal human principle: Everyone has friends, including any person–who–has–the–power–to–hire–you. You are simply approaching them through *their* friends.

My favorite (true) story about using this technique concerns a job-hunter I know, in Virginia. He decided he wanted to work for a particular health-care organization in that State, and not knowing any better, he approached them by visiting their Human Resources Department. After dutifully filling out a job application, and talking to someone there in that department, he was told there were no jobs available. Stop. Period. End of story.

Approximately three months later he learned about this technique of approaching your favorite organization by using contacts, and insiders. He explored his contacts diligently, got the name of an insider, and that person got him an interview with the person–who–had–the–power–to–hire–him for the position he was interested in. The employer and he hit it off, immediately. The appointment went swimmingly. "You're hired," said the person–who–had–the–power–to–hire–him. "I'll call Human Resources and tell them I just hired you, and you'll be down to fill out the necessary stuff."

Our job-hunter never once mentioned that he had previously approached that same organization through that same Human Resources Department, and been turned down cold.

Wild Life by John Kovalic, © 1989 Shetland Productions. Reprinted with permission.

How

To Prepare for
The Interview

When you are asking for the interview with the boss, tell them you only need twenty minutes; and be prepared to stick to your word about this. Don't stay one minute longer! This will always impress an employer tremendously! *(The only exception is if the employer at the end of the twenty minutes begs you to stay longer. And I mean, begs!)*

Research the organization ahead of time, before going in for an interview. In the employer's mind, this will put you way ahead of the other people they may be interviewing.

An employer said to me, "I'm so tired of job-hunters who come in, and say, *'Uh, what do you guys do here?'* that the next time someone walks in who already knows something about us, I'm going to hire him or her, on the spot." And he did, within the week.

So, when you first set up the appointment, ask them right then and there if they have anything *in writing* about their organization; if so, request they mail it to you, so you'll have time to read it before the interview. Or, if the interview is the next day, offer to come down today and pick it up, yourself.

Visit also your local library, and ask the librarian for help in locating any newspaper articles or other information about that organization.

Finally, ask all your friends if they know anyone who is working there, or used to work there; if they do, ask them to put you in contact with them, *please*. Tell them you have a job-interview there, and you'd like to know anything they can tell you about the place.

All organizations, be they large or small, profit or nonprofit, love to be loved. If you have gone to all this trouble, to learn so much about them - - before you ever walk in their doors, they will be impressed, believe me, because most job-hunters never go to this trouble. *They* walk in knowing little or nothing about the organization. This drives employers *nuts.*

An IBM college recruiter was wont to ask a graduating senior, "What do the initials IBM stand for?" The senior didn't know, and the interview was over.

Picture how you're going to conduct the interview. The most important rule you will need to pay attention to is the 50/50, 2 minute max rule.

The 50/50 rule means that throughout the interview you will listen half the time, speak half the time. Reason? It seems they did a study at M.I.T. to see why people got hired. Turned out, job-hunters who talked half the time, and let the employer talk the other half of the time, were the ones who got hired. People who didn't follow that mix, were the ones who didn't get hired. My hunch as to *why* this is so, is that if you talk too much about yourself, you come across as one who is self-absorbed, and blind to the needs of the organization; while if you talk too little, you come across as one who is trying to hide something about their history.

The 2 minute max rule means that when you are asked a question, you try never to speak for more than two minutes, in answering it. Twenty seconds may be sufficient. Reason? Studies have confirmed that this makes a *very good* impression on an interviewer.[12] People who ramble on and on don't get hired.

Be aware ahead of time of what the employer will be listening for. They want any evidence they can find that you would be a good employee, were they to hire you.

They are scared, of course, that they will hire a bad employee. So, think out before the interview how a bad employee would behave in the position you're seeking: such things as -- *comes in late, takes too much time off, follows his or her own agenda*

---

12. This one was conducted by my colleague, Daniel Porot, in Geneva, Switzerland.

"I'm hoping to find something in a meaningful, humanist, outreach kind of bag, with flexible hours, non-sexist bosses, and fabulous fringes."

instead of the employer's, etc. Then emphasize to the employer how much you are the very opposite.

Let me emphasize, here, what are the marks of a good employee in almost any job (this is what the employer will be listening for).

A good employee these days is one who: wants more than a paycheck; is dependable, self-motivated, with drive, energy, and enthusiasm; is self-disciplined, and good at managing their own time; gives 150%; is punctual, arriving at work on time or early, and staying until quitting time, or later; loves to learn, is very trainable, is flexible, and can respond to novel situations, or adapt when circumstances at work change.

Most employers will also be listening for any signs that you are a person who can handle people well; that you use language effectively; can work with a computer; are committed to teamwork; are project-oriented, and goal-oriented; have creativity and are good at problem solving; you are able to identify opportunities, markets, coming trends. And, above all, they are listening to see if you have a good attitude, integrity, and would be loyal to that organization.

So, plan to demonstrate or claim as many of these as you *legitimately* can, during the hiring interview.

Just be sure that whatever you claim is illustrated by your job-hunt. For example, if you claim you are very *thorough* in all your work, be sure your job-hunt looks truly thorough. (Hint: research the company, before going in there for the job-interview.)

Employers know this simple truth: Most people job-hunt the way they live their lives.

Plan to take into the interview-room with you any evidence you can, of past accomplishments. A portfolio, photographs, documents, etc. If you are an artist, craftsperson or anyone who produces a product, try to bring a sample of what you have made or produced -- either in 'the flesh,' or in photos, or videotapes.

Determine ahead of time not to bad-mouth your previous employer(s) or place(s) of work. Employers often feel as though they are a fraternity or sorority. During the interview you want to come across as one who displays courtesy toward all members of that fraternity or sorority. Bad-mouthing a previous employer only makes this employer worry that were they to hire you, you would end up bad-mouthing *them.*

If you know the previous employer is going to give you a very bad recommendation, just say something simple like, "I usually get along with everybody; but for some reason, my past employer and I just didn't get along. Don't know why. It's never happened to me before. Hope it never happens again."

If you think the employer will not only bad-mouth you, but claim you did something bad that you didn't do, you can add: "When I left there, false claims were made against me; I thought *I* should tell you that, rather than wait for you to discover it and wonder why I hadn't mentioned it." (Point this out only at the end of the interview, or interviews, after the employer has indicated they really want you.)

Determine not to drag out all the dirty laundry from the past, all the injustices done to you, all the wrong treatment you suffered. Be gracious toward your past employers, even as this employer hopes you would be gracious to them.

Decide what image you're going to try to convey: job-beggar, or resource person? The attitude with which you enter the interview room is important. Do not go wimpishly, as one coming to beg a favor. Go helpfully, as one offering them resources they need. Go as resource person, not job-beggar.

I cannot tell you the number of employers I have known over the years, who can't figure out how to find the right employee. That even includes employers who are 'human resource experts!' It is absolutely mind-boggling. But it's the nature of our Neanderthal job-hunting system.

You're having trouble finding the employer. The employer is having trouble finding you. You may pass each other in the dark. *What a great country!*

By coming there you solve this problem. You are not just answering your own prayers; you are answering the employer's as well -- if that employer was looking for You, needed you, your skills, your knowledge, but didn't know how to find you -- and suddenly, here you are!

Of course, you don't know for sure that they need you; that remains for this hiring-interview to uncover.

But at least by choosing them only after you've done all the homework described in our previous two chapters, there's a good chance you are in the right place -- whether they have an announced vacancy or not.

Decide you're going to make them both an 'oral proposal' and a 'written proposal.' Determine to make clear during the interview that you are concerned what *you can do for them*, to help them with *their* problems. You will see immediately what a switch this is from the way most job-hunters approach an employer! *("How much do you pay, and how much time off will I have?")* Will he or she be glad to see you, with this different emphasis? In most cases, you bet they will. They *want* a resource person, and a problem-solver. Determine to summarize, orally, at the end of the interview what it is you have to offer them; send a written summary of that, the next day.

How
To Conduct An Interview

Okay, you're in. The interview is about to begin. And now you're starting to sweat bullets. Face-to-face at last with the person-who-actually-has-the-power-to-hire-you. Stop sweating! There are six comforting thoughts you can console yourself with:

COMFORTING THOUGHT #1:

In a hiring-interview, you're still doing research.

Your natural question, as you approach any job-interview, often is, "How do I convince this employer to hire me?" Wrong question. It implies that you have already made up your mind that this would be a grand place to work at, and this boss a grand person to work for, so that all that remains is for you to sell yourself. This is rarely the case.

In most cases, despite your best attempts to research the place thoroughly, you don't know enough about it yet, to say that. You have *got* to use the hiring-interview as a chance to gather further information about this place, and this boss.

If you understand *this* about an interview, you will be ahead of 98% of all job-hunters -- who all too often go to the hiring-interview as a lamb to the slaughter. Or you may prefer the metaphor of a criminal on trial before a judge.

You *are* on trial, of course, in the employer's eyes.

But, so is that employer and that organization on trial, in *your* eyes.

You are studying everything about this employer, at the same time that they are studying everything about you.

Two people, both sizing each other up. You know what this should remind you of. Dating, of course.

Well, the job interview is every bit like 'the dating game.' Both of you have to like each other, before you can even discuss the question of *'going steady,'* i.e., a job. So, you're sitting there, sizing each other up. *Great!*

The importance of your doing your own weighing of this person, this organization, and this job, *during* the hiring-interview, cannot be overstated. The tradition in the U.S., and throughout the world for that matter, is to find a job, take it, and *then* try to figure out during the first three months that you're in the job, whether you like it or not -- and quitting if you decide you don't.

By using the hiring-interview to screen the organization *before you go to work there* you can save yourself time, money, grief, and guilt.

If you learn enough in the hiring-interview to 'quit' the job even before it's offered to you, instead of *quitting three months after you've taken the job*, the employer will thank you, your Mother will thank you, your spouse or partner will thank you, and of course you will thank yourself, for being so intelligent and mature.

The end of the matter: don't think of this as a hiring-interview. Think of it as 'further research.'

COMFORTING THOUGHT #2:

Hiring-interviews are not a science.

As you go to the interview, do remember that the person-who-has-the-power-to-hire-you is sweating too. Why? Because, the hiring-interview is not a very reliable way to choose an employee.

In a survey conducted among a dozen top United Kingdom employers,[13] it was discovered that the chances of an employer finding a good employee through the hiring interview was only *3% better* than if they had picked a name out of a hat. In a further ironic finding, it was discovered that if the interview were conducted by someone who would be working directly with the candidate, the success rate dropped to *2% below* that of

---

13. Reported in the *Financial Times Career Guide 1989* in the United Kingdom.

picking a name out of a hat. And if the interview were conducted by a so-called personnel expert, the success rate dropped
to *10% below* that of picking a name out of a hat.

No, I don't know how they came up with these figures. But
they are totally consistent with what I know of the whole hiring
process. I have watched so-called personnel or human resources experts make *wretchedly* bad choices about hiring for
their own office, and when they would morosely confess this to
me some months later, over lunch, I would gently tease them
with, "If you don't even know how to hire well, yourself, how
do you keep a straight face when you're called in as a hiring
consultant by another organization?" And they would ruefully
reply, "We act as if it were a science."

Well, let me tell you, dear friend, the hiring-interview is *not*
a science. It is a very very hazy art, done badly by most of its
employer-practitioners, even when they have a kind heart and
carloads of good intentions.

COMFORTING THOUGHT #3:

Oftentimes the employer is as scared as you are.

So, you are sitting there with sweaty palms, but you are probably assuming that the person–who–has–the–power–to–hire–
you is sitting there *enjoying* this whole masochistic process.
Well, sure, sometimes that's true. But more often than not, the
employer is sitting there scared.

So, you have not one but two individuals (*you* and *the employer*) sitting there, scared to death. It's just that the employer
has learned to *hide* his or her fears better than you have, because they've had more practice.

But he or she is, after all, a human being just as you are. He
or she may *never* have been hired to do *this*. *This* just got
thrown in with all their other duties. And they may *know*
they're not very good at it.

So, what is going on in an employer's head, while they're interviewing you? Oh, things like this:

A. That you won't be able to do the job: that you lack the
necessary skills or experience, and the hiring-interview didn't
uncover this.

B. That if hired, you won't put in a full working day, regularly.

C. That if hired, you'll be frequently "out sick," or otherwise absent whole days.

D. That if hired, you'll only stay around for a few weeks or at most a few months, and then quit without advance warning.

E. That it will take you too long to master the job, and thus it will be too long before you're profitable to that organization.

F. That you won't get along with the other workers there, or that you will develop a personality conflict with the boss himself (or herself).

G. That you will do only the minimum that you can get away with, rather than the maximum that they hired you for.

H. That you will always have to be told what to do next, rather than displaying initiative - - always in a responding mode, rather than an initiating mode (and mood).

I. That you will have a work-disrupting character flaw, and turn out to be: dishonest, or totally irresponsible, a spreader of dissention at work, lazy, an embezzler, a gossip, a sexual harasser, a drug-user or substance abuser, a drunk, a liar, incompetent, or - - in a word - - bad news.

J. *(If this is a large organization, and your would-be boss is not the top person)*: that you will bring discredit upon them, and upon their department/section/division, etc., for ever hiring you in the first place - - making them lose face, possibly also costing your would-be boss a raise or promotion.

K. That you will cost a lot of money, if they make a mistake by hiring you. Currently, in the U.S. the cost to an employer of a bad hire can run $50,000 or more, including relocation costs, lost pay for the period for work not done or aborted, and severance pay - - if *they* let you go.

No wonder the employer is scared . . . anxious . . . worried . . . or whatever word you prefer.

Moreover, the hiring interview has become *everything*. In the old days, an employer might have gotten useful information to guide them in the hiring decision outside the interview, from your previous employers. No more. In the past decade, as job-hunters started filing lawsuits left and right alleging 'unlawful discharge,' or 'being deprived of an ability to make a living,' most Previous Employers adopted the policy of refusing to volunteer *any* information about Previous Employees, except name, rank and serial number -- i.e., the person's job-title and dates of employment. And that is even more true today.

So, the interviewer is completely on his own -- or her own -- in trying to figure out whether to hire you or not. They're just as nervous as you are.

COMFORTING THOUGHT #4:

You don't have to memorize a lot of answers to difficult interview questions. Books on interviewing, of which there are many, often publish lists of the kind of questions they think employers might ask you, such as:

- Tell me about yourself.
- Why are you applying for this job?
- What do you know about this job or company?
- How would you describe yourself?
- What are your major strengths?
- What is your greatest weakness?
- What type of work do you like to do best?
- What are your interests outside of work?
- What accomplishment gave you the greatest satisfaction?
- What was your worst mistake in previous jobs?
- Why did you leave your last job?
- Why were you fired (if you were)?
- How does your education or experience relate to this job?
- Where do you see yourself five years from now?
- What are your goals in life?
- How much did you make at your last job?

Well, the list goes on and on. It sometimes totals eighty-nine questions -- or more.

You are then told that you should prepare for a hiring-interview by writing out, practicing, and memorizing some clever answers to *all* these questions -- answers which these books furnish for you. They're sometimes very clever; but let me tell you, my friend, your preparation for the hiring-interview doesn't need to be so complicated.

Beneath the dozens and dozens of possible questions like those above, there are really only *five basic questions* that underlie all the rest.

Five. Just five. Whether they're ever put into words or not, the person-who-has-the-power-to-hire-you wants to know:

1. **"Why are you here?"** *They mean by this, "Why are you knocking on my door, rather than someone else's door?"*

Then, the person-who-has-the-power-to-hire-you wants to know:

2. **"What can you do for us?"** *They mean by this, "If I were to hire you would you be part of the problems I already have, or would you be a part of the solution to those problems? What are your skills, and how much do you know about some subject or field that is of interest to us here?"*

Then, the person-who-has-the-power-to-hire-you wants to know:

3. **"What kind of person are you?"** *They mean by this, "Do you have the kind of personality that makes it easy for people to work with you, and do you share the values which we have at this place?"*

Then, the person-who-has-the-power-to-hire-you wants to know:

4. **"What distinguishes you from nineteen other people who have the same skills as you have?"** *They mean by this, "Do you have better work habits than the nineteen others, do you show up earlier, stay later, work more thoroughly, work faster, maintain higher standards, go the extra mile, or . . . what?"*

Lastly, the person-who-has-the-power-to-hire-you wants to know:

5. **"Can I afford you?"** *They mean by this, "If we decide we want you here, how much will it take to get you, and are we willing and able to pay that amount -- governed as we are by our budget, and our inability to pay you as much as the person who would be above you, on the organizational chart?"*

Since there are really only five basic questions on the employer's mind, and not eighty-nine, there are really only five answers you need to know.

But, you had *better* know those five. If you've done your homework, you will. If you haven't, you won't. Period. End of story.

You, of course, have the right -- nay, the duty -- to be asking yourself the same five questions, though in a slightly different form:

1. **What does this job involve?**

2. **Do my skills truly match this job?**

3. **Are these the kind of people I would like to work with, or not?** *Do not ignore your intuition if it tells you that you would not be comfortable working with these people!!*

4. **If we like each other, and both want to work together, can I persuade them there is something unique about me, that makes me different from nineteen other people who can do the same tasks?**

5. **Can I persuade them to hire me at the salary I need or want?**

And that's it!

You don't, necessarily ask these questions out loud, except perhaps the first one. But finding answers to them should be your goal during the interview.

To get at them, you might begin your part of the interview by reporting to them just exactly how you've been conducting your job-hunt, and what impressed you so much about *their* organization during your research, that you decided to come in and talk to them about a job. Then you can devote your attention, during the remainder of the interview, to exploring the five questions above, in your own way.[14]

If the job you want doesn't really exist there - - yet - - but you hope they'll *create* such a job for you, then your five questions get changed into five *statements*, that you make to this person-who-has-the-power-to-hire-you. You tell them:

1. **What you like about this organization.**

2. **What sorts of needs you find intriguing in this field and in this organization** (don't ever use the word "*problems*," as most employers prefer synonyms, such as '*needs*' - - unless you first hear the word '*problems*' coming out of their mouth).

3. **What skills seem to you to be needed in order to meet such needs.**

---

14. Additional questions you may want to ask, to elaborate upon these five:
    What significant changes has this company gone through in the last five years?
    What values are sacred to this company?
    What characterizes the most successful employees this company has?
    What future changes do you see in the work here?
    Who do you see as your allies, colleagues or competitors in this business?

> IT'S WHAT I'VE ALWAYS HEARD..
> TIMING IS EVERYTHING..

4. Evidence **from your past experience that demonstrates you have the very skills in question, and that you perform them in the manner or style you claim.** And, finally:

5. **What is** unique **about the way** *you* **perform those skills.** As I said before, every prospective employer wants to know *what makes you different* from nineteen other people who can do the same kind of work as you do. You *have* to know what that is. And then not only talk about it, but actually demonstrate it, by the way you conduct your part of the hiring-interview. *e.g.,* *"I am very thorough in the way I would do the job for you"* = be thorough in the way you have researched the place before you go in for the hiring-interview.

Try to put your finger on the 'style' or 'manner' in which you do your work, that is distinctive and sets you apart from the others who might be approaching this employer.

COMFORTING THOUGHT #5:

The employer doesn't *really* care about your past.

In most cases, as I have been emphasizing, the person-who-has-the-power-to-hire-you is *scared* not about the past but about the future. No employer cares about your past. In fact, in the U.S., employers can only legally ask you questions that are related to the requirements and expectations of the job. They cannot ask about such things in your past (or present) as your creed, religion, race, age, sex or marital status.

The employer cares only about your future . . . with *them*. But that future is difficult to predict, so they usually try to guess your future behavior by asking about your past behavior on the job.

Do not be fooled by questions about your past. There is a fear about the future, that lies beneath all of an employer's questions. Let me illustrate:

Employer's Question	The Fear Behind The Question	The Point You Try To Get Across	Phrases You Might Use To Get This Across
"Tell me about yourself"	The employer is afraid he/she isn't going to conduct a very good interview, by failing to ask the right questions. Or is afraid there is something wrong with you, and is hoping you will blurt it out.	You are a good employee, as you have proved in the past at your other jobs. (Give the briefest history of who you are, where born, raised, interests, hobbies, and kind of work you have enjoyed the most to date.) *Keep it to two minutes, max.*	In describing your past work history, use any *honest* phrases you can about your work history, that are self-complimentary: "Hard worker." "Came in early, left late." "Always did more than was expected of me." Etc.
"What kind of work are you looking for?"	The employer is afraid that you are looking for a different job than that which the employer is trying to fill. E.g., he/she wants a secretary, but you want to be an office manager, etc.	You are looking for precisely the kind of work the employer is offering (but don't say that, if it isn't true). Repeat back to the employer, in your own words, what he/she has said about the job, and emphasize the skills you have to do *that*.	If the employer hasn't described the job at all, say, "I'd be happy to answer that, but first I need to understand exactly what kind of work this job involves." *Then* answer, as at left.
"Have you ever done this kind of work before?"	The employer is afraid you don't possess the necessary skills and experience to do this job.	You have skills that are transferable, from whatever you used to do; and you did it well.	"I pick up stuff very quickly." "I have quickly mastered any job I have ever done."

Employer's Question	The Fear Behind The Question	The Point You Try To Get Across	Phrases You Might Use To Get This Across
"When did you leave your last job?" *-- or* **"How did you get along with your former boss and co-workers?"**	The employer is afraid you don't get along well with people, especially bosses, and is just waiting for you to 'bad-mouth' your previous boss or co-workers, as proof of that.	Say whatever positive things you possibly can about your former boss and co-workers (*without telling lies*). Emphasize you usually get along very well with people -- and then let your gracious attitude toward your previous boss(es) and co-workers prove it, right before this employer's very eyes (and ears).	If you left voluntarily: "*My boss and I* both felt I would be happier and more effective in a job where [here describe your strong points, such as] I would have more room to use my initiative and creativity." If you were fired: "Usually, I get along well with everyone, but in this particular case the boss and I just didn't get along with each other. Difficult to say why." *You don't need to say any more than that.* If you were laid off and your job wasn't filled after you left: "My *job* was terminated."
"How is your health?" *-- or* **"How much were you absent from work during your last job?"**	The employer is afraid you will be absent from work a lot, if they hire you.	You will not be absent. If you have a health problem, you want to emphasize that it is one which will not keep you from being at work, daily. Your productivity, compared to other workers', is excellent.	If you were *not* absent a lot at your last job: "I believe it's an employee's job to show up every work day. Period." If you *were* absent a lot, say why, and stress that it was due to a difficulty that is now *past.*

Employer's Question	The Fear Behind The Question	The Point You Try To Get Across	Phrases You Might Use To Get This Across
"Can you explain why you've been out of work so long?" -- *or* **"Can you tell me why there are these gaps in your work history?"** *(Usually said after studying your resume.)*	The employer is afraid that you are the kind of person who quits a job the minute he/she doesn't like something at it; in other words, that you have no 'stick-to-it-iveness.'	You love to work, and you regard times when things aren't going well as challenges, which you enjoy learning how to conquer.	"During the gaps in my work record, I was studying/doing volunteer work/doing some hard thinking about my mission in life/finding redirection." (Choose one.)
"Wouldn't this job represent a step down for you?" -- *or* **"I think this job would be way beneath your talents and experience."** -- *or* **"Don't you think you would be underemployed if you took this job?"**	The employer is afraid you could command a bigger salary, somewhere else, and will therefore leave him/her as soon as something better turns up.	You will stick with this job as long as you and the employer agree this is where you should be.	"This job isn't a step down for me. It's a step up -- from welfare." "We have mutual fears: every employer is afraid a good employee will leave too soon, and every employee is afraid the employer might fire him/her, for no good reason." "I like to work, and I give my best to every job I've ever had."
And, lastly: **"Tell me, what is your greatest weakness?"**	The employer is afraid you have some character flaw, and hopes you will now rashly blurt it out, or confess it.	You have limitations just like anyone else but you work constantly to improve yourself and be a more and more effective worker.	Mention a weakness and then stress its positive aspect, e.g., "I don't like to be oversupervised, because I have a great deal of initiative, and I like to anticipate problems before they even arise."

As the interview proceeds, you want to quietly notice *(but not comment on)* the time-frame of the questions the employer is asking.

Because, when the interview is going well for you, the time-sequence of the employer's questions will usually move -- however slowly -- through the following stages.

1. **Distant past**: *e.g., "Where did you attend high school?"*

2. **Immediate past**: *e.g., "Tell me about your most recent job."*

3. **Present**: *e.g., "What kind of a job are you looking for?"*

4. **Immediate future**: *e.g., "Would you be able to come back for another interview next week?"*

5. [*Optional:* **Distant future**: *e.g., "Where would you like to be five years from now?"*]

The more the interviewer's questions move from the past to the future, the more favorably the interview is going for you. On the other hand, if the interviewer's questions stay firmly in the past, the outlook is not so good. *Ah well, y' can't win 'em all!*

If the time-frame of the interviewer's questions moves firmly into the future, then experts suggest you ask -- now -- some essential questions *about the organization.*

The research you're doing here concerns what you can do for the company, not what the company can do for you. Don't ask -- at this point -- about their health plan, days off, vacation time, benefits or salary; page 221 will tell you when.)

What is the job, specifically, that I am being considered for?

If I were hired, what duties would I be performing?

What responsibilities would I have?

What would you be hiring me to accomplish?

Would I be working with a team, or group? To whom would I report?

Whose responsibility is it to see that I get the training I need, here, to get up to speed?

How would I be evaluated, how often, and by whom?

What were the strengths and weaknesses of previous people in this position?

Why did *you* yourself decide to work here?

What do you wish you had known about this company before you started here? What particular characteristics do you think have made you successful in your job here?

May I meet the person I would be working for (if it isn't you)?

Remember, as job-expert Nathan Azrin has said for years, *The hiring process is more like choosing a mate, than it is like deciding whether or not to buy a new car.*

'Choosing a mate' is of course a metaphor: it means that *the mechanisms* by which human nature decides to hire someone, are *similar to* the mechanisms by which we decide whether or not to marry someone.

In hiring, as in dating, both people are scared of making a mistake.

COMFORTING THOUGHT #6:

No matter what handicap you have, it will not keep you from getting hired. It will only keep you from getting hired at *some* places.

Most of us think that when we go job-hunting we have some special handicap (hidden or obvious), that's going to keep us from getting a job. Forever.

The handicaps that bother us are such things as:

I have a physical handicap
I have a mental handicap
I never graduated from high school
I never graduated from college
I am just graduating
I just graduated a year ago
I graduated too long ago
I am a self-made man
I am a self-made woman
I am too handsome
I am too beautiful
I am too ugly
I am too thin
I am too fat
I am too young
I am too old
I am too new to the job-market
I am too near retirement
I have a prison record
I have a psychiatric history
I have never held a job before
I have held too many jobs before
I have only had one employer
I am Hispanic
I am Black
I am Asian
I am a foreigner
I have not had enough education
I have had too much education
I am too much of a generalist

I am too much of a specialist
I am a clergyperson
I am just coming out of the military
I've only worked for volunteer organizations
I have only worked for large employers
I have only worked for small employers
I am too shy
I am too assertive
I come from a very different kind of background
I come from another industry
I come from another planet

I guess the true meaning of the above comprehensive list is that there are about three weeks of your life when you're employable.

Many of us think we need a special book to teach us how to job-hunt with our handicap. Actually, all we really need is to keep firmly in mind this one simple truth:

> There are two kinds of employers out there: those who will be put off by your handicap, and therefore won't hire you;
>
> AND
>
> Those who will not be put off by your handicap, and therefore will hire you, if you are qualified for the job.

You are not interested in the former kind of employer, no matter how many of them there are - - except as a source of referrals.

You are only looking for the second kind of employer.

So: if the employer you are talking to in a particular interview is obviously bothered by your (supposed) handicap, you want to quietly bring that interview to a conclusion, and ask them - - in parting - - if they know of anyone else who might be interested in your skills. Keep going, until you find that second kind of employer.

It doesn't matter what skills-you-don't-have, as long as the skills-that-you-do-have exactly match those-needed-in-the-job.

How
To End The Interview

At some point this interview has to come to a close. Not that you may not be back for further interviews. But this interview should end with you asking six, maybe seven, questions. In most cases, if you don't ask for this information, the employer won't volunteer it, believe me:

#1. **"Given my skills and experience, is there work here that you would consider me for?"** This is if you haven't honed in on a specific job, from the beginning. Otherwise you begin with #2.

#2. **"Can you offer me this job?"** It is astonishing how many job-hunters have secured a job simply by being bold enough to ask for it, at the end of the interview, either with the words above or something similar. I don't know *why* this is so. I only know *that* it is so.

So, if after hearing all about this job at this place, you decide you'd really like to have it, *ask for it.* The worst thing the employer can say is "No," or "We need some time to think about all the interviews we're conducting with various people." In which case you move on to #3. (Or #7, if they turn you down flat.)

#3. **"Do you want me to come back for another interview?"** If the employer is seriously considering you, this interview will very likely be only the first in a series; there usually is a second round of interviews, and often a third and fourth.

You, of course, want to be in those subsequent rounds. Indeed, many experts say the *only* purpose you should have in mind for the first interview at a particular place, is to be invited back for a second interview.

If you've secured *that,* say they, the first interview was a ringing success.

#4. **"When may I expect to hear from you?"** You *never* want to leave control of the ensuing steps in this process in the hands of the employer. You want it in your own hands. Even if the employer says, *"We need time to think about this,"* or *"We will be calling you for a second interview,"* you don't want to leave that as just a good intention on the employer's part. You want to nail it down.

#5. **"What would be the latest I can expect to hear from you?"** The employer has probably given you their *best* guess, in answer to your previous question. Now you want to know *what is the worse case* scenario? One employer, when I asked him the *worse case* scenario replied, *"Never!"* I thought he had a great sense of humor. Turned out he wasn't joking.

#6. **"May I contact you after that date, if for any reason you haven't had a chance to get back to me by that time?"** Some employers will not appreciate this question; you'll know that's the case if you get some retort like, *"Don't you trust me?"*

Most employers, however, appreciate your offering them what is in essence a safety-net. They know they can get busy, become overwhelmed with other things, forget how long a time has elapsed. It's reassuring, in such a case, that you offer them a backup fail-safe strategy -- particularly if they really are interested in you. (If they dislike this question, it may be a clue that they're not really interested in you, and are just 'blowing you off' -- as they say.)

[#7. **Optional: "Can you think of anyone else who might be interested in hiring me?"** This question is asked *only* if they replied *"No,"* to your first question, above.]

When you've got the answers to the first six questions here, jotting down any answers you may need to, you stand up, thank them sincerely for their time, give a firm handshake, and leave.

In the following days, rigorously keep to this covenant, and don't contact them (except with a thank-you note) until after the *latest* deadline you two agreed upon, in answer to question #6, above.

If you do contact them after that date, and if they tell you things are still up in the air, you ask questions #4, #5, and #6, all over again. And so on, and so forth.

Incidentally, it is entirely appropriate for you to insert a thank-you note into the running stream after *each* interview or telephone contact. That will help them remember you, without your bugging them.

BACK HOME:
THE IMPORTANCE OF
THANK-YOU NOTES

You're home that night. Putting your feet up. Relaxing. The job-hunt is over for the day. *Oops,* no it's not. You've still got work to do: thank-you notes.

Every expert on interviewing will tell you three things:

(1) **Thank-you notes *must* be sent after *every* interview**, by every job-hunter, that same day or the next morning at the latest;

(2) **Most job-hunters ignore this advice** -- indeed, it is the most overlooked step in the entire job-hunting process; and

(3) **Therefore you will stand out from all the other interviewees** if you remember to send a thank-you note to the person who interviewed you (and to their secretary, or anyone else you made contact with while you were there).

If you need any additional encouragement, here are seven reasons for sending a thank-you note to the employer who interviewed you:

You are giving evidence that you have good people skills. Sending a thank-you note backs up any claim you made to that effect, during the interview. From this they know: you *are* good with people, 'cause you remember to thank them.

It helps the employer to remember you. If they had a very busy schedule the day you were there, you may be just a blur in their mind by next morning. The thank-you note helps to correct that.

It gives the interviewer something to show to other members of the committee, if more than one person is going to be involved in the hiring decision.

It gives you a chance to emphasize your interest in further talks, if the first interview went well. "I'd love to talk further with you, at your convenience."

It gives you an opportunity to correct any wrong impression you left behind you. You can correct any wrong impressions, add anything you forgot to tell them, and underline the main two or three points that you want to stand out in their minds as they weigh whether or not to hire you.

It may cause them to give you the job. One baseball team hired a woman for a public relations job *solely* because she was the only one (out of 35 job-hunters interviewed) who sent them a thank-you note.

If you don't get the job, it gives you a chance to ask them for further leads that they may hear of from other colleagues, who might need someone with your skills.

Says one human resources manager: "A prompt, brief, faxed business letter thanking me for my time along with a (brief!) synopsis of his/her unique qualities communicates to me that this person is an assertive, motivated, customer service-oriented salesperson who utilizes technology and knows the rules of the 'game.' These are qualities I am looking for . . . At the moment I receive approximately one letter . . . for every fifteen candidates interviewed."

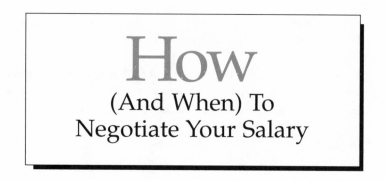

How
(And When) To Negotiate Your Salary

When the interviewing process is almost all over, and it's gone well, it's time to deal with the question that is inevitably on the employer's mind: *how much is this person going to cost me?* and also on yours: *how much does this job pay?*

The rules are simple:

(1) **Before you go to the interview, figure out how much you need to make from this job, if it's offered to you.** The job-hunter's nightmare is that you just love the prospect of working here, but: *What if their highest figure is so far below your lowest figure, that you will starve if you accept it?*

Let's say you need $14 an hour, just to survive, but the highest they're willing to pay is $8 an hour.

You see the problem. You've *got* to know, beforehand, just how much you need to make, at a minimum.

You can deal with this in one of two ways: a) take a wild guess -- and risk finding out after you take the job that it's simply impossible for you to live on that salary *(the favorite strategy in this country, and most others)*; or, b) do some figuring, so you'll know what you're talking about. Exercises to help you do this are on pages 299–301.

(2) **In the interview, never discuss salary until the end, after they've definitely said they want you.**

The left-brained way of putting this is:

Never Discuss Salary

Until *all* of the following conditions have been fulfilled:
- Until you're in the final interview at that place, for that job.
- Until they've gotten to know you, at your best, so they can see how you stand out above the other applicants.
- Until you've gotten to know them, as completely as you can, so you can tell when they're being firm, or when they're flexible.
- Until you've found out exactly what the job entails.
- Until they've had a chance to find out how well you match the job-requirements.
- Until you've decided, "I'd really like to work here."
- Until they've said, "We want you."
- Until they've said or implied, "We've *got* to have you."

The right-brained way of putting the same thing is:[15]

When To Negotiate Salary

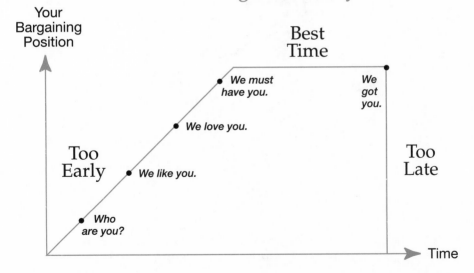

---

15. Reprinted, by permission of the publisher, from *Ready, Aim, You're Hired*, by Paul Hellman, © 1986 Paul Hellman. Published by AMACOM, a division of American Management Association, New York. All rights reserved.

Why is it to your advantage to delay salary discussion? Because, if you really *shine* during the hiring-interview, they may -- at the end -- mention a higher salary than they originally had in mind when the interview started.

So, don't raise it earlier. And if it is the employer who raises the salary question too early in the process, your gentle reply should be: "I'll gladly come to that, but could you first help me to understand what this job involves?" *or* "Until you've decided you definitely want me, and I've decided I definitely could help you with your tasks here, I feel discussion of salary is a bit premature." That will work, in most cases.

Of course if they're asking you too early because they're determined to give the job to the one who's willing to work for the lowest salary, you'll have to decide how badly you want the job; and if the answer is, "Very badly," you're going to have to give a reply -- hopefully in terms of a *range* -- and just pray.

(3) **You'll have to *negotiate* for your salary, because the employer will rarely begin by telling you the most they are willing to pay.** Salary negotiation would never happen if *every* employer in *every* hiring-interview mentioned, right from the start, the top figure they are willing to pay for that position.

Some employers do start there. And that's the end of any salary negotiation with them!

But most employers don't. Hoping they'll be able to get you for less, they start *lower* than they're ultimately willing to go. This creates *a range*. And that range is what salary negotiation is all about.

For example, if the employer wants to hire somebody for no more than $12 an hour, they may start *the bidding* at $8 an hour. In which case, their range is from $8 to $12 an hour. Or if they want to pay no more than $20 an hour, they may start the bidding at $16 an hour. In which case their range runs from $16 to $20 an hour.

If a range *is* thus involved, you have every right to try to negotiate the highest salary possible *within that range.*

The employer is trying to save money. You're trying to get the most money you can, for the sake of your loved ones as well as yourself. Nothing is wrong with either goal. But if the employer starts low, salary negotiation is proper, and expected.

(4) **To win at salary negotiation, don't be the first one to mention a figure.** Experienced interviewers will always try to get you to mention a figure before they do, by asking some innocent-sounding question, such as: "What kind of salary are you looking for?" *Well, how kind of them to ask me what I want --* you may be thinking. No, no, no. Kindness has nothing to do with it.

They are hoping *you* will be the first to mention a figure, because they know a weird truth about salary negotiation, borne out by many years' experience. It is: *whoever mentions a salary figure first, generally loses salary negotiation, in the end.*

So of course, you will *always* want to respond to that innocent-sounding question with some reply like: "Well, you created this position, so you must have some figure in mind, and I'd be interested in knowing what that is."

(5) **To win at salary negotiation, know what a top salary offer would be, in this field.** Okay, the employer mentions a figure: how do you tell whether it's the *starting bid*, or their *top* offer?

Well, you can't really tell. But you can make a guess *if* you have some idea of what jobs pay in that field or industry -- generally speaking. And that means research.

Oh, come on! I can hear you say. *Isn't this more trouble than it's worth?* Well, sure, if you think it is. But if you're determined to get this job, salary research can pay off *handsomely.*

Let's say it takes you from one to three days to run down this sort of information on the three or four organizations that interest you the most. And when you finally get to salary negotiation, you realize their bid is low for the industry. So, you quote the industry figures, and ask for (let's say) a salary that is $2 an hour more than they originally intended to pay you. And they agree to give you that, because you know what the industry standard is. What does that add up to?

Well, if you work a forty-hour week for 50 weeks a year, $2 an hour would add up to $4,000 more for you each year, than you would otherwise have gotten. In just the next three years, you would be earning $12,000 extra, or more, because of your salary research. *Not bad pay, for one to three days' work!*

I know *many* job-hunters and career-changers to whom this has happened.

So, to put this another way: if you don't do this research, it'll cost ya!

Okay then, how do you do it? Well, there's a simple rule: **abandon books, and go talk to people**.

I'll give some examples from various industries, so you can see how it goes:

> First Example: *Working at your first entry-level job, say at a fast-food place.*

They pay what they pay. You can walk in, ask for a job application, and interview with the manager. He or she will usually tell you the pay, outright. It's usually *inflexible.* But at least you'll find how easy it is to discover what the pay is. (Incidentally, filling out an application, or having an interview there, doesn't commit you to take the job -- but you probably already know that. You can always decline an offer from *any place.* That's what makes this research harmless.)

> Second Example: *Working at a place where you can't discover what the pay is, say at a construction company.*

If that construction company where you would hope to get a job is difficult to research, go visit a different construction company in the same town -- one that isn't of much interest to you -- and ask what they make there. Fill out one of their applications, and talk to the hiring person about what kinds of jobs they have (or might have in the future), at which time prospective wages is a legitimate subject of discussion. Then, having done this research on a place you don't care about, go back to the place that really interests you, and apply. You still don't know exactly what they pay, but you do know what their competitor pays -- which will usually be close.

> Third Example: *Working in a one-person office, say as a secretary.*

Here you can often find useful salary information by perusing the *Help Wanted* ads in the local paper for a week or two. Most of the ads probably won't mention a salary figure, but a few *may.* Among those that do, note what the lowest salary offering is, and what the highest is, and see if the ad reveals some reasons for the difference. It's interesting how much you can learn about salaries, with this approach.

Another way to do salary research is to find a *Temporary Work Agency* that places secretaries, and let yourself be farmed out to various offices: the more, the merrier. It's relatively easy to do salary research when you're *inside* the place. (Study what that place pays *the agency*, not what the agency pays *you.*) If it's an office where the other workers *like* you, you'll be able to ask questions about a lot of other jobs there besides secretarial ones, including salary issues. It's like *summertime*, where the research is easy.

Before you finish your research, before you go in to that organization for your final interview, you want to discover what the range is, for that job. In any organization which has more than five employees, that range is relatively easy to figure out. It will be less than what the person above you makes, and more than what the person below you makes, viz:

If The Person Who Would Be Below You Makes	And The Person Who Would Be Above You Makes	The Range For Your Job Would Be
$37,000	$42,000	$38,000–$41,000
$22,000	$27,000	$23,000–$26,000
$10,000	$13,500	$10,500–$12,500

One teensy-tiny little problem: *how* do you find out the salary of those who would be above and below you? Well, first you have to find out their *names* or the names of their *positions*. If it is a small organization you are going after - - one with twenty or less employees - - finding this information out should be *duck soup*. Any employee who works there is likely to know the answer, and you can usually get in touch with one of those employees, or even an ex-employee, through your contacts. Since two-thirds of all new jobs are created by companies of that size, that's the size organization you are likely to be researching, anyway.

If you are going after a larger organization, then you have our familiar life-preserver to fall back on, namely, every contact you have (family, friend, relative, business, or church acquaintance) who might know the company, and therefore, the information you seek. You are looking for Someone Who Knows Someone who either is working, or has worked, at the particular place or places that interest you, who therefore has or can get this information for you.

If you absolutely run into a blank wall on a particular organization (everyone who works there is pledged to secrecy, and they have shipped all their ex-employees to Siberia), then seek out information on their nearest *competitor* in the same geographic area. *For example,* let us say you were researching Bank X, and they were proving to be inscrutable about what they pay their managers. You would then try Bank Y as your research base, to see if the information is easier to come by, there. You make an assumption, and that is that the two are probably similar in their pay scales, and that what you learned about Bank Y was applicable also to Bank X.

Also experts point out that in researching salaries, you should take note of the fact that most governmental agencies have civil service positions *which match or almost match* those in private industry. Their job descriptions and pay ranges are available to the public. Go to the nearest City, County, Regional, State or Federal Civil Service office, find the job description nearest what you are seeking in private industry, and then ask for the starting salary.

Also, if you have access to the Internet, you can go to the site run by Mary Ellen Mort called JobStar

(`http://jobstar.org/`)

which has the most extensive collection of salary surveys by industry or position, that exists on the Web.

When all this research is done, when you are in the actual hiring-interview, and the employer mentions the figure *they* have in mind, you are then ready to respond: "I understand of course the constraints under which all organizations are operating in the current business environment, but I believe my productivity is such that it would *justify* a salary in the range of . . ." -- *and here you mention a figure near the top of their range.*

It will help a lot if during this discussion, you are prepared to show in what ways you will *make money* or in what ways you will *save money* for that organization, such as would justify the higher salary you are seeking. Hopefully, this will succeed in getting you the salary you want.[16]

---

16. Daniel Porot, in Europe, suggests that if you and an employer really hit it off, and you're *dying* to work there, but they cannot afford the salary you need, consider offering them part of your time. If you need, and believe you deserve, say $25,000, but they can only afford $15,000, you might consider offering them three days a week of your time for that $15,000 (15/25 = 3/5). This leaves you free to take other work those other two days.

FRANK & ERNEST reprinted by permission of NEA, Inc.

Once all salary negotiation is concluded to your satisfaction, do remember to ask to have it summed up in a letter of agreement -- or employment contract -- that they give to you. It may be you cannot get it in writing, but do try! The Road to Hell is paved with oral promises that went unwritten, and -- later -- unfulfilled.

Many executives unfortunately 'forget' what they told you during the hiring-interview, or even deny they ever said such a thing.

Also, many executives leave the company (willingly or unwillingly) and their successor or a new top boss may disown any *unwritten* promises: *"I don't know what caused them to say that to you, but they clearly exceeded their authority, and of course we can't be held to that."*

There's also the matter of raises, down the road. You should plan on asking for one annually, unless they are regularly offering one to you without your having to ask.

When you ask for a raise, a year from now -- or *whenever* -- you will need to justify it. Toward this end, once you are in the job, plan to keep track of your accomplishments there, on a weekly basis -- jotting them down, every weekend, in your own private journal. Career experts, such as Bernard Haldane, recommend you do this without fail. You can then *summarize* these accomplishments annually on a one-page sheet, for your boss's eyes, when raise or promotion is the subject under discussion.[17]

---

17. In any good-sized organization, you will often be amazed at how little attention your superiors pay to your noteworthy accomplishments, and how little they are aware at the end of the year that you really are *entitled* to a raise. Noteworthy your accomplishments may be, but no one is taking notes . . . unless *you* do.

Fringe Benefits

During your salary negotiation, do not forget to pay attention to so-called fringe benefits. 'Fringes' such as life insurance, health benefits or health plans, vacation or holiday plans, and retirement programs typically add another 30% to many workers' salaries. That is to say, if an employee receives $800 salary per month, the fringe benefits are worth another $240 per month.

If your job is at a higher level, benefits may include but not be limited to: health, life, dental, disability, malpractice insurance; insurance for dependents; sick leave; vacation; personal leave/personal days; educational leave; educational cost reimbursement for coursework related to the job; maternity and or parental leave; health leave to care for dependents; bonus system or profit sharing; stock options; expense accounts for entertaining clients; dues to professional associations; travel reimbursement; fee sharing arrangements for clients that the employee generates; organizational memberships; parking; automobile allowance; relocation costs; sabbaticals; professional conference costs; time for community service; flextime work schedules; fitness center memberships.

You should therefore remember to ask what benefits are offered, and -- if they want you badly enough -- negotiate for the benefits you want.

How
To React, When Employers Never Offer You A Job

WHEN IT'S NOT YOUR FAULT

I hear regularly from job-hunters who report that they followed all the advice in this chapter, and were quite successful at getting interviews -- but they still didn't get hired. And they want to know what they're doing wrong. Well, unfortunately, the answer *sometimes* is: Nothing.

A few -- very few -- employers play games, and invite you in for an interview despite the fact that they have already hired someone for the position in question!

You are cheered, of course, by the ease with which you get these interviews. But unbeknownst to you, the manager who is interviewing you *(we'll say it's a he)* has a personal friend he already agreed to give the job to. Of course, there's one small hurdle to get over, namely that the State or the Federal government gives funds to this organization, and has mandated that this position be advertised and open to all.

So this manager must pretend to comply. He chooses ten candidates, including his favorite, and pretends to interview them all with an open mind. Then he does what he always intended to do: he rejects the first nine out of hand and chooses his favorite. You're automatically rejected -- even if you are a better candidate. This tenth person is, after all, his *friend*. The manager ends this charade by claiming he followed the mandated hiring procedures *to the letter.*

I don't know *how often* this happens, but I know it does happen -- first of all, because more than one employer has actually confessed it to me. And, secondly, because at one point in my life it actually happened to me.

If you are one of the nine allegedly interviewed in this charade, you will always be baffled as to *why* you got turned down. *"What did I do wrong,"* you'll cry. The answer may be: Nothing.

WHEN IT IS YOUR FAULT

But, ah, what if no games are being played? You are getting rejected at place after place, because there is something really wrong with the way you are coming across, during these hiring-interviews.

And, it doesn't have to be a big thing. For example, you could have all the skills in the world, have researched this organization to death, have practiced *interviewing* until you are a master at giving precisely the 'right answers,' be absolutely the perfect person (skillwise) for this job, and yet lose the hiring-interview because . . . *your breath smells terrible.*

You're ready to fight dragons, and you're getting destroyed by a mosquito?!

Yes, and there are a lot of other 'mosquitoes' that can fly in -- often during the first 30 seconds to two minutes of your interview -- and cause *the person-who-has-the-power-to-hire-you* to start thinking, *"I sure hope we have some other candidates besides this one"*: These 'interview-killers' fall into five basic categories:

1. **Nervous mannerisms**: *it is a turn-off for employers if* --
• you give a limp handshake, *or*
• you slouch in your chair, or endlessly fidget in your seat, during the interview, *or*
• you continually avoid eye contact with the employer, *or*
• you crack your knuckles, *or* are constantly playing with your hands, or your hair.

2. **Lack of self-confidence**: *it is a turn-off for employers if* --
• you are continuously being extremely self-critical,
• you are downplaying your achievements or abilities,
• you are speaking so softly you cannot be heard, or so loudly you can be heard two rooms away,
• you are giving one-word-answers to all the employer's questions,

- you are constantly interrupting the employer,
- or you are giving answers in an extremely hesitant fashion.

3. **Inconsiderateness toward other people**: *it is a turn-off for employers if --*
- you show a lack of courtesy to the receptionist, secretary, and (at lunch) to the waiter or waitress,
- you display extreme-criticalness toward your previous employers and places of work,
- you drink strong stuff (ordering a drink if and when the employer takes you to lunch is always a bad idea, as it raises the question in the employer's mind, *Do they normally stop with one, or do they normally keep on going?* Don't. . . . do. . . . it!)

4. **Your values**: *it is a turn-off for employers, if they see in you --*
- any signs of dishonesty or lying, on your resume or in the interview;
- any signs of irresponsibility or tendency to goof off;
- any sign of arrogance or excessive aggressiveness; any sign of tardiness or failure to keep appointments and commitments on time, including the hiring-interview;
- any sign of not following instructions or obeying rules;
- any sign of constant complaining or blaming things on others;
- any sign of laziness or lack of motivation;
- any sign of a lack of enthusiasm for this organization and what it is trying to do; *or*
- any sign of instability, inappropriate response, and the like.
- the other ways in which you evidence your *values*, such as: what things impress you or don't impress you in the office; what you are willing to sacrifice in order to get this job *and* what you are *not* willing to sacrifice in order to get this job; your enthusiasm for work;
the carefulness with which you did or didn't research this company before you came in;
and blah, blah, blah.

5. **Your appearance and personal habits**: interview after in-terview has revealed that if you are a male, *you are much more likely to get the job if:*

• you have freshly bathed, have your face freshly shaved or your hair and beard freshly trimmed, have clean fingernails; and are using a deodorant;

• you have on freshly laundered clothes, and a suit rather than a sports outfit, pants with a sharp crease, and shoes freshly polished;

• you do not have bad breath, do not dispense gallons of garlic, onion, stale tobacco, or the odor of strong drink, into the enclosed office air; but have brushed and flossed your teeth, plus used a mouthwash if necessary;

• you are not wafting tons of after-shave cologne fifteen feet ahead of you, as you enter the room.

If you are a female, interview after interview has revealed that *you are much more likely to get the job if --*

• you have freshly bathed, have not got tons of makeup on your face; have had your hair newly 'permed' or 'coiffed'; have clean or nicely manicured fingernails, that don't stick out ten inches from your fingers; and are using a deodorant;

• you wear a bra, have on freshly cleaned clothes, a suit or sophisticated-looking dress, shoes not sandals, and ones which don't call *a lot* of attention to themselves;

• you do not have bad breath, do not dispense gallons of garlic, onion, stale tobacco, or the odor of strong drink, into the enclosed office air; but have brushed and flossed your teeth, plus used a mouthwash if necessary;

• you are not wafting tons of perfume fifteen feet ahead of you, as you enter the room.

Remember, since the hiring process is more like choosing a mate, than deciding whether or not to buy a new house, the employer is simply trying to determine if they like you. In which case, these 'mosquitoes' can kill you, no matter how qualified you may otherwise be.

P.S. In the U.S. at least, *many* an employer watches to see if you smoke, either in the interview or at lunch. *(In a race between two equally qualified people, the nonsmoker will win out over the smoker 94% of the time, according to a study done by a professor of business at Seattle University.)*

Some experts counsel job-hunters who smoke to try to hide it during the interview. Personally, I think all such attempts to deceive the employer are ill-advised. So what if you do pull it off? It will come out that you smoke, after you are hired, and the employer who hates smoking can always manage to fire you, on one pretext or another. My advice: don't try to hide it.

But, I do think it is legitimate to *delay* revealing it until the employer has decided they really want you. Once a job-offer has been made, *then* I think it is crucial for you to tell the employer you smoke, and offer an easy way out: "If this is a truly offensive habit to you, and one you don't want in any of your employees, I'd rather bow out gracefully now, than have it become an issue between us down the road." Such consideration, thoughtfulness, and graciousness on your part may go a long way to soften the employer's resistance to the fact that you are a smoker. Many places, in fact, allow employees who smoke to go outside for a 'smoke break' at stated intervals.

You may take this list of 'interview-killers' to heart, or just ignore it. If you do decide to ignore it, and then - - despite interview after interview - - you continue not to get hired, you might want to rethink your position on all of this.

It may indeed be the mosquitoes, not the dragons, that are killing you. And if that is the case, you can fix any or all of these things; they're all within your control. Once fixed, your next interviews may go much much better.

But if they don't, then I would recommend you go to a career counselor who charges by the hour, and put yourself in their tender knowledgeable hands. Role-play an interview, and see what advice they have to give you.

CONCLUSION

We have covered now the techniques of successful job-hunters. We have seen that the three secrets of successful career-change or systematic job-hunting are: WHAT, WHERE and HOW.

If you are having great trouble in finding work, you must not merely read these chapters and exercises, but *do it all.*

Here is one job-hunter's experience with all of this:

"Before I read this book, I was depressed and lost in the futile job-hunt using Want Ads Only. I did not receive even one phone call from any ad I answered, over a total of 4 months. I felt that I was the most useless person on earth. I am female, with a 2½-year-old daughter, former professor in China, with no working experience at all in the U.S. We came here seven months ago because my husband had a job offer here.

"Then, on June 11th of this year, I saw your book in a local bookstore. Subsequently, I spent 3 weeks, 10 hours a day except Sunday, reading every single word of your book and doing all of the exercises. After getting to know myself much better, I felt I was ready to try the job-hunt again. I used Parachute throughout as my guide, from the very beginning to the very end, namely, salary negotiation.

"In just two weeks I secured (you guessed it) two job offers, one of which I am taking, as it is an excellent job, with very good pay. It is (you guessed it again) a small company, with 20 or so employees. It is also a career-change: I was a professor of English; now I am to be a controller!

"I am so glad I believed your advice: there are jobs out there, and there are two types of employers out there, and truly there are!

"I hope you will be happy to hear my story."

With a little bit of luck, these techniques should work for you as they have worked for her.

You have a precious kind of knowledge, now: how to get hired. And to paraphrase something Dick Lathrop first said many years ago, in his book *Who's Hiring Who:*

BEING ABLE to do the job well will not necessarily get you hired; The person who gets hired is often the one who knows the most about how to get hired.

How To Find Your Mission In Life

God and One's Vocation

Foreword

As I started writing this section, I toyed at first with the idea of following what might be described as an "all-paths approach" to religion. But, after much thought, I decided not to try that. This, because I have read many other writers who tried, and I felt the approach failed miserably. An "all-paths" approach to religion ends up being a "no-paths" approach, even as a woman or man who tries to please everyone ends up pleasing no one. It is the old story of the "universal" vs. the "particular."

Those of us who do career counseling could predict, ahead of time, that trying to stay universal is not likely to be helpful, in writing about religion. We know well from our own field that truly helpful career counseling depends upon defining the **particularity** or uniqueness of each person we try to help. No employer wants to know only what you have in common with everyone else. He or she wants to know what makes you unique and individual. As I have argued throughout this book, the identification and inventory of your uniqueness or *particularity* is crucial if you are ever to find meaningful work.

This particularity invades and carries over to *everything* a person does; it is not suddenly "jettisonable" when he or she turns to religion. Therefore, when I or anyone else writes about religion I believe we **must** write out of our own particularity -- which *starts*, in my case, with the fact that I write, and think, and breathe as a Christian -- as you might expect from the fact that I have been an ordained Episcopalian minister for the last forty-seven years. Understandably, then, this article speaks from a Christian perspective. I want you to be aware of that, at the outset.

Balanced against this is the fact that I have always been acutely sensitive to the fact that this is a pluralistic society in which we live, and that I owe a great deal to my readers who may have religious convictions quite different from my own. It has turned out that the people who work or have worked here in my office with me, over the years, have been predominantly of other faiths, mainly Jewish. Furthermore, **Parachute's** more than 6 million readers have not only included Christians of every variety and persuasion, Mormons, Christian Scientists, Jews, members of the Baha'i faith, Hindus, Buddhists, adherents of Islam, but also believers in 'new age' religions, secularists, humanists, agnostics, atheists, and many others. I have therefore tried to be very courteous toward the feelings of all my readers, *while at the same time* counting on them to translate my Christian thought forms into their own thought forms. This ability to thus translate is the indispensable *sine qua non* of anyone who wants to communicate helpfully with others, these days.

In the Judeo-Christian tradition from which I come, one of the indignant Biblical questions is, "Has God forgotten to be gracious?" The answer was a clear No. I think it is important *for all of us* also to seek the same goal. I have therefore labored to make this section gracious as well as helpful.

R.N.B

TURNING POINT

For many of us, the job-hunt offers a chance to make some fundamental changes in our whole life. It marks a turning point in how we live our life.

It gives us a chance to ponder and reflect, to extend our mental horizons, to go deeper into the sub-soil of our soul.

It gives us a chance to wrestle with the question, "Why am I here on Earth?" We don't want to feel that we are just another grain of sand lying on the beach called humanity, unnumbered and lost in the 5 billion other human beings.

We want to do more than plod through life, going to work, coming home from work. We want to find that special joy, "that no one can take from us," which comes from having a sense of Mission in our life.

We want to feel we were put here on Earth for some special purpose, to do some unique work that only we can accomplish.

We want to know what our Mission is.

THE MEANING OF THE WORD 'MISSION'

When used with respect to our life and work *Mission* has always been a religious concept, from beginning to end. It is defined by Webster's as "a continuing task or responsibility that one is destined or fitted to do or specially called upon to undertake," and historically has had two major synonyms: *Calling* and *Vocation*. These, of course, are the same word in two different languages, English and Latin. Both imply God. To be given a Vocation or Calling implies *Someone who* calls. To have a Destiny implies *Someone who determined the destination for us.* Thus, the concept of Mission lands us inevitably in the lap of God, before we have hardly begun.

I emphasize this, because there is an increasing trend in our culture to try to speak about religious subjects without reference to God. This is true of "spirituality," "soul," and "Mission," in particular. More and more books talk about Mission as though it were simply "a purpose you choose for your own life, by identifying your enthusiasms."

This attempt to obliterate all reference to God from the originally-religious concept of Mission, is particularly ironic because the proposed substitute word - - enthusiasms - - is derived from two Greek words, 'en theos,' and means "God in us."

In the midst of this "redefining culture" we find an oasis called "the job-hunting field." It is a field that was raised on a firm concept of "God." That's because most of its inventors, most of its leaders over the years - - the late John Crystal, Arthur Miller, Ralph Mattson, Tom and Ellie Jackson, Bernard Haldane, Arthur and Marie Kirn, myself and many others - - have been people who believe firmly in God, and came into this field because we think about Him a lot, in connection with meaningful work.

Nor are we alone. Many many job-hunters also think about God a lot. In the U.S., 94% of us believe in God, 90% of us pray, 88% of us believe God loves us, and 33% of us report we have had a life-changing religious experience - - and these figures have remained virtually unchanged for the past fifty years, according to opinion polls conducted by the Gallup Organization. (*The People's Religion: American Faith in the 90s.* Macmillan & Co. 1989).

What is not so clear is whether we think about God in connection with our work. Often these two subjects - - spiritual beliefs and Work - - live in separate mental ghettos within the same person's head.

But unemployment offers us a chance to fix all that: to marry our work and our religious beliefs together, to talk about Calling, and Vocation, and Mission in life - - to think out why we are here, and what plans God has for us.

That's why a period of unemployment can absolutely change our life.

THE SECRET OF
FINDING YOUR MISSION
IN LIFE:
TAKING IT IN STAGES

> I will explain the steps toward finding your mission in life that I have learned in my seventy years on Earth. Just remember two things. First, I speak from a Christian perspective, and trust you to translate this into your own thought-forms.
>
> Secondly, I know that these steps are not the only Way -- by any means. Many people have discovered their Mission by taking other paths. And you may, too. But hopefully what I have to say may shed some light upon whatever path you take.

I have learned that if you want to figure out what your Mission in life is, it will likely take some time. It is not a *problem* to be solved in a day and a night. It is a *learning process* which has steps to it, much like the process by which we all learned to eat. As a baby we did not tackle adult food right off. As we all recall, there were three stages: first there had to be the mother's milk or bottle, then strained baby foods, and finally -- after teeth and time -- the stuff that grown-ups chew. Three stages -- and the two earlier stages were not to be disparaged. It was all Eating, just different forms of Eating -- appropriate to our development at the time. But each stage had to be mastered, in turn, before the next could be approached.

There are usually three stages also to learning what your Mission in life is, and the two earlier stages are likewise not to be disparaged. It is all "Mission" -- just different forms of Mission, appropriate to your development at the time. But each stage has to be mastered, in turn, before the next can be approached.

Of course, there is a sense in which you never master any of these stages, but are always growing in understanding and mastery of them, throughout your whole life here on Earth.

As it has been impressed on me by observing many people over the years (admittedly through *Christian spectacles*), it appears that the three parts to your Mission here on Earth can be defined generally as follows:

(1) *Your first Mission here on Earth* is one which you share with the rest of the human race, but it is no less your individual Mission for the fact that it is shared: and it is, **to seek to stand hour by hour in the conscious presence of God, the One from whom your Mission is derived**. *The Missioner before the Mission,* is the rule. In religious language, your Mission here is: *to know God, and enjoy Him forever, and to see His hand in all His works.*

(2) Secondly, once you have begun doing that in an earnest way, *your second Mission here on Earth* is also one which you share with the rest of the human race, but it is no less your individual mission for the fact that it is shared: and that is, **to do what you can, moment by moment, day by day, step by step, to make this world a better place, following the leading and guidance of God's Spirit within you and around you**.

(3) Thirdly, once you have begun doing that in a serious way, *your third Mission here on Earth* is one which is uniquely yours, and that is:

a) **to exercise that Talent which you particularly came to Earth to use -- your greatest gift, which you most delight to use,**

b) **in the place(s) or setting(s) which God has caused to appeal to you the most,**

c) **and for those purposes which God most needs to have done in the world.**

When fleshed out, and spelled out, I think you will find that there you have the definition of your Mission in life. Or, to put it another way, these are the three Missions which you have in life.

The Two Rhythms of the Dance of Mission:
Unlearning, Learning,
Unlearning, Learning

The distinctive characteristic of these three stages is that in each we are forced to *let go* of some fundamental assumptions which the world has *falsely* taught us, about the nature of our Mission. In other words, throughout this quest and at each stage we find ourselves engaged not merely in a process of *Learning.* We are also engaged in a process of *Un*learning. Thus, we can restate the above three Learnings, in terms of what we also need to *un*learn at each stage:

• We need in the first Stage to *un*learn the idea that our Mission is primarily to keep busy *doing* something (here on Earth), and learn instead that our Mission is first of all to keep busy *being* something (here on Earth). In Christian language (and others as well), we might say that we were sent here to learn how *to be* sons of God, and daughters of God, before anything else. *"Our Father, who art in heaven . . ."*

• In the second stage, "Being" issues into "Doing." At this stage, we need to *un*learn the idea that everything about our Mission must be *unique* to us, and learn instead that some parts of our Mission here on Earth are *shared* by all human beings: e.g., we were all sent here to bring more gratitude, more kindness, more forgiveness, and more love, into the world. We share this Mission because the task is too large to be accomplished by just one individual.

• We need in the third stage to *un*learn the idea that that part of our Mission which is truly unique, and most truly ours, is something Our Creator just *orders* us to do, without any agreement from our spirit, mind, and heart. (On the other hand, neither is it something that each of us chooses and then merely asks God to bless.) We need to learn that God so honors our free will, that He has ordained our unique Mission be something which we have some part in choosing.

• In this third stage we need also to *un*learn the idea that our unique Mission must consist of some achievement which all the world will see, -- and learn instead that as the stone does not always know what ripples it has caused in the pond whose surface it impacts, so neither we nor those who watch our life will always know *what we have achieved* by our life and by our Mission. *It may be* that by the grace of God we helped bring about a profound change for the better in the lives of other souls around us, but it also may be that this takes place beyond our sight, or after we have gone on. And we may never know what we have accomplished, until we see Him face-to-face after this life is past.

* Most finally, we need to *un*learn the idea that what we have accomplished is our doing, and ours alone. It is God's Spirit breathing in us and through us which helps us to do whatever we do, and so the singular first person pronoun is never appropriate, but only the plural. Not "*I* accomplished this" but "*We* accomplished this, God and I, working together . . ."

That should give you a general overview. But I would like to add some random comments on my part about each of these three Missions of ours here on Earth.

Some Random Comments About Your First Mission in Life

Your first Mission here on Earth is one which you share with the rest of the human race, but it is no less your individual Mission for the fact that it is shared: and that is, **to seek to stand hour by hour in the conscious presence of God, the One from whom your Mission is derived**. The Missioner before the Mission, is the rule. In religious language, your Mission is: to know God, and enjoy Him forever, and to see His hand in all His works.

Comment 1: How We Might Think of God

Each of us has to go about this primary Mission according to the tenets of his or her own particular religion. But I will speak what I know out of the context of my own particular faith, and you may perhaps translate and apply it to yours. I will speak as a Christian, who believes (passionately) that Christ is the Way and the Truth and the Life. But I also believe, with St. Peter, "that God shows no partiality, but in every nation any one who fears him and does what is right is acceptable to him." (Acts 10:34-35)

Now, Jesus claimed many unique things about Himself and His Mission; but He also spoke of Himself as the great prototype for us all. He called himself "the Son of Man," and He said, "I assure you that the man who believes in me will do the same things that I have done, yes, and he will do even greater things than these . . ." (John 14:12)

Emboldened by His identification of us with His life and His Mission, we might want to remember how He spoke about His Life here on Earth. He put it in this context: "**I came from the Father and have come into the world; again, I am leaving the world and going to the Father.**" (John 16:28)

If there is a sense in which this is, in even the faintest way, true also of our lives (and I shall say in a moment in what sense I think it is true), then instead of calling our great Creator "God" or "Father" right off, we might begin our approach to the subject of religion by referring to the One Who gave us our Mission and sent us to this planet not as "God" or "Father" but -- *just to help our thinking* -- as: "**The One From Whom We Came and The One To Whom We Shall Return**," when this life is done.

If our life here on Earth be at all like Christ's, then this is a true way to think about the One Who gave us our Mission. We are not some kind of eternal, pre-existent *being*. We are **creatures**, who once did not exist, and then came into Being, and continue to have our Being, only at the will of our great Creator. But as creatures we are both body and soul; and although we know our body was created in our mother's womb, our soul's origin is a great mystery. Where it came from, at what moment the Lord created it, is something we cannot know. It is not unreasonable to suppose, however, that the great God created our *soul* before it entered our body, and in that sense we did indeed stand before God before we were born; and He is indeed "**The One From Whom We Came and The One To Whom We Shall Return.**"

Therefore, before we go searching for "what work was I sent here to do?" we need to establish or in a truer sense *reestablish* -- contact with this "**One From Whom We Came and The One To Whom We Shall Return.**" Without this reaching out of the creature to the great Creator, without this reaching out of *the creature with a Mission* to *the One Who Gave Us That Mission*, the question *what is my Mission in life?* is void and null. The *what* is rooted in the *Who*; absent the Personal, one cannot meaningfully discuss The Thing. It is like the adult who cries, "I want to get married," without giving any consideration to *who* it is they want to marry.

Comment 2: How We Might Think of Religion or Faith

In light of this larger view of our creatureliness, we can see that *religion* or *faith* is not a question of whether or not we choose to (*as it is so commonly put*) "have a relationship with God." Looking at our life in a larger context than just our life here on Earth, it becomes apparent that some sort of relationship with God is a given for us, about which we have absolutely no choice. God and we **were and are** related, during the time of our soul's existence before our birth and in the time of our soul's continued existence after our death. The only choice we have is what to do about **The Time In Between**, i.e., what we want the nature of our relationship with God to be during our time here on Earth and how that will affect the *nature* of the relationship, then, after death.

One of the corollaries of all this is that by the very act of being born into a human body, it is an inevitable that we undergo a kind of *amnesia* -- an amnesia which typically embraces not only our nine months in the womb, our baby years, and almost one-third of each day (sleeping), but more importantly any memory of our origin or our destiny. We wander on Earth as an amnesia victim. To seek after Faith, therefore, is to seek to climb back out of that amnesia. Religion or faith is **the hard reclaiming of knowledge we once knew as a certainty**.

Comment 3: The First Obstacle to Executing This Mission

This first Mission of ours here on Earth is not the easiest of Missions, simply because it is the first. Indeed, in many ways, it is the most difficult. All can see that our life here on Earth is a very physical life. We eat, we drink, we sleep, we long to be held, and to hold. We inherit a physical body, with very physical appetites, we walk on the physical earth, and we acquire physical possessions. It is the most alluring of temptations, *in our amnesia*, to come up with just a *Physical* interpretation of this life: to think that the Universe is merely interested in the survival of species. Given this interpretation, the story of our individual life could be simply told: we are born, grow up, procreate, and die.

But we are ever recalled to do what we came here to do: that without rejecting the joy of the Physicalness of this life, such as the love of the blue sky and the green grass, we are to reach out beyond all this to **recall** and recover a *Spiritual* interpretation of our life. *Beyond* the physical and *within* the physicalness of this life, to detect a Spirit and a Person from beyond this Earth who is with us and in us -- the very real and loving and awesome Presence of the great Creator from whom we came -- and the One to whom we once again shall go.

Comment 4: The Second Obstacle to Executing This Mission

It is one of the conditions of our earthly amnesia and our creatureliness that, sadly enough, some very *human* and very *rebellious* part of us *likes* the idea of living in a world where we can be our own god -- and therefore loves the purely Physical interpretation of life, and finds it *anguish* to relinquish it. Traditional Christian vocabulary calls this **"sin"** and has a lot to say about the difficulty it poses for this first part of our Mission. All who live a thoughtful life know that it is true: our greatest enemy in carrying out this first Mission of ours is indeed *our own* heart and our own rebellion.

Comment 5: Further Thoughts About What Makes Us Special and Unique

As I said earlier, many of us come to this issue of our Mission in life, because we want to feel that we are unique. And what we mean by that, is that we hope to discover some "specialness" intrinsic to us, which is our birthright, and which no one can take from us. What we, however, discover from a thorough exploration of this topic, is that we are indeed special -- but only because God thinks us so. Our specialness and uniqueness reside in Him, and His love, rather than in anything intrinsic to our own *being*. The proper appreciation of this distinction causes our feet to carry us in the end not to the City called Pride, but to the Temple called Gratitude.

> What is religion? Religion is the service of God
> out of grateful love for what God has done for
> us. The Christian religion, more particularly, is
> the service of God out of grateful love for what
> God has done for us in Christ.
>
> Phillips Brooks, author of
> *O Little Town of Bethlehem*

Comment 6: The Unconscious Doing of The Work We Came To Do

You may have *already* wrestled with this first part of your Mission here on Earth. You may not have called it that. You may have called it simply "learning to believe in God." But if you ask what your Mission is in life, this one was and is the precondition of all else that you came here to do. Absent this Mission, and it is folly to talk about the rest. So, if you have been seeking faith, or seeking to strengthen your faith, you have -- willy nilly -- already been about *the doing of the Mission you were given*. Born into **This Time In Between**, you have found His hand again, and reclasped it. You are therefore ready to go on with His Spirit to tackle together what you came here to do -- the other parts of your Mission.

Some Random Comments About
Your Second Mission in Life

Your second Mission here on Earth is also one which you share with the rest of the human race, but it is no less your individual mission for the fact that it is shared: and that is, **to do what you can moment by moment, day by day, step by step, to make this world a better place -- following the leading and guidance of God's Spirit within you and around you**.

Comment 1: The Uncomfortableness of One Step at a Time

Imagine yourself out walking in your neighborhood one night, and suddenly you find yourself surrounded by such a dense fog, that you have lost your bearings and cannot find your way. Suddenly, a friend appears out of the fog, and asks you to put your hand in theirs, and they will lead you home. And you, not being able to tell where you are going, trustingly follow them, even though you can only see one step at a time. Eventually you arrive safely home, filled with gratitude. But as you reflect upon the experience the next day, you realize how unsettling it was to have to keep walking when you could see only one step at a time, even though you had guidance in which you knew you could trust.

Now I have asked you to imagine all of this, because this is the essence of the second Mission to which *you* are called -- and *I* am called -- in this life. It is all very different than we had imagined. When the question, *"What is your Mission in life?"* is first broached, and we have put our hand in God's, as it were, we imagine that we will be taken up to *some mountaintop*, from which we can see far into the distance. And that we will hear a voice in our ear, saying, "Look, look, see that distant city? That is the goal of your Mission; that is where everything is leading, every step of your way."

But instead of the mountaintop, we find ourself in *the valley* -- wandering often in a fog. And the voice in our ear says something quite different from what we thought we would hear. It says, **"Your Mission is to take one step at a time, even when you don't yet see where it all is leading, or what the Grand Plan is, or what your overall Mission in life is. Trust Me; I will lead you."**

Comment 2: The Nature of This Step-by-Step Mission

As I said, in every situation you find yourself, you have been sent here to do whatever you can -- moment by moment -- that will bring more gratitude, more kindness, more forgiveness, more honesty, and more love into this world.

There are dozens of such moments every day. Moments when you stand -- as it were -- at a spiritual crossroads, with two ways lying before you. Such moments are typically called "**moments of decision.**" It does not matter what the frame or content of each particular decision is. It all devolves, in the end, into just two roads before you, *every time*. **The one** will lead to *less* gratitude, *less* kindness, *less* forgiveness, *less* honesty, or *less* love in the world. **The other** will lead to *more* gratitude, *more* kindness, *more* forgiveness, *more* honesty, or *more* love in the world. Your Mission, each moment, is to seek to choose the latter spiritual road, rather than the former, *every time*.

Comment 3: Some Examples of This Step-by-Step Mission

I will give a few examples, so that the nature of this part of your Mission may be unmistakably clear.

You are out on the freeway, in your car. Someone has gotten into the wrong lane, to the right of *your* lane, and needs to move over into the lane you are in. You *see* their need to cut in, ahead of you. **Decision time.** In your mind's eye you see two spiritual roads lying before you: the one leading to less kindness in the world (you speed up, to shut this driver out, and don't let them move over), the other leading to more kindness in the world (you let the driver cut in). **Since you know this is part of your Mission, part of the reason why you came to Earth, your calling is clear. You know which road to take, which decision to make.**

You are hard at work at your desk, when suddenly an interruption comes. The phone rings, or someone is at the door. They need something from you, a question of some of your time and attention. **Decision time.** In your mind's eye you see two spiritual roads lying before you: the one leading to less love in the world (you tell them you're just too busy to be bothered), the other leading to more love in the world (you put aside your work, decide that God may have sent this person to you, and say, "Yes, what can I do to help you?"). **Since you know this is part of your Mission, part of the reason why you came to Earth, your calling is clear. You know which road to take, which decision to make.**

Your mate does something that hurts your feelings. **Decision time.** In your mind's eye you see two spiritual roads lying before you: the one leading to less forgiveness in the world (you institute an icy silence between the two of you, and think of how you can punish them or otherwise get even), the other leading to more forgiveness in the

world (you go over and take them in your arms, speak the truth about your hurt feelings, and assure them of your love). **Since you know this is part of your Mission, part of the reason why you came to Earth, your calling is clear. You know which road to take, which decision to make.**

You have not behaved at your most noble, recently. And now you are face-to-face with someone who asks you a question about what happened. **Decision time.** In your mind's eye you see two spiritual roads lying before you: the one leading to less honesty in the world (you lie about what happened, or what you were feeling, because you fear losing their respect or their love), the other leading to more honesty in the world (you tell the truth, together with how you feel about it, in retrospect). **Since you know this is part of your Mission, part of the reason why you came to Earth, your calling is clear. You know which road to take, which decision to make.**

Comment 4: The Spectacle Which Makes the Angels Laugh

It is necessary to explain this part of our Mission in some detail, because so many times you will see people wringing their hands, and saying, "*I want to know what my Mission in life is,*" all the while they are cutting people off on the highway, refusing to give time to people, punishing their mate for having hurt their feelings, and lying about what they did. And it will seem to you that the angels must laugh to see this spectacle. *For these people wringing their hands*, their Mission was right there, on the freeway, in the interruption, in the hurt, and at the confrontation.

Comment 5: The Valley vs. The Mountaintop

At some point in your life your Mission may involve some grand *mountaintop experience*, where you say to yourself, "This, this, is why I came into the world. I know it. I know it." *But until then*, your Mission is here in *the valley*, and the fog, and the little callings moment by moment, day by day. More to the point, it is likely you cannot ever get to your mountaintop Mission unless you have first exercised your stewardship faithfully in the valley.

It is an ancient principle, to which Jesus alluded often, that if you don't use the information the Universe has already given you, you cannot expect it will give you any more. If you aren't being faithful in small things, how can you expect to be given charge over larger things? (Luke 16:10,11,12; 19:11–24) If you aren't trying to bring more gratitude, kindness, forgiveness, honesty, and love into the world each day, you can hardly expect that you will be entrusted with the Mission to help bring peace into the world or anything else large and important. If we do not live out our day-by-day Mission in the valley, we cannot expect we are yet ready for a larger *mountaintop* Mission.

Comment 6: The Importance of Not Thinking of This Mission As 'Just A Training Camp'

The valley is not just a kind of "training camp." There is in your imagination even now an invisible *spiritual* mountaintop to which you may go, if you wish to see where all this is leading. And what will you see there, in the imagination of your heart, but the goal toward which all this is pointed: **that Earth might be more like heaven. That human's life might be more like God's**. That is the large achievement toward which all our day-by-day Missions *in the valley* are moving. This is a *large* order, but it is accomplished by faithful attention to the doing of our great Creator's **will** in little things as well as in large. It is much like the building of the pyramids in Egypt, which was accomplished by the dragging of a lot of individual pieces of stone by a lot of individual men.

The valley, the fog, the going step-by-step, is no mere training camp. The goal is real, however large. "**Thy Kingdom come, Thy will be done, on Earth, as it is in heaven.**"

Some Random Comments About Your Third Mission in Life

Your third Mission here on Earth is one which is uniquely yours, and that is:

a) **to exercise that Talent which you particularly came to Earth to use -- your greatest gift which you most delight to use**

b) **in those place(s) or setting(s) which God has caused to appeal to you the most,**

c) **and for those purposes which God most needs to have done in the world.**

Comment 1: Our Mission Is Already Written, "in Our Members"

It is customary in trying to identify this part of our Mission, to advise that we should ask God, in prayer, to speak to us -- and **tell us** plainly what our Mission is. We look for a voice in the air, a thought in our head, a dream in the night, a sign in the events of the day, to reveal this thing which is otherwise *(it is said)* completely hidden. Sometimes, from just such answered prayer, people do indeed discover what their Mission is, beyond all doubt and uncertainty.

But having to wait for the voice of God to reveal what our Mission is, is not the truest picture of our situation. St. Paul, in Romans, speaks of a law "written in our members," -- and this phrase has a telling application to the question of **how** God reveals to each of us our unique Mission in life. Read again the definition of our third Mission (above) and you will see: the clear implication of the definition is that God has **already** revealed His will to us concerning our vocation and Mission, by causing it to be "**written in our members.**" We are to begin deciphering our unique Mission by studying our talents and skills, and more particularly which ones (or One) we most rejoice to use.

God actually has written His will *twice* in our members: *first in the talents* which He lodged there, and secondly *in His guidance of our heart*, as to which talent gives us the greatest pleasure from its exercise (**it is usually the one which, when we use it, causes us to lose all sense of time**).

Even as the anthropologist can examine ancient inscriptions, and divine from them the daily life of a long lost people, so we by examining **our talents** and **our heart** can *more often than we dream* divine the Will of the Living God. For true it is, our Mission is not something He **will** reveal; it is something He **has already** revealed. It is not to be found written in the sky; it is to be found written in our members.

Comment 2: Career Counseling: We Need You

Arguably, our first two Missions in life could be learned from religion alone -- without any reference whatsoever to career counseling, the subject of this book. Why then should career counseling claim that this question about our Mission in life is its proper concern, *in any way?*

It is when we come to this third Mission, which hinges so crucially on the question of our Talents, skills, and gifts, that we see the answer. If you've read the body of this book, before turning to this Epilogue, you know without my even saying it, how much the identification of Talents, gifts, or skills is the province of career counseling. Its expertise, indeed its *raison d'etre*, lies precisely in the identification, classification, and (forgive me) "prioritization" of Talents, skills, and gifts. To put the matter quite simply, career counseling knows how to do this better than any other discipline -- **including** traditional religion. This is not a defect of religion, but the fulfillment of something Jesus promised: "When the Spirit of truth comes, He will guide you into all truth." (John 16:12) Career counseling is part (we may hope) of that promised late-coming truth. It can therefore be of inestimable help to the pilgrim who is trying to figure out what their greatest, and most enjoyable, talent is, as a step toward identifying their unique Mission in life.

If career counseling needs religion as its helpmate in the first two stages of identifying our Mission in life, religion repays the compliment by clearly needing career counseling as **its** helpmate here in the third stage.

And this place where you are in your life right now -- facing the job-hunt and all its anxiety -- is the perfect time to seek the union within your own mind and heart of both career counseling (as in the pages of this book) and your faith in God.

Comment 3: How Our Mission Got Chosen: A Scenario for the Romantic

It is a mystery which we cannot fathom, in this life at least, as to why one of us has this talent, and the other one has that; why God chose to give one gift -- and Mission -- to one person, and a different gift -- and Mission -- to another. Since we do not know, and in some degree cannot know, we are certainly left free to speculate, and imagine.

We may imagine that before we came to Earth, our souls, *our Breath, our Light*, stood before the great Creator and volunteered for this Mission. And God and we, together, chose what that Mission would be and what particular gifts would be needed, which He then agreed to give us, after our birth. Thus, our Mission was not a command given preemptorily by an unloving Creator to a reluctant slave without a vote, but was a task jointly designed by us both, in which as fast as the great Creator said, **"I wish"** our hearts responded, **"Oh, yes."** As mentioned in an earlier Comment, it may be helpful to think of the condition of our becoming human as that we became amnesiac about any consciousness our soul had before birth -- and therefore amnesiac about the nature or manner in which our Mission was designed.

Our searching for our Mission now is therefore a searching to recover the memory of something we ourselves had a part in designing.

I am admittedly a hopeless romantic, so of course I like this picture. If you also are a hopeless romantic, you may like it too. There's also the chance that it just may be true. We will not know until we see Him face-to-face.

Comment 4: Mission As Intersection

There are all different kinds of voices calling you to all different kinds of work, and the problem is to find out which is the voice of God rather than that of society, say, or the superego, or self-interest. By and large a good rule for finding out is this: the kind of work God usually calls you to is the kind of work (a) that you need most to do and (b) the world most needs to have done. If you really get a kick out of your work, you've presumably met requirement (a), but if your work is writing TV deodorant commercials, the chances are you've missed requirement (b). On the other hand, if your work is being a doctor in a leper colony, you have probably met (b), but if most of the time you're bored and depressed by it, the chances are you haven't only bypassed (a) but probably aren't helping your patients much either. Neither the hair shirt nor the soft birth will do. **The place God calls you to is the place where your deep gladness and the world's deep hunger meet.**

Fred Buechner
Wishful Thinking -- A Theological ABC

Excerpted from *Wishful Thinking – A Theological ABC* by Frederick Buechner. Copyright ©1973 by Frederick Buechner. Reprinted with permission of HarperCollins, Inc.

Comment 5: Examples of Mission As Intersection

Your unique and individual mission will most likely turn out to be a mission of Love, acted out in one or all of three arenas: either in the Kingdom of the Mind, whose goal is to bring more Truth into the world; or in the Kingdom of the Heart, whose goal is to bring more Beauty into the world; or in the Kingdom of the Will, whose goal is to bring more Perfection into the world, through Service.

Here are some examples:

"My mission is, out of the rich reservoir of love which God seems to have given me, to nurture and show love to others -- most particularly to those who are suffering from incurable diseases."

"My mission is to draw maps for people to show them how to get to God."

"My mission is to create the purest foods I can, to help people's bodies not get in the way of their spiritual growth."

"My mission is to make the finest harps I can so that people can hear the voice of God in the wind."

"My mission is to make people laugh, so that the travail of this earthly life doesn't seem quite so hard to them."

"My mission is to help people know the truth, in love, about what is happening out in the world, so that there will be more honesty in the world."

"My mission is to weep with those who weep, so that in my arms they may feel themselves in the arms of that Eternal Love which sent me and which created them."

"My mission is to create beautiful gardens, so that in the lilies of the field people may behold the Beauty of God and be reminded of the Beauty of Holiness."

Comment 6: Life As Long As Your Mission Requires

Knowing that you came to Earth for a reason, and knowing what that Mission is, throws an entirely different light upon your life from now on. You are, generally speaking, delivered from any further fear about how long you have to live. You may settle it in your heart that you are here until God chooses to think that you have accomplished your Mission, or until God has a greater Mission for you in another Realm. You need to be a good steward of what He has given you, while you are here; but you do not need to be an anxious steward or stewardess.

You need to attend to your health, *but you do not need to constantly worry about it*. You need to meditate on your death, *but you do not need to be constantly preoccupied with it*. To paraphrase the glorious words of G. K. Chesterton: "**We now have a strong desire for living combined with a strange carelessness about dying. We desire life like water and yet are ready to drink death like wine.**" We know that we are here to do what we came to do, and we need not worry about anything else.

Final Comment: A Job-Hunt Done Well

If you approach your job-hunt as an opportunity to work on this issue as well as the issue of how you will keep body and soul together, then hopefully your job-hunt will end with your being able to say: "Life has deep meaning to me, now. I have discovered more than my ideal job; I have found my Mission, and the reason why I am here on Earth."

EXERCISES

The Flower

A PICTURE OF THE JOB OF YOUR DREAMS

YOUR FLOWER

IN ORDER TO HUNT FOR YOUR IDEAL JOB, or even something close to your ideal job, you must have a picture of it, in your head. The clearer the picture, the easier it will be to hunt for it. The purpose of this booklet is to guide you as you draw that picture.

We have chosen a "Flower" as the model for that picture. While such expressions as "plugging in," "turning on," and other common phrases portray you (implicitly) as a machine, you are actually much more like a Flower than a machine. That is to say, you flourish in some job-environments, but wither in others. Therefore, the purpose of putting together this Flower Picture of yourself is to help you identify what kind of a work climate you will flourish in, and thus do your very best work. Your twin goals should be to be as happy as you can be at your job, while at the same time you do your most effective work.

There is a picture of the Flower on pages 264–265, that you can use as your worksheet.

As you can see, skills are at the center of the Flower, even as they are at the center of your mission, career, or job. They are listed in order of priority.

Surrounding them are six petals. Listed in the order in which you will work on them, they are:

1. Geography
2. Interests (Special Knowledges)
3. People Environments
4. Values, Purposes, and Goals
5. Working Conditions
6. Salary & Responsibility

When you are done filling in these skills and petals, you will have the complete Flower picture of your Ideal Job. Okay? Then, get out your pen or pencil and let's get started.

The Flower

A Picture of The Job of Your Dreams

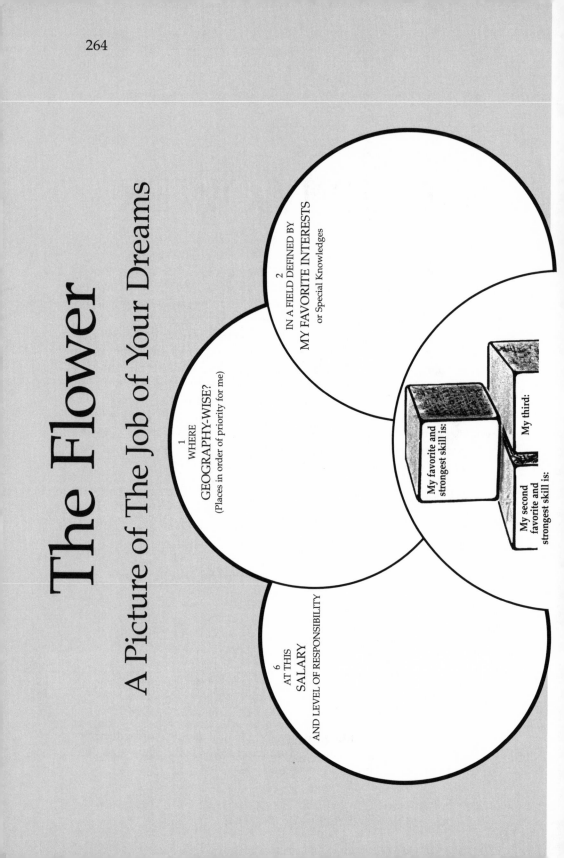

1
WHERE
GEOGRAPHY-WISE?
(Places in order of priority for me)

2
IN A FIELD DEFINED BY
MY FAVORITE INTERESTS
or Special Knowledges

6
AT THIS
SALARY
AND LEVEL OF RESPONSIBILITY

My favorite and strongest skill is:

My second favorite and strongest skill is:

My third:

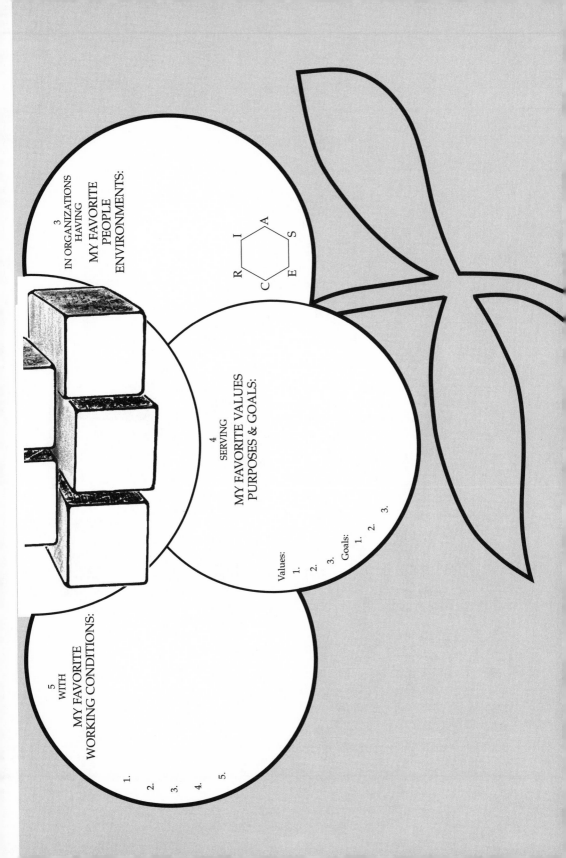

3
IN ORGANIZATIONS
HAVING
MY FAVORITE
PEOPLE
ENVIRONMENTS:

R — I — A — S — E — C

4
SERVING
MY FAVORITE VALUES
PURPOSES & GOALS:

Values:
1.
2.
3.

Goals:
1.
2.
3.

5
WITH
MY FAVORITE
WORKING CONDITIONS:

1.
2.
3.
4.
5.

Example

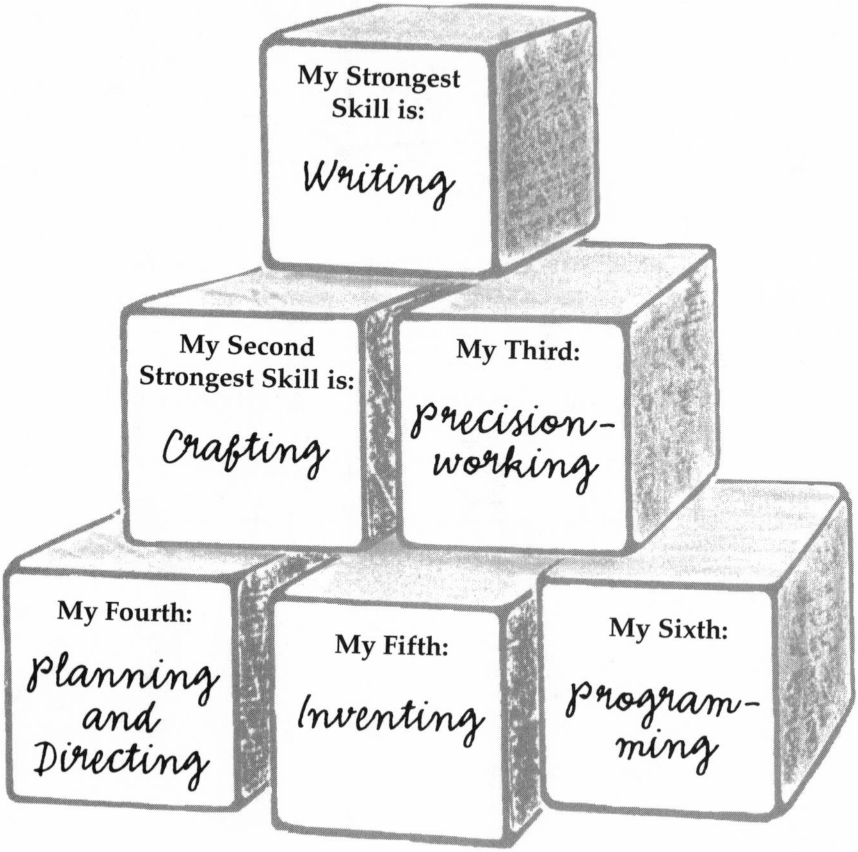

My Strongest
Skill is:

Writing

My Second
Strongest Skill is:

Crafting

My Third:

*precision-
working*

My Fourth:

*Planning
and
Directing*

My Fifth:

Inventing

My Sixth:

*program-
ming*

Your Favorite
Transferable Skills

We begin with skills. You must, first of all, identify your favorite (transferable) skills that you most enjoy using, *in order of priority or importance to you.* Here are the five steps to accomplishing that.

1. Write Your First Story

To do this, you will need to write **seven stories** about things you did just because they were fun, or because they gave you a sense of adventure, or gave you a sense of accomplishment. It does not matter whether anyone else ever knew about this accomplishment, or not. Each story can be about something you did at work, or in school, or at play -- and can be from any time period of your life. It should not be more than two or three paragraphs, in length.

> Below is a form to help you write each of your Seven Stories. *(You will obviously want to go down to Kinko's or your local copy shop and make seven copies of this form* before *you begin filling it out, for the first time. The copies work best if you make them on seven pieces of $8\frac{1}{2}" \times 11"$ paper,* turned sideways.*)*

If you need an example of what to put in each of the five columns, turn back to page 80ff here in *Parachute.* After you have written your first story, we will show you how to analyze it for the transferable skills that you used therein.

My Seven Life Stories

Column 1	Column 2	Column 3	Column 4	Column 5
Your Goal: What You Want to Accomplish	Some Kind of Obstacle (or limit, hurdle or restraint you had to overcome before it could be accomplished)	What You Did Step-by-Step (It may help if you pretend you are telling this story to a whining 4-year-old child, who keeps asking, after each of your sentences, "An' then whadja do? An' then whadja do?")	Description of the Result (What you accomplished)	Any Measure or Quantities To Prove Your Achievement

2. Analyze The Story for Transferable Skills

Once you have written Story #1 (and before you write the other six), you will want to analyze it for the transferable skills you *used*. (You can decide later if you loved those skills or not. For now, just do an inventory.)

To do this inventory, go to the list of Skills Keys found on pages 270–275, which resemble a series of typewriter keys. Transferable skills divide into:

1. Physical Skills: the transferable skills you enjoy, using primarily *your hands or body* -- with things, or nature;

2. Mental Skills: the transferable skills you enjoy, using primarily *your mind* -- with data/information, ideas, or subjects;

3. Your Interpersonal Skills: the transferable skills you enjoy, involving primarily *personal relationships* -- as you serve or help people or animals, and their needs or problems.[1]

Therefore you will find three sets of Skills Keys, labeled accordingly.

As you look at each key in the three sets, the question you need to ask yourself, is: "Did I use this transferable skill *in this Story* (#1)?"

That is the *only* question you ask yourself (at the moment). Then you go to the little box named #1 (under each Skill Key), and this is what you do:

If the answer is "Yes", fill in the little box, as shown below:

Taking
Instructions,
Serving,
Or Helping

Did I Use This Skill in Story

Yes ▮ | #2? | #3? | #4? | #5? | #6? | #7?

Ignore the other little boxes for the time being; they belong to your other stories (all the little boxes named #2 belong to Story #2, all the little boxes named #3 belong to Story #3, etc.)

My Physical Skills

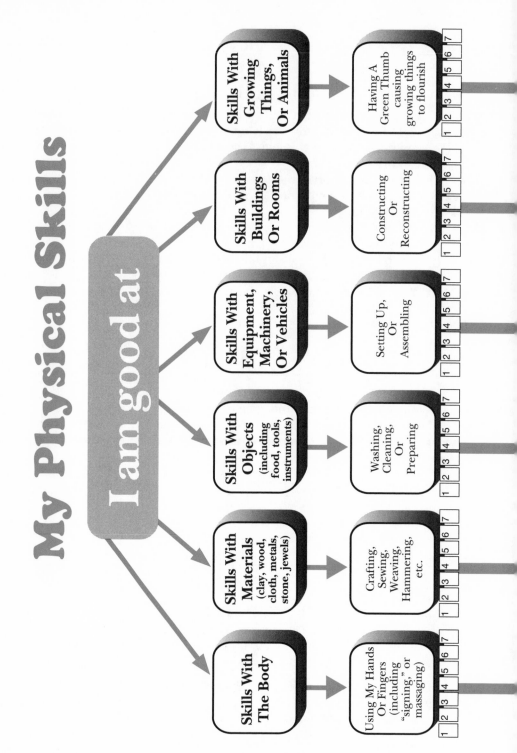

I am good at

Skills With Growing Things, Or Animals
Having A Green Thumb causing growing things to flourish
1 2 3 4 5 6 7

Skills With Buildings Or Rooms
Constructing Or Reconstructing
1 2 3 4 5 6 7

Skills With Equipment, Machinery, Or Vehicles
Setting Up, Or Assembling
1 2 3 4 5 6 7

Skills With Objects (including food, tools, instruments)
Washing, Cleaning, Or Preparing
1 2 3 4 5 6 7

Skills With Materials (clay, wood, cloth, metals, stone, jewels)
Crafting, Sewing, Weaving, Hammering, etc.
1 2 3 4 5 6 7

Skills With The Body
Using My Hands Or Fingers (including "signing," or massaging)
1 2 3 4 5 6 7

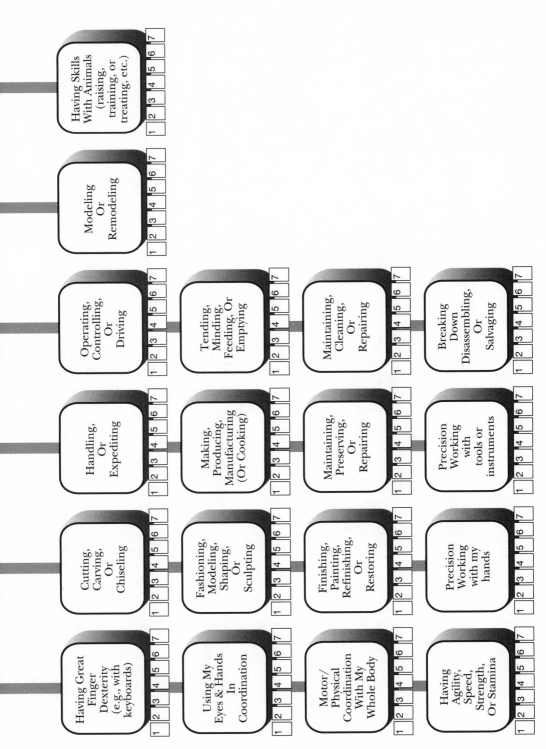

Having Skills With Animals (raising, training, or treating, etc.)
1 2 3 4 5 6 7

Modeling Or Remodeling
1 2 3 4 5 6 7

Operating, Controlling, Or Driving
1 2 3 4 5 6 7

Tending, Minding, Feeding, Or Emptying
1 2 3 4 5 6 7

Maintaining, Cleaning, Or Repairing
1 2 3 4 5 6 7

Breaking Down Disassembling, Or Salvaging
1 2 3 4 5 6 7

Handling, Or Expediting
1 2 3 4 5 6 7

Making, Producing, Manufacturing (Or Cooking)
1 2 3 4 5 6 7

Maintaining, Preserving, Or Repairing
1 2 3 4 5 6 7

Precision Working with tools or instruments
1 2 3 4 5 6 7

Cutting, Carving, Or Chiseling
1 2 3 4 5 6 7

Fashioning, Modeling, Shaping, Or Sculpting
1 2 3 4 5 6 7

Finishing, Painting, Refinishing, Or Restoring
1 2 3 4 5 6 7

Precision Working with my hands
1 2 3 4 5 6 7

Having Great Finger Dexterity (e.g., with keyboards)
1 2 3 4 5 6 7

Using My Eyes & Hands In Coordination
1 2 3 4 5 6 7

Motor/ Physical Coordination With My Whole Body
1 2 3 4 5 6 7

Having Agility, Speed, Strength, Or Stamina
1 2 3 4 5 6 7

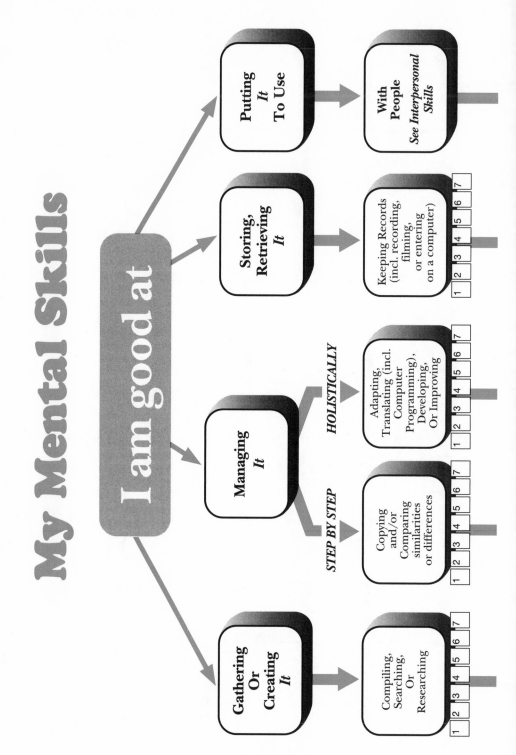

272

My Mental Skills

I am good at

Gathering Or Creating *It*

Compiling, Searching, Or Researching

| 1 | 2 | 3 | 4 | 5 | 6 | 7 |

Managing *It*

STEP BY STEP

Copying and/or Comparing similarities or differences

| 1 | 2 | 3 | 4 | 5 | 6 | 7 |

HOLISTICALLY

Adapting, Translating (incl. Computer Programming), Developing, Or Improving

| 1 | 2 | 3 | 4 | 5 | 6 | 7 |

Storing, Retrieving *It*

Keeping Records (incl. recording, filming, or entering on a computer)

| 1 | 2 | 3 | 4 | 5 | 6 | 7 |

Putting *It* **To Use**

With People *See Interpersonal Skills*

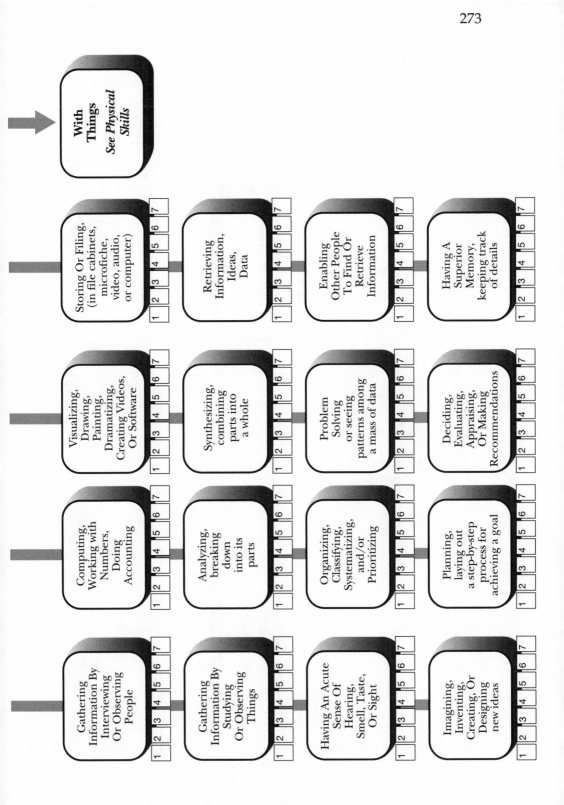

With Things
See Physical Skills

Storing Or Filing, (in file cabinets, microfiche, video, audio, or computer)
1 2 3 4 5 6 7

Retrieving Information, Ideas, Data
1 2 3 4 5 6 7

Enabling Other People To Find Or Retrieve Information
1 2 3 4 5 6 7

Having A Superior Memory, keeping track of details
1 2 3 4 5 6 7

Visualizing, Drawing, Painting, Dramatizing, Creating Videos, Or Software
1 2 3 4 5 6 7

Synthesizing, combining parts into a whole
1 2 3 4 5 6 7

Problem Solving or seeing patterns among a mass of data
1 2 3 4 5 6 7

Deciding, Evaluating, Appraising, Or Making Recommendations
1 2 3 4 5 6 7

Computing, Working with Numbers, Doing Accounting
1 2 3 4 5 6 7

Analyzing, breaking down into its parts
1 2 3 4 5 6 7

Organizing, Classifying, Systematizing, and/or Prioritizing
1 2 3 4 5 6 7

Planning, laying out a step-by-step process for achieving a goal
1 2 3 4 5 6 7

Gathering Information By Interviewing Or Observing People
1 2 3 4 5 6 7

Gathering Information By Studying Or Observing Things
1 2 3 4 5 6 7

Having An Acute Sense Of Hearing, Smell, Taste, Or Sight
1 2 3 4 5 6 7

Imagining, Inventing, Creating, Or Designing new ideas
1 2 3 4 5 6 7

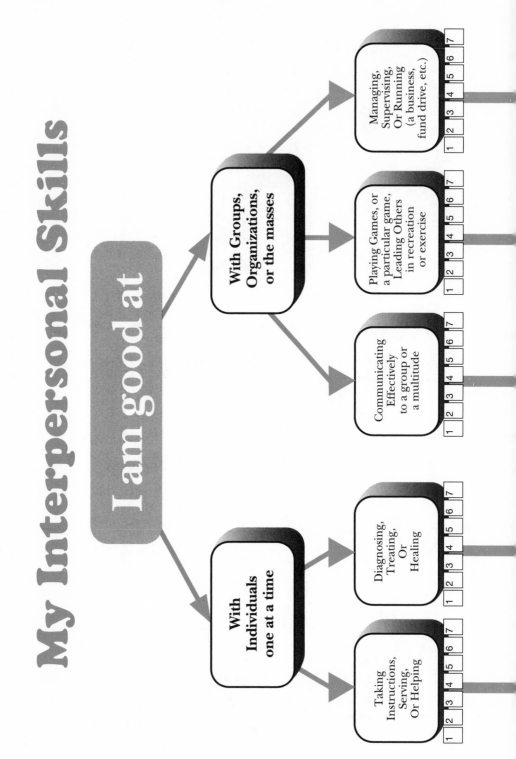

Following Through, Getting Things Done, Producing
1 2 3 4 5 6 7

Leading, Taking The Lead, Being A Pioneer
1 2 3 4 5 6 7

Initiating, Starting Up, Founding, Or Establishing
1 2 3 4 5 6 7

Negotiating between two parties, or Resolving Conflicts
1 2 3 4 5 6 7

Teaching, Training, or designing educational events
1 2 3 4 5 6 7

Guiding A Group Discussion, conveying warmth
1 2 3 4 5 6 7

Persuading A Group, Debating, Motivating, Or Selling
1 2 3 4 5 6 7

Consulting, Giving Advice to groups in your area of expertise
1 2 3 4 5 6 7

By Using Words Expressively in speaking or writing
1 2 3 4 5 6 7

By Making Presentations in person, or on TV or film
1 2 3 4 5 6 7

By Performing, Entertaining, Amusing, or Inspiring
1 2 3 4 5 6 7

"Signing," Miming, Acting, Singing, Or Playing an Instrument
1 2 3 4 5 6 7

Referring People, or helping two people to link up
1 2 3 4 5 6 7

Assessing, Evaluating, Screening, Or Selecting Individuals
1 2 3 4 5 6 7

Persuading, Motivating, Recruiting, Or Selling To Individuals
1 2 3 4 5 6 7

Representing Others, Interpreting Others' Ideas or Language
1 2 3 4 5 6 7

Communicating Well in conversation, in person, or on the phone
1 2 3 4 5 6 7

Communicating Well in writing (e.g., excellent letters)
1 2 3 4 5 6 7

Instructing, Teaching, Tutoring, Or Training Individuals
1 2 3 4 5 6 7

Advising, Coaching, Counseling, Mentoring, Empowering
1 2 3 4 5 6 7

If the answer is "No", leave the box labeled #1 blank, as shown below:

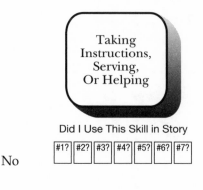

Did I Use This Skill in Story

| #1? | #2? | #3? | #4? | #5? | #6? | #7? |

No

---

3. Write Six Other Stories, and Analyze Them for Transferable Skills

Voila! You are done with Story #1. However, 'one swallow doth not a summer make,' so the fact that you used certain skills in this first Story doesn't tell you much. What you are looking for is **patterns** -- transferable skills that keep re-appearing in story after story. They keep reappearing because they are your favorites (assuming you chose stories where you were *really* enjoying yourself).

So, now, write Story #2, from any period in your life, analyze it using the keys, etc., etc. And keep this process up, until you have written, and analyzed, seven stories.

---

4. Decide Which Skills Are Your Favorites, and Prioritize Them

When you're done writing and analyzing all Seven Stories, you should now go back and look over the six pages of "Skills Keys" to see which skills got used the most often. Make a list.

Cross out any that you don't enjoy using.

Prioritize the remainder, using the Prioritizing Grids on the next two pages.

1	1	1	1	1	1	1	1	1	1	1	1	1	1	1	1	1	1	1	1	1	1	1
2	3	4	5	6	7	8	9	10	11	12	13	14	15	16	17	18	19	20	21	22	23	24

2 2 2 2 2 2 2 2 2 2 2 2 2 2 2 2 2 2 2 2 2 2
3 4 5 6 7 8 9 10 11 12 13 14 15 16 17 18 19 20 21 22 23 24

3 3 3 3 3 3 3 3 3 3 3 3 3 3 3 3 3 3 3 3 3
4 5 6 7 8 9 10 11 12 13 14 15 16 17 18 19 20 21 22 23 24

4 4 4 4 4 4 4 4 4 4 4 4 4 4 4 4 4 4 4 4
5 6 7 8 9 10 11 12 13 14 15 16 17 18 19 20 21 22 23 24

5 5 5 5 5 5 5 5 5 5 5 5 5 5 5 5 5 5 5
6 7 8 9 10 11 12 13 14 15 16 17 18 19 20 21 22 23 24

6 6 6 6 6 6 6 6 6 6 6 6 6 6 6 6 6 6
7 8 9 10 11 12 13 14 15 16 17 18 19 20 21 22 23 24

7 7 7 7 7 7 7 7 7 7 7 7 7 7 7 7 7
8 9 10 11 12 13 14 15 16 17 18 19 20 21 22 23 24

8 8 8 8 8 8 8 8 8 8 8 8 8 8 8 8
9 10 11 12 13 14 15 16 17 18 19 20 21 22 23 24

9 9 9 9 9 9 9 9 9 9 9 9 9 9 9
10 11 12 13 14 15 16 17 18 19 20 21 22 23 24

10 10 10 10 10 10 10 10 10 10 10 10 10 10
11 12 13 14 15 16 17 18 19 20 21 22 23 24

11 11 11 11 11 11 11 11 11 11 11 11 11
12 13 14 15 16 17 18 19 20 21 22 23 24

12 12 12 12 12 12 12 12 12 12 12 12
13 14 15 16 17 18 19 20 21 22 23 24

13 13 13 13 13 13 13 13 13 13
14 15 16 17 18 19 20 21 22 23 24

14 14 14 14 14 14 14 14 14 14
15 16 17 18 19 20 21 22 23 24

15 15 15 15 15 15 15 15 15
16 17 18 19 20 21 22 23 24

16 16 16 16 16 16 16 16
17 18 19 20 21 22 23 24

17 17 17 17 17 17 17
18 19 20 21 22 23 24

18 18 18 18 18 18
19 20 21 22 23 24

19 19 19 19 19
20 21 22 23 24

20 20 20 20
21 22 23 24

21 21 21
22 23 24

22 22
23 24

23
24

Total times each number got circled

1	2	3	4	5	6
7	8	9	10	11	12
13	14	15	16	17	18
19	20	21	22	23	24

Prioritizing Grid
for 24 Items

SECTION D—
*After Prioritizing—
Items in final order*

SECTION A—
*Before Prioritizing—
Items in any order*

SECTION B

SECTION C

1	2	3	4	5	6	7	8	9	10

◁ Item **number**
◁ How many **times** circled
◁ Final **rank**

Prioritzing Grid
for 10 Items

The Prioritizing Grid

How to Prioritize Your Lists of Anything

Here is a method for taking (say) ten items, and figuring out which one is most important to you, which is next most important, etc.

• Insert the items to be prioritized, in any order, in Section A. Then compare two items at a time, circling the one you prefer -- between the two -- in Section B. Which one is more important to you? State the question any way you want to: In the case of geographical factors, you might ask. "If I were being offered two jobs, one in an area that had factor #1, but not factor #2; the other in an area that had factor #2, but not factor #1, all other things being equal, which job would I take? Circle it. Then go on to the next pair, etc.

• When you are all done, count up the number of times each number got circled, all told. Enter these totals on the TIMES line in Section C. Then notice the number of times each item was circled ("Times" = "Times Circled"). This determines the item's ranking. Most circled = #1, next most circled = #2, etc. Enter this ranking on the RANK line in Section C. If two items are circled the same number of times, look back in Section B to see -- when those two were compared there -- which one you preferred. Give that one an extra half point. List the items, now in their proper rank, in Section D.

Since you will be using this Prioritizing Grid more than once in these exercises you will want to go down to Kinko's or your local copy shop and make a number of copies of this form before you begin filling it in, for the first time.

The question to ask yourself, on the Grid, as you confront each 'pair' is: "If I were offered two jobs, and in one job I could use the first skill, but not the second; while in the other job, I could use the second skill, but not the first, which job would I choose?" When you've got your ten favorite transferable skills, in order, copy the top six onto the Flower diagram on page 264.

5. 'Flesh Out' Your Favorite Transferable Skills With Your Traits (see page 84)

In general, traits describe:
How you deal with time, and promptness.
How you deal with people and emotions.
How you deal with authority, and being told what to do at your job.
How you deal with supervision, and being told how to do your job.
How you deal with impulse vs. self-discipline, within yourself.
How you deal with initiative vs. response, within yourself.
How you deal with crises or problems.

A Check-List of My Strongest Traits

I am very. . .

- ❏ Accurate
- ❏ Achievement-oriented
- ❏ Adaptable
- ❏ Adept
- ❏ Adept at having fun
- ❏ Adventuresome
- ❏ Alert
- ❏ Appreciative
- ❏ Assertive
- ❏ Astute
- ❏ Authoritative
- ❏ Calm
- ❏ Cautious
- ❏ Charismatic
- ❏ Competent
- ❏ Consistent
- ❏ Contagious in my enthusiasm
- ❏ Cooperative
- ❏ Courageous
- ❏ Creative
- ❏ Decisive
- ❏ Deliberate
- ❏ Dependable/have dependability
- ❏ Diligent
- ❏ Diplomatic

- ❏ Discreet
- ❏ Driving
- ❏ Dynamic
- ❏ Extremely economical
- ❏ Effective
- ❏ Energetic
- ❏ Enthusiastic
- ❏ Exceptional
- ❏ Exhaustive
- ❏ Experienced
- ❏ Expert
- ❏ Firm
- ❏ Flexible
- ❏ Humanly oriented
- ❏ Impulsive
- ❏ Independent
- ❏ Innovative
- ❏ Knowledgeable
- ❏ Loyal
- ❏ Methodical
- ❏ Objective
- ❏ Open-minded
- ❏ Outgoing
- ❏ Outstanding
- ❏ Patient
- ❏ Penetrating
- ❏ Perceptive

- ❏ Persevering
- ❏ Persistent
- ❏ Pioneering
- ❏ Practical
- ❏ Professional
- ❏ Protective
- ❏ Punctual
- ❏ Quick/work quickly
- ❏ Rational
- ❏ Realistic
- ❏ Reliable
- ❏ Resourceful
- ❏ Responsible
- ❏ Responsive
- ❏ Safeguarding
- ❏ Self-motivated
- ❏ Self-reliant
- ❏ Sensitive
- ❏ Sophisticated, very sophisticated
- ❏ Strong
- ❏ Supportive
- ❏ Tactful
- ❏ Thorough
- ❏ Unique
- ❏ Unusual
- ❏ Versatile
- ❏ Vigorous

Once you've checked off your favorites, prioritize them (using another copy of the Prioritizing Grid if necessary), and then integrate your favorites into the building blocks of transferable skills, as described on page 84.

SOME PROBLEMS YOU MAY RUN INTO, WHILE DOING YOUR SKILL-IDENTIFICATION

In trying to identify your skills, it will not be surprising if you run into some problems. Let us look at the five most common ones that have arisen for job-hunters in the past:

1. *"When I write my skill stories, I don't know exactly what is an achievement."*

When you're looking for a story/achievement to illustrate one of your skills, you're *not* looking for something that only you have done, in the history of the world. What you're looking for is a lot simpler than that. You're looking for *any* time in your life when you did something that was, at that time of your life, a source of pride and accomplishment *for you*. It might have been learning to ride a bike. It might be achieving your first quota, at work. It might be a particularly significant project that you designed, in mid-life. It doesn't matter whether or not it pleased anybody else; it only matters that it pleased you.

I like Bernard Haldane's definition of an achievement. He says it is: something you yourself feel you have done well, that you also enjoyed doing and felt proud of. In other words you are looking for an accomplishment which gave you two pleasures: enjoyment while doing it, and satisfaction from the outcome. That doesn't mean you may not have sweated as you did it, or hated *some parts* of the process, but it does mean that basically you enjoyed *most of* the process. The pleasure was not simply in the outcome, but along the way as well. Generally speaking, an achievement will have all the parts outlined on page 81f.

2. *"I don't see why I should look for skills I enjoy; it seems to me that employers will only want to know what skills I do well. They will not care whether I enjoy using the skill or not."*

Well, sure, it is important for you to find the skills you do well, above all else. But, generally speaking, that is hard for you to evaluate about yourself. *Do I do this well, or not? Compared to whom?* Even aptitude tests can't resolve this dilemma for you. So it's better to take the following circular equation, which experience has shown to be true:

If it is a skill you do well, you will generally enjoy it.

If it is a skill you enjoy, it is generally because you do it well.

With these equations in hand, you will see that - - since they are equal anyway - - it is much more useful to ask yourself, "Do I enjoy doing it?" instead of hunting for the elusive "Do I do it well?" I repeat: listing the skills you most *enjoy* is - - in most cases - - just another way of listing the skills you do *best*.

The reason why this idea - - of making *enjoyment* the key - - causes such feelings of uncomfortableness in so many of us is that we have an old historical tradition in this country which insinuates you shouldn't really enjoy yourself in life. To suffer is virtuous.

Sample: Two girls do babysitting. One hates it. One enjoys it thoroughly. Which is more virtuous in God's sight? According to that old tradition, the one who hates it is more virtuous. Some of us feel this instinctively, even if more logical thought says, Whoa!

We have this subconscious fear that if we are caught enjoying life, punishment looms. Thus, the story of two Scotsmen who met on the street one day: "Isn't this a beautiful day?" said one. "Aye," said the other, "but we'll pay for it."

We feel it is okay to talk about our failures, but not about our successes. To talk about our successes appears to be boasting, and that is manifestly a sin. Or so we think. We shouldn't be enjoying so much about ourselves.

But look at the birds of the air, or watch your pets at play. You will notice one distinctive fact about that part of God's creation: when a bird or a pet does what it is meant to do, by God and nature, it manifests true joy.

Joy is so clearly a part of God's plan for us. God wants us to eat; therefore He made eating enjoyable. God wants us to sleep; therefore He made sleeping enjoyable. God wants us to procreate, love, and make love; therefore He made sex enjoyable, and love even more so.

Likewise, God gives to each of us unique combinations of skills and talents which He wants us to contribute to His general plan -- to the symphony of the world, and the music of the spheres. Therefore, **when we use the talents He most wants each of us to use, He attends it with a feeling of great joy.** Everywhere in God's plan for His creation, joy rewards right action.

Bad employers will not care whether you enjoy a particular task, or not. But good employers will care greatly. They know that unless a would-be employee has **enthusiasm** for his or her work, the quality of that work will always suffer.

3. *"I have no difficulty finding stories to write up, from my life, that I consider to be enjoyable achievements; but once these are written, I have great difficulty in seeing what the skills are -- even if I stare at the skills keys in the Exercises for hours. I need somebody else's insight."*

You may want to consider getting two friends or two other members of your family to sit down with you, and do skill identification through the practice of 'Trioing' which I invented some twenty years ago to help with this very problem. This practice is fully described in my book, *Where Do I Go From Here With My Life?* But to save you the trouble of reading it, here is -- in general -- how it goes:

a. Each of the three of you quietly writes up some story of an accomplishment in their life that was enjoyable.

b. Each of the three of you quietly analyzes just your own story to see what skills you see there; you jot these down.

c. One of you then volunteers to go first. You read your story aloud. The other two jot down on a piece of paper whatever skills they hear you using. They ask you to pause if they're having trouble keeping up. You finish your story. You read aloud the skills *you* picked out in that story.

d. Then the second person tells you what's on their list: what skills *they* heard you use in your story. You copy them down, below your own list, even if you don't agree with every one of them.

e. Then the third person tells you what's on their list; what skills *they* heard you use in your story. You copy them down, below your own list, even if you don't agree with every one of them.

f. When they're both done, you ask them any questions for further elaboration that you may have. *"What did you mean by this skill? Where did you think you heard me using it?"*

g. Now it is the next person's turn, and you repeat steps 'c' through 'f' with them. Then it is the third person's turn, and you repeat steps 'c' through 'f' with them.

h. Now it is time to move on to a second story for each of you, so you begin with steps 'a' through 'g' all over again, except that each of you writes a new story. And so on, through seven stories.

4. *"I don't like the skill words you offer in the Exercises. Can't I use my own words, the ones I'm familiar with from my past profession?"*

It's okay to invent your own words for your skills, but it is not useful to state your transferable skills in the jargon of your old profession, such as (in the case of ex-clergy), *"I am good at preaching."* If you are going to choose a new career, out there in what people call the secular world, you must not use language that locks you into the past -- or suggests that you were good in one profession but in one profession only. Therefore, it is important to take jargon words such as *preaching* and ask yourself what is its larger form? *"Teaching?"* Perhaps. *"Motivating people?"* Perhaps. *"Inspiring people to the depths of their being?"* Perhaps. Only you can say what is true, for you. But in one way or another be sure to get your skills out of any jargon that locks you into your past career.

5. *"Once I've listed my favorite transferable skills, I see immediately a job-title that they point to. Is that okay?"*

Nope. Once you've finished your skill-identification, steer clear of prematurely putting a job-title on the skills you see. Skills can point to *many* different jobs, which have a multitude of titles. Therefore, don't lock yourself in, prematurely. *"I'm looking for a job where I can use the following skills,"* is fine. But, *"I'm looking for a job where I can be a (job-title)"* is a no-no, at this point in your job-hunt. Always define WHAT you want to do with your life and WHAT you have, to offer to the world, in terms of your favorite talents/gifts/skills -- not in terms of a job-title. That way, you can stay mobile in the midst of this constantly-changing economy, where you never know what's going to happen next.

Petal #1
Geography

Even if you *love* where you are now, or even if you're *stuck* where you are now, you never know when an opportunity may suddenly open up for you, down the road. You want to be ready. Don't wait until then to do this exercise; do it now!

The question you need to answer is: Where would you most like to live and work, if you had a choice (besides where you are now)? In answering this question, it is important -- before you come to names -- to list the geographical *factors* that are important to you.

To help you do this, fill out the accompanying chart. *(You may copy it on to a larger piece of paper if you wish, before you begin working on it. And, if you are doing this exercise with a partner, make a copy of the chart, for them also, before you start filling it out, so that each of you may have a 'clean' copy of your own.)*

My Geographical Preferences
Decision Making for Just You

Column 1 Names of Places I Have Lived	Column 2 From the Past: Negatives	Column 3 Translating the Negatives into Positives	Column 4 Ranking of My Positives
	Factors I Disliked and Still Dislike about That Place		1. 2. 3. 4. 5. 6. 7. 8. 9. 10. 11. 12.
		Factors I Liked and Still Like about That Place	13. 14. 15.

Our Geographical Preferences
Decision Making for You and A Partner

Column 5 Places Which Fit These Criteria	Column 6 Ranking of His/Her Preferences	Column 7 Combining Our Two Lists (Column 4 & 6)	Column 8 Places Which Fit These Criteria
	a.	a. 1.	
	b.	b. 2.	
	c.	c. 3.	
	d.	d. 4.	
	e.	e. 5.	
	f.	f. 6.	
	g.	g. 7.	
	h.	h. 8.	
	i.	i. 9.	
	j.	j. 10.	
	k.	k. 11.	
	l.	l. 12.	
	m.	m. 13.	
	n.	n. 14.	
	o.	o. 15.	

Then, this is how you use the chart. There are seven easy steps:

1. List all the places (towns, cities, etc.) where you have ever lived.
These go in Column 1.

2. List the factors you *disliked* and still dislike about each place.
Naturally, there will be some repetition. In which case, just put an extra check mark in front of any factor you already have written down, when it comes up again. All of these negative factors go in Column 2.

3. Then take each of those negative factors and translate the negatives into positives.
This will not *necessarily* be the opposite. For example, "rains all the time" does not necessarily translate into "sunny all the time." It might be more like: "sunny at least 200 days a year." *It's your call.* All these positive factors go in Column 3. Feel free to add at the bottom of the column here, any positive factors you remember, off the top of your head, about the places in Column 1.

4. Now, rank your positive factors list (Column 3) in their order of importance, to you.
They will be things like: "has cultural opportunities," "skiing in the winter," "good newspaper," etc. List your top 10 positive factors, in exact order, in Column 4.

If you are baffled as to how to prioritize these factors in exact order, use the Prioritizing Grid on page 278. In using that grid, the question to ask yourself as you confront each 'pair' is: "If I could live in a place that had this first 'factor', but not the second; or if I could live in another place that had the second 'factor,' but not the first, in which place would I choose to live?"

5. When you are done, show this list of ten prioritized, positive factors to everyone you know, and ask them what cities, towns, or places they know of that have all or most of these factors.
You want to particularly emphasize the top factors, the ones that are the most important to you. If there is only a partial overlap between your factors and the places your friends suggest, be sure the overlap is in the factors you placed first on your list.

6. From all the names your friends suggest to you, choose the three that look most intriguing to you, in order of your personal preference, based on what you now know.

This goes in Column 5. These are the places you will want to find out more about, until you are sure which is your absolute first preference, second, and third.

N.B. If you are doing this with a partner, you will not use Column 5. Instead, copy *their* Column 4 into your Column 6. Then alternately combine *their* first five factors and *your* first five factors, until you wind up with a list of ten altogether. (First you list their top one, then your top one, then their second preference, then your second preference, etc.) *This goes in Column 7.* It is *this* list of ten positive factors which you both then show to *everyone* you know, to ask them what cities, towns, or places they know of that have all or most of these factors, *beginning with the top ones.* From all the names those friends suggest to you, you then choose the three places that look the most intriguing to both of you, and rank them in order. This goes in Column 8.

---

7. Now, go back to the Flower diagram on page 264, and copy Column 5 (or 8) onto the Geography petal.

You may also, if you wish, copy the first three to five Positives, from column 4 or 7. Voila! You are done with Geography. You now know the place(s) to find out more about, through their Chamber of Commerce, the Internet, a summer visit, etc.

Petal #2
Your Favorite Interests

You will find the instructions for inventorying these in chapter 5, on pages 96–101. You may have already done the exercises there.

When you have, come back to the Flower diagram on page 264, and copy the Field(s) you selected, plus your strongest interests (favorite knowledges) on to the Interests petal, in order of priority for you.

Petal #3
Your Favorite People

With the great emphasis upon the importance of the environment, in recent years, it has become increasingly realized that jobs are environments too. The most important environmental factor always turns out to be people, since every job, except possibly that of a full-fledged hermit, surrounds us with people to one degree or another.

Indeed, many a good job has been ruined by the people one is surrounded by. Many a mundane job has been made delightful, by the people one is surrounded by. Therefore, it is important to think out what kinds of people you want to be surrounded by.

Dr. John L. Holland offers the best description of people environments. He says there are six principal ones:

1. The **Realistic** People-Environment: filled with people who prefer activities involving "the explicit, ordered, or systematic manipulation of objects, tools, machines, and animals." 'Realistic,' incidentally, refers to Plato's conception of "the real" as that which one can apprehend through the senses.

I summarize this as: R = people who like nature, or athletics, or tools & machinery.

2. The **Investigative** People-Environment: filled with people who prefer activities involving "the observation and symbolic, systematic, creative investigation of physical, biological or cultural phenomena."

I summarize this as: I = people who are very curious, liking to investigate or analyze things.

3. The **Artistic** People-Environment: filled with people who prefer activities involving "ambiguous, free, unsystematized activities and competencies to create art forms or products."

I summarize this as: A = people who are very artistic, imaginative and innovative.

4. The **Social** People-Environment: filled with people who prefer activities involving "the manipulation of others to inform, train, develop, cure or enlighten."

I summarize this as: S = people who are bent on trying to help, teach, or serve people.

5. The **Enterprising** People-Environment: filled with people who prefer activities involving "the manipulation of others to attain organizational or self-interest goals."

I summarize this as: E = people who like to start up projects or organizations, and/or influence or persuade people.

6. The **Conventional** People-Environment: filled with people who prefer activities involving "the explicit, ordered, systematic manipulation of data, such as keeping records, filing materials, reproducing materials, organizing written and numerical data according to a prescribed plan, operating business and data processing machines." 'Conventional,' incidentally, refers to the "values" which people in this environment usually hold -- representing the broad mainstream of the culture.

I summarize this as: C = people who like detailed work, and like to complete tasks or projects.

According to John's theory and findings everyone has three preferred people-environments, from among these six. The letters for your three preferred people-environments gives you what is called "your Holland Code."

There is, incidentally, a relationship between the people you like to be surrounded by *and* your skills *and* your values. See John Holland's book, *Making Vocational Choices (3rd. ed., 1997).* You can procure it by writing to Psychological Assessment Resources, Inc., Box 998, Odessa, FL 33556. Phone: 1-800-331-8378. *The book is $29.95 at this writing.* PAR also has John Holland's instrument, called *The Self-Directed Search* (or SDS, for short) for discovering what your Holland code is. PAR says you can take the test online for a small fee (if you have Internet access) at `http://www.self-directed-search.com`

For those who don't have Internet access (or are in a hurry) I invented (many years ago) a quick and easy way to get an *approximation* of your 'Holland Code,' as it's called. I call it "The Party Exercise." Here is how the exercise goes (do it!):

On the next page is an aerial view of a room in which a two-day (!) party is taking place. At this party, people with the same or similar interests have (for some reason) all gathered in the same corner of the room.

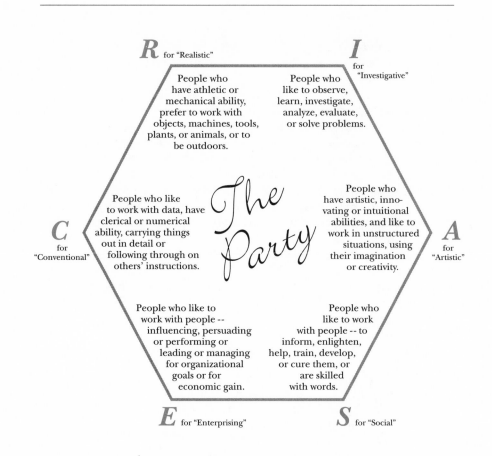

R for "Realistic"

I for "Investigative"

People who have athletic or mechanical ability, prefer to work with objects, machines, tools, plants, or animals, or to be outdoors.

People who like to observe, learn, investigate, analyze, evaluate, or solve problems.

The Party

People who like to work with data, have clerical or numerical ability, carrying things out in detail or following through on others' instructions.

People who have artistic, innovating or intuitional abilities, and like to work in unstructured situations, using their imagination or creativity.

C for "Conventional"

A for "Artistic"

People who like to work with people -- influencing, persuading or performing or leading or managing for organizational goals or for economic gain.

People who like to work with people -- to inform, enlighten, help, train, develop, or cure them, or are skilled with words.

E for "Enterprising"

S for "Social"

(1) Which corner of the room would you instinctively be drawn to, as the group of people you would most enjoy being with for the longest time? (Leave aside any question of shyness, or whether you would have to talk to them.) Write the letter for that corner here:

(2) After fifteen minutes, everyone in the corner you have chosen leaves for another party crosstown, except you. Of the groups that still remain now, which corner or group would you be drawn to the most, as the people you would most enjoy being with for the longest time? Write the letter for that corner here:

(3) After fifteen minutes, this group too leaves for another party, except you. Of the corners, and groups, which remain now, which one would you most enjoy being with for the longest time? Write the letter for that corner here:

The three letters you just chose, in the three steps, are called your "Holland Code." Here is what you should now do:

1. Circle them on the People petal, on page 265.
Put three circles around your favorite corner; two circles around your next favorite; and one circle around your third favorite.

2. Once the corners are circled, you may wish to write up (for yourself and your eyes only) a temporary statement about your future job or career, using the descriptors above.
If your "Code" turned out to be IAS, for example, you might write: *"I would like a job or career best if I was surrounded by people who are very curious, and like to investigate or analyze things (I); who are also very innovative (A); and who are bent on trying to help or serve people (S)."*

3. Finally, here, look over the skills you have just described *in others*, and see how much of this is also true of *you*.
What I call "The Mirror Theory" holds that we often see *ourselves* best by looking into the faces of others. Hence, once we have described the people we would most like to be surrounded by, in many cases we have also described ourselves. ("Birds of a feather flock together.") So, look over the circled items on your People petal. Are these, perchance, *your* favorite proclivities, skills, tasks, etc.? Or not?

Petal #4
Your Favorite Values
& Goals

1. Values are a matter of what guides you through every day, every task, every encounter with another human being. Yet, we are often unaware of what our values are.

One way to bring values to your consciousness is to imagine that shortly before the end of your life you are invited to dinner -- and to your great surprise people have secretly come in from all over the country and all over the world, to attend a surprise testimonial dinner for You.

At the dinner, to your great embarrassment, there is one testimonial after another about the good things you did, or the good person that you were, in your lifetime. No mention of any parts of your life that you don't want to have remembered. Just the good stuff.

So, this brings us to some questions. If you get the life you really want between now and then, what would you hope you would hear at that dinner, as they looked back on your life?

If you do achieve what you want with your life, what about you would you like to have remembered, after you are gone from this earth? Here is a checklist to help you[2]:

It would be a good life, if at its end here, people remembered me as one who: (check as many items as are important to you)

- ❑ Served or helped those who were in need.
- ❑ Impressed people with my going the second mile, in meeting their needs.
- ❑ Was always a great listener.
- ❑ Was always good at carrying out orders, or bringing projects to a successful conclusion.
- ❑ Mastered some technique, or field.
- ❑ Did something that everyone said couldn't be done.
- ❑ Did something that no one had ever done before.
- ❑ Excelled and was the best at whatever it is I did.
- ❑ Pioneered or explored some new technology.
- ❑ Fixed something that was broken.

❏ Made something work, when everyone else had failed or
   given up.
❏ Improved something, made it better, or perfected it.
❏ Combatted some bad idea/philosophy/ force/influence/
   pervasive trend -- and I persevered and/or prevailed.
❏ Influenced people and gained a tremendous response from
   them.
❏ Had an impact, and caused change.
❏ Did work which brought more information/truth into the world.
❏ Did work which brought more beauty into the world, through
   gardens, or painting, or decorating, or designing, or whatever.
❏ Did work which brought more justice, truth, and ethical behav-
   ior into the world.
❏ Brought people closer to God.
❏ Growing in wisdom and compassion was my great goal all
   my life.
❏ Had a vision of what something could be, and helped that
   vision to come true.
❏ Developed or built something, where there was nothing.
❏ Began a new business, or did some project from start to finish.
❏ Exploited, shaped and influenced some situation, market,
   before others saw the potential.
❏ Put together a great team, which made a huge difference in
   its field, industry, or community.
❏ Was a good decision-maker.
❏ Was acknowledged by everyone as a leader, and was in charge
   of whatever it was that I was doing.
❏ Had status in my field, industry, or community.
❏ Was in the spotlight, gained recognition, and was well-known.
❏ Made it into a higher echelon than I was, in terms of reputation,
   and/or prestige, and/or membership, and/or salary.
❏ Was able to acquire possessions, things or money.

❏ Other goals which occur to me:_____

_____

When you're done checking off all the values that are important to
you, go back, and pick out the ten that you care the most about, and
then prioritize them in exact order of importance to you. As always, if
you just can't prioritize them by guess and by gosh, then use the Prioritizing Grid on page 278.

The question to ask yourself, there, as you confront each 'pair' on the Grid is: "If I could only have this true about me, at the end of my life, but not the other, which would I prefer?" *Try not to pay attention to what others might or might not think of you, if they knew this was your heart's desire. This is just between you and God.*

Put your top three values on the Values & Goals petal, in the Flower diagram on page 265.

We turn, now from values to goals.

2. Goals are a matter of what you hope to accomplish before you die. Figuring out now, what we'd like to achieve before our life is over, gives us greater direction in our present career choices. Here are some questions, in the form of a check-list, that may prove helpful in surfacing what your goals in life are:

My goal, before I die, is to be able to help people with their need for:

❑ **Clothing** (people's need to find and choose appropriate and affordable clothing); *and in my case what interests me particularly is*_____.

❑ **Food** (people's need to be fed, to be saved from starvation or poor nutrition) *and in my case what interests me particularly is*_____.

❑ **Housing** and **Real estate** (people's need to find appropriate and affordable housing, office or land); *and in my case what interests me particularly is*_____.

❑ **Language** (people's need for literacy, to be able to read, or to learn a new language); *and in my case what interests me particularly is*_____.

❑ **Personal services** (people's need to have someone do tasks they can't do, or haven't time to do, or don't want to do, for themselves -- ranging from childcare to helping run a farm); *and in my case what interests me particularly is*_____.

❑ **Finances** (people's need to have help with budgeting, taxes, financial planning, money management, etc.); *and in my case what interests me particularly is*_____.

❑ **Acquisition** (people's need for help in buying something); *and in my case what interests me particularly is*_____.

❑ **Transportation** (people's need for travel locally or elsewise); *and in my case what interests me particularly is*_____.

❑ **Legal services** (people's need for expert counseling concerning the legal implications of things they are doing, or things that have been done to them); *and in my case what interests me particularly is_____.*

❑ **Child development** (people's need for help with various problems as their children are moving from infancy through childhood, including behavioral disabilities); *and in my case what interests me particularly is_____.*

❑ **Physical fitness** (people's need to get their body in tune through physical or occupational therapy, 'body-work,' exercise or diet); *and in my case what interests me particularly is_____.*

❑ **Health services** (people's need to have preventative medicine or help with ailments, allergies and disease); *and in my case what interests me particularly is_____ .*

❑ **Healing** including **Alternative medicine** and **Holistic health** (people's need to have various injuries, ailments, maladies or diseases healed); *and in my case what interests me particularly is_____.*

❑ **Medicine** (people's need to have help with diagnosing, treating various diseases, or removing diseased or badly-injured parts of their body, etc.); *and in my case what interests me particularly is_____.*

❑ **Mental health** (people's need for help with stress, depression, insomnia or other forms of emotional or mental disturbance); *and in my case what interests me particularly is_____.*

❑ **Personal counseling and guidance**, (people's need for help with family relations, with dysfunctions, or with various crises in their life, including a lack of balance in their use of time); *and in my case what interests me particularly is_____.*

❑ **Job-hunting, job-placement or vocational rehabilitation** (people's need to have help in finding the work they have chosen, particularly when handicapped, or unemployed, or enrolling for welfare under the new regulations); *and in my case what interests me particularly is_____.*

❑ **Life/work planning** (people's need for help in choosing a career or planning a holistic life); *and in my case what interests me particularly is_____.*

❑ **Learning or training** (people's need to learn more about something, at work or outside of work); *and in my case what interests me particularly is_____.*

❑ **Entertainment** (people's need to be entertained, by laughter, wit, intelligence, or beauty); *and in my case what interests me particularly is_____.*

❑ **Spirituality** or **religion** (people's need to learn as much as they can about God, character, and their own soul, including their values and principles); *and in my case what interests me particularly is*_____.

❑ **The needs of animals or plants** (their need for nurturing, growth, health and other life cycles which require the kinds of sensitivities often referred to as 'interpersonal skills'); *and in my case what interests me particularly is*_____.

❑ **The creating, making, marketing, handling of things**, such as: airplanes, antiques, bicycles, blueprints, books, bridges, buildings, bushes, cameras, campers, cars, catalogs, chemicals, cooking utensils, clothing, computers, crops, diagrams, electricity, electronics, drugs, farms, farm machinery, fish, flowers, gardens, groceries, guidebooks, houses, kitchens appliances, lawns, machines, magazines, makeup, manuals, medicines, minerals, money, music, musical instruments, newspapers, office machines, paints, paper, plants, radios, rivers, rooms, sailboats, security systems, sewing machines, skiing equipment, soil, telephones, toiletries, tools, toys, trains, trees, valuable objects , videotapes, wine, wood, etc.; *and in my case what interests me particularly is*_____.

❑ **Other goals** not listed above, that fascinate me are:_____.

When you're done checking off all the goals that are important to you, go back, and pick out the ten that you care the most about, and then prioritize them in exact order of importance to you. As always, if you just can't prioritize them by guess and by gosh, then use the Prioritizing Grid on page 278.

Put your top three Goals on the Values & Goals petal, in the Flower diagram on page 265.

Petal #5

Your Favorite
Working Conditions

Plants that grow beautifully at sea level, often perish if they're taken ten thousand feet up the mountain. Likewise, we do our best work under certain conditions, but not under others. Thus, the question: What are your favorite 'working conditions'? actually is a question about "Under what circumstances do you do your most effective work?"

The best way to approach this is by starting with the things you *disliked* about all your previous jobs, using the following chart to list these. The chart, as you can see, has three columns, and you fill them out in the same order, and manner, that you filled out the geography chart earlier. Here too, you may copy this chart on to a larger piece of paper if you wish, before you begin filling it out. *Column A may begin with such factors as: "too noisy," "too much supervision," "no windows in my workplace," "having to be at work by 6 a.m.," etc.*

Of course, when you get to Column B, you must rank these factors that are in Column A, in their exact order of importance, to you.

As always, if you are baffled as to how to prioritize these factors in exact order, use the Prioritizing Grid on page 277 or 278.

The question to ask yourself, there, as you confront each 'pair' is: "If I were offered two jobs, and in the first job I would be rid of this first distasteful working condition, but not the second; while in the second job, I would be rid of the second distasteful working condition, but not the first, which distasteful working condition would I choose to get rid of?"

Note that when you later come to Column C, the factors will be already prioritized. Your only job, there, is to think of the "positive" form of that factor that you hated so much (in Column B). (It is not always "the exact opposite." For example, *too much supervision* (listed in Column B) does not always mean *no supervision* (in Column C). It *might* mean: *a moderate amount of supervision, once or twice a day.*)

Once you've finished Column C, enter the top five factors from there on the Working Conditions petal of the Flower diagram, on page 265.

DISTASTEFUL WORKING CONDITIONS

	Column A — Distasteful Working Conditions	*Column B* — Distasteful Working Conditions Ranked	*Column C* + The Keys to My Effectiveness At Work
Places I Have Worked Thus Far In My Life	*I Have Learned From the Past that My Effectiveness at Work is Decreased When I Have To Work Under These Conditions:*	*Among the Factors or Qualities Listed in Column A, These Are The Ones I Dislike Absolutely The Most (in order of Decreasing Dislike):*	*The Opposite of These Qualities, in order:* *"I Believe My Effectiveness Would Be At An Absolute Maximum, If I Could Work Under These Conditions:"*

Petal #6

Level & Salary

As you saw in chapter 6, on page 220, salary is something you must think out ahead of time, when you're contemplating your ideal job or career. Level goes hand-in-hand with salary, of course.

1. The first question here is at what level would you like to work, in your ideal job?

Level is a matter of how much responsibility you want, in an organization:

- ❑ Boss or CEO (this may mean you'll have to form your own business)
- ❑ Manager or someone under the boss who carries out orders, but also gives them
- ❑ The head of a team
- ❑ A member of a team of equals
- ❑ One who works in tandem with one other partner
- ❑ One who works alone, either as an employee or as a consultant to an organization, or as a one-person business.

Enter a two- or three-word summary of your answer, on the Salary and Level petal of your Flower diagram, on page 264.

2. The second question here is what salary would you like to be aiming at?

Here you have to think in terms of minimum or maximum. Minimum is what you would need to make, if you were just barely 'getting by.' And you need to know this *before* you go in for a job interview with anyone *(or before you form your own business, and need to know how much profit you must make, just to survive).*

Maximum could be any astronomical figure you can think of, but it is more useful here to put down the salary you realistically think you could make, with your present competency and experience, were you working for a real, *but generous,* boss. (If this maximum figure is still depressingly low, then put down the salary you would like to be making five years from now.)

Make out a detailed outline of your estimated expenses *now,* listing what you need *monthly* in the following categories:[3]

Housing
  Rent or mortgage payments. . . . . $ _____
  Electricity/gas. . . . . $ _____
  Water. . . . . $ _____
  Telephone . . . . $ _____
  Garbage removal . . . . $ _____
  Cleaning, maintenance, repairs[4] . . . . $ _____
Food
  What you spend at the supermarket
  and/or meat market, etc. . . . . $ _____
  Eating out . . . . $ _____
Clothing
  Purchase of new or used clothing . . . . $ _____
  Cleaning, dry cleaning, laundry . . . . $ _____
Automobile/transportation[5]
  Car payments . . . . $ _____
  Gas. . . . . $ _____
  Repairs. . . . . $ _____
  Public transportation (bus, train, plane). . . . . . . $ _____
Insurance
  Car . . . . $ _____
  Medical or health-care . . . . $ _____
  House and personal possessions . . . . $ _____
  Life . . . . $ _____
Medical expenses
  Doctors' visits. . . . . $ _____
  Prescriptions. . . . . $ _____
  Fitness costs . . . . $ _____
Support for Other Family Members
  Child-care costs (if you have children) . . . . $ _____
  Child-support (if you're paying that) . . . . $ _____
  Support for your parents (if you're helping out) . . . . $ _____
Charity giving/tithe (to help others) . . . . $ _____
School/learning
  Children's costs (if you have children in school) . . . . . $ _____
  Your learning costs (adult education,
  job-hunting classes, etc.) . . . . $ _____
Pet care (if you have pets). . . . . $ _____

Bills and debts *(Usual monthly payments)*

    Credit cards . . . . $ _____

    Local stores . . . . $ _____

    Other obligations you pay off monthly . . . . $ _____

Taxes

    Federal[6] *(next April's due, divided by*

    months remaining until then) . . . . $ _____

    State *(likewise)* . . . . $ _____

    Local/property *(next amount due, divided by*

    months remaining until then) . . . . $ _____

    Tax-help *(if you ever use an accountant,*

    pay a friend to help you with taxes, etc.). . . . . $ _____

Savings

Retirement (Keogh, IRA, Sep, etc.)

Amusement/discretionary spending

    Movies, video rentals, etc. . . . . $ _____

    Other kinds of entertainment . . . . $ _____

    Reading, newspapers, magazines, books . . . . $ _____

    Gifts *(birthday, Christmas, etc.)* . . . . $ _____

Total Amount You Need Each Month . . . . $ _____

Multiply the total amount you need each month by 12, to get the yearly figure. Divide the yearly figure by 2000, and you will be reasonably near the *minimum* hourly wage that you need. Thus, if you need $3333 per month, multiplied by 12 that's $40,000 a year, and then divided by 2,000, that's $20 an hour.

Parenthetically, you may want to prepare two different versions of the above budget: one with the expenses you'd ideally *like* to make, and the other a minimum budget, which will give you what you are looking for, here: the floor, below which you simply cannot afford to go.

Enter the maximum, and minimum, on your Salary & Level petal on the Flower diagram on page 264.

Optional Exercise: You may wish to put down other rewards, besides money, that you would hope for, from your next job or career. These might be:

❏ Adventure
❏ Challenge
❏ Respect
❏ Influence
❏ Popularity
❏ Fame
❏ Power
❏ Intellectual stimulation from the other workers there
❏ A chance to exercise leadership
❏ A chance to be creative
❏ A chance to make decisions
❏ A chance to use my expertise
❏ A chance to help others
❏ A chance to bring others closer to God
❏ Other:

If you do check off things on this list, arrange your answers in order of importance to you, and then add them to the Salary & Level petal on page 264.

Done!

Voila! Your flower should now be complete. At this point, go to chapter 5, on page 134f, and see how this new knowledge of yourself and your ideal job helps you to narrow down what it is you are looking for.

Footnotes

1. For the curious, "animals" are placed in this category with "people," because **the skills** required to deal with animals are more like those used with people, than like those used with "things."

2. I am indebted to Arthur Miller, of People Management, Inc., for many of these ideas.

3. If this kind of financial figuring is not your cup of tea, find a buddy, friend, relative, family member, or *anyone*, who can help you do this. If you don't know anyone who could do this, go to your local church, synagogue, religious centre, social club, gym, or wherever you hang out, and ask the leader or manager there, to help you find someone. If there's a bulletin board, put up a notice on the bulletin board.

4. If you have extra household expenses, such as a security system for example, be sure and include the quarterly (or whatever) expenses here, divided by three.

5. Your checkbook stubs will tell you a lot of this stuff. But you may be vague about your cash or credit card expenditures. For example, you may not know how much you spend at the supermarket, or how much you spend on gas, etc. But there is a simple way to find out. Just carry a little notepad and pen around with you for two weeks or more, and jot down *everything* you pay cash *(or use credit cards)* for -- on the spot, right after you pay it. At the end of those two weeks, you'll be able to take that notepad and make a realistic guess of what should be put down in these categories that now puzzle you. *(Multiply the two-weeks figure by two, and you'll have the monthly figure.)*

6. Incidentally, looking ahead to next April 15th, be sure and check with your local IRS office or a reputable accountant to find out if you can deduct the expenses of your job-hunt on your Federal (and State) income tax returns. At this writing, some job-hunters can, if -- big IF -- this is not your first job that you're looking for, if you haven't been unemployed too long, and if you aren't making a career-change. Do go find out what the latest "ifs" are. If IRS tells you you are eligible, keep careful receipts of everything related to your job-hunt, as you go along: telephone calls, stationery, printing, postage, travel, etc.

*T*wo are better than one;
  for if they fall,
  the one will lift up his fellow;

  but woe to him that is alone when he falleth,
  and hath not another to lift him up.

            Ecclesiastes

LOOK BEFORE YOU LEAP:

How to Choose
A Career Counselor,
If You Decide
You Need One

YES, THERE'S A CERTAIN AMOUNT OF PRIDE IN BEING A SELF-MADE MAN, BUT TO TELL THE TRUTH, IF I HAD IT ALL TO DO OVER AGAIN I WOULD GET A LITTLE HELP.

THAVES

HOW TO CHOOSE
A CAREER COUNSELOR,
IF YOU DECIDE
YOU NEED ONE

I wish I could say that everyone who hangs out a sign saying they are now a career counselor could be completely trusted. Nope, they can't all be. As is the case in many professions, they divide into: a) those who are honest and know what they're doing; b) those who are honest but inept; and c) those who are dishonest, and merely want your money -- in lump sums, up front.

You, of course, want a list of those who are honest and know what they're doing. Well, unfortunately, no one (including me) has such a list. You've got to do your own homework, or research, here, and your own interviewing, in your own geographical area, or you will deserve what you get.

Why do *you* have to do it? You, you, and nobody else but you? Well, let's say a friend tells you to go see so-and-so. He's a wonderful counselor, but unhappily he reminds you of your Uncle Harry. No one but you knows that you've always **hated** your Uncle Harry. That's why no one else can do this research for you -- because the real question is not "Who is best?" but "Who is best **for you**?" Those last two words demand that it be you who 'makes the call,' that it is you who does the research.

Of course, you're tempted to skip over this research, aren't you?

"Well, I'll just call up one place, and if I like the sound of them, I'll sign up. I'm a pretty good judge of character." Right. I hear many a sad tale from people who had this overconfidence in their ability to detect a phony, and then found out too late that they had been *taken*, by slicker sales-people than they had ever run into before. As they tell me their stories, they *cry* over the telephone. My reply usually is, "I'm sorry indeed to hear that you had a very disappointing experience; that is very unfortunate, but -- as the Scots would say -- "Ya dinna do your homework." Often you could easily have discovered whether a partic-ular counselor was competent or not, before you ever gave them any of your money, simply by asking the right questions during your pre-liminary research."

Another way people try to avoid this research is by saying, "Well, I'll just see who Bolles recommends." That's a stretch, because I never ever recommend anyone. Some try to claim I do, because they're in the book here. Nice try! Inclusion in this book does *not* constitute an endorsement or recommendation by me -- as I have been at great pains to make clear for the past twenty-five years. Never has. Never will.

You must do your own homework. You must do your own research.

So, how do you go about finding a good counselor? Well, you start by collecting three names of career counselors in your geographical area.

How do you find those names? Several ways:

First, you can get names from your friends: ask if any of them have ever used a career counselor. And if so, did they like 'em? And if so, what is that counselor's name?

Secondly, you can get names from the *Sampler* that begins on page 316. See if there are any career counselors who are near you. They may know how you can find still other names in your community. But I re-peat what I said above: just because they're listed in the Sampler *doesn't* mean I recommend them. It only means they asked to be listed, and professed familiarity with the contents of this book (current edition).

Still haven't got three names? Then try your telephone book's Yellow Pages, under such headings as: *Aptitude and Employment Testing, Career and Vocational Counseling, Personnel Consultants* and (if you are a woman) *Women's Organizations and Services.*

You will discover that even the Yellow Pages can't keep up with the additional groups that spring up daily, weekly, and monthly -- including job clubs and other group activities. The most comprehensive list of these, in the U.S., is to be found in the National Business Employment Weekly, on its pages called "Calendar of Career Events." It is an extensive listing. It's available on many newsstands, $3.95 an issue, or you can order six issues for $19 directly from: National Business Employment Weekly, P.O. Box 435, Chicopee, MA 01021-0435. Their phone is: 800-JOB-HUNT (that's 562-4868) ext. 193.

Once you have three names, you need to go do some comparison shopping. You want to go talk with all three of them, and decide which of the three (if any) you want to hook up with.

Don't try to do this over the telephone, *please!* There is so much more you can tell, when you're looking the person straight in the eyes.

Cost: if this is a firm, trying to sell you a package, they will almost certainly give you the initial interview for free. On the other hand, if it's an individual counselor, who charges by the hour, you are going to have to pay them for this exploratory hour, or part of an hour -- even if it's only five or ten minutes. Do not expect that individual counselors can afford to give you this exploratory interview for nothing! If they did that, and got a lot of requests like yours, they would never be able to make a living. You do have the right, however, to inquire *ahead of time* how much they are going to have to charge you for the exploratory interview.

When you are face-to-face with the firm or with the individual counselor, you ask each of them the same questions, listed on the form below. (Keep a little pad or notebook with you, so you can write their answers down.)

MY SEARCH FOR A GOOD CAREER COUNSELOR

Questions I Will Ask Them	Answer from counselor #1	Answer from counselor #2	Answer from counselor #3
1. What is your program?			
2. Who will be doing it? And how long have you been doing it?			
3. What is your success rate?			
4. What is the cost of your services?			
5. Is there a contract?			

After visiting the three places you chose for your comparison shopping, you have to go home, sit down, put your feet up, look over your notes, and compare those places. You need to decide a) whether you want none of the three, or b) one of the three (and if so, which one). Remember, you don't have to choose any of the three counselors, if you didn't really care for any of them. If that is the case, then choose three new counselors, dust off the notebook, and go out again. It may take a few more hours to find what you want. But the wallet, the purse, the job-hunt, the life, you save will be your own.

As you look over your notes, you will realize there is no definitive way for you to determine a career counselor's expertise. It's something you'll have to smell out, as you go along. But here are some clues:

BAD ANSWERS

If they give you the feeling that everything will be done for you, by them (including interpretation of tests, and decision making about what this means you should do, or where you should do it) -- rather than you having to do all the work, with their basically assuming the role of coach,

(15 bad points)

You want to learn how to do this for yourself; you're going to be job-hunting again, you know.

If they say they are not the person who will be doing the program with you, but deny you any chance to meet the counselor you would be working with,

(75 bad points)

You're talking to a salesperson. Avoid any firm that has a salesperson.

If you do get a chance to meet the counselor, but you don't like the counselor as a person,

(150 bad points)

I don't care what their expertise is, if you don't like them, you're going to have a rough time getting what you want. I guarantee it. Rapport is everything.

If you ask how long the counselor has been doing this, and they get huffy or give a double-barreled answer, such as: "I've had eighteen years' experience in the business and career counseling world,"

(20 bad points)

What that may mean is: seventeen and a half years as a fertilizer salesman, and one half year doing career counseling. Persist. "How long have you been with this firm, and how long have you been doing formal career counseling, as you are here?" You might be interested to know that some executive or career counseling firms hire yesterday's clients as today's new staff. Such new staff are sometimes given training only after they're "on-the-job." They are practicing on you.

If they try to answer the question of their experience by pointing to their degrees or credentials,

(3 bad points)

Degrees or credentials tell you they've passed certain tests of their qualifications, but often these tests bear more on their expertise at career assessment than on their knowledge of creative job-hunting.

If, when you ask about their success rate, they say they have never had a client that failed to find a job, no matter what,

(15 bad points)

They're lying. I have studied career counseling programs for over twenty years, have attended many, have studied records at State and Federal offices, and I have hardly ever seen a program that placed more than 86% of their clients, tops, in their best years. And it goes downhill from there. A prominent executive counseling firm was reported by the Attorney General's Office of New York State to have placed only 38 out of 550 clients (a 93% failure rate).[1] If they make it clear that they have had a good success rate, but if you fail to work hard at the whole process, then there is no guarantee you are going to find a job, give them three stars.

If they show you letters from ecstatically-happy former clients, but when you ask to talk to some of those clients, you get stone-walled.

(45 bad points)

I quote from one job-hunter's letter to me: "I asked to speak to a former client or clients. You would of thought I asked to speak to Elvis. The Counselor stammered and stuttered and gave me a million excuses why I couldn't talk to some of these 'satisfied' former clients. None of the excuses sounded legitimate to me. We went back and forth for about thirty minutes. Finally, he excused himself and went to speak to his boss, the owner. The next thing I knew I was called into the owner's office for a more 'personal' sales pitch. We spoke for about 45 minutes as he tried to convince me to use his service. When I told him I was not ready to sign up, he became angry and asked my Counselor why I had been put before 'the committee' if I wasn't ready to commit? The Counselor claimed I had given a verbal commitment at our last meeting. The owner then turned to me and said I seemed to have a problem

---

1. For further details, go to your local library and look up "Career Counselors: Will They Lead You Down The Primrose Path?" by Lee Guthrie, in the December 1981 issue of *Savvy Magazine*, pp. 60ff.

making a decision and that he did not want to do business with me. I was shocked. They had turned the whole story around to make it look like it was my fault. I felt humiliated. In retrospect, the whole process felt like dealing with a used car salesman. They used pressure tactics and intimidation to try to get what they wanted. As you have probably gathered, more than anything else this experience made me angry."

If they claim they only accept 5 clients out of every hundred who apply, and your name will have to be put before 'The Committee' before you can be accepted.

(1000 bad points)

This is one of the oldest tricks in the book. You're supposed to feel 'special' before they lift those thousands of dollars out of your wallet. Personally, the minute I heard this at a particular agency or service, I would run for the door and never look back.

If you ask what is the cost of their services, and they reply that it is a lump sum that must all be paid "up front" before you start or shortly after you start, either all at once or in installments,

(100 bad points)

For twenty-five years I've tried to avoid saying this, but I have grown weary of the tears of job-hunters who 'got taken.' So now I say it without reservation: if the firm charges a lump sum for their services, rather than allowing you to simply pay for each hour as you go, go elsewhere. Every insincere and inept counselor or firm charges a lump sum. So, of course, do some sincere and good counselors and firms. Trouble is: you won't know which kind you've signed up with, until they've got all your money. The risk is too great, the cost is too high. If you really like to gamble that much, go to Las Vegas. They give better odds.

If they asked you to bring in your partner or spouse with you,

(45 bad points)

This is a well-known tactic of some of the slickest salespeople in the world, who want your spouse or partner there so they can manipulate one or the other or both of you to reach a decision on the spot, while they have you in their 'grasp.'

If they ask you to sign a contract,

(1000 bad points)

With insincere and inept firms or counselors, there is always a written contract. And you must sign it, before they will help you. (Often, your partner or spouse will be asked to sign it, too.) The fee normally ranges from $1000 on up to $10,000 or more.

You may think the purpose of that firm's contract is that they are promis-

ing you something, that they can be held to. Uh-uh! *More often, the main purpose of the contract is to get you to promise them something. Like, your money. Don't. . . . . . do. . . . . it.*

You will sometimes be told that, "Of course, you can get your money back, or a portion of it, at any time, should you be dissatisfied with the career counselor's services." Nine times out of ten, however, you are told this verbally, and it is not in the written contract. Verbal promises, without witnesses, are difficult if not impossible for you to later try to enforce. The written contract is binding.

Sometimes the written contract will claim to provide for a partial refund, at any time, until you reach a cut-off date in the program, which the contract specifies. Unfortunately, many crafty fraudulent firms bend over backwards to be extra nice, extra available, and extra helpful to you until that cut-off point is reached. So, when the cut-off point for getting a refund has been reached, you let it pass because you are very satisfied with their past services, and believe there will be many more weeks of the same. Only, there aren't. At fraudulent firms, once the cut-off point is passed, the career counselor becomes virtually impossible for you to get ahold of. Call after call will not be returned. You will say to yourself "What happened?" Well, what happened, my friend, is that you paid up in full, they have all the money they're ever going to get out of you, and now they don't want to give you any more time.

You may think I am exaggerating: I mean, can there possibly be such mean men and women, who would prey on job-hunters, when they're down and out. Yes, ma'am, and yes, sir, there are. That's why you have to do this preliminary research so thoroughly.

I quote from the late Robert Wegmann, former director of the UHCL Center for Labor Market Studies: "One high-charging career counseling firm went bankrupt a few years ago. They left many of their materials behind in their former office. A box of what they abandoned has come into my possession. Going through the contents of the box has been fascinating.

"Particularly interesting are several scripts used to train their salespeople. The goal of the sales pitch is to convince the unemployed (or unhappily employed) person that he or she can't find a good job alone, but can do it with professional help. Hiring us, they argue, is just like hiring a lawyer . . .

"Then, at the end of the pitch, comes the 'takeaway.' The firm may not accept your money, you are warned! There will have to be a review board meeting at which your application is considered. Only a minority of applicants are accepted. The firm only wants the right kind of clients.

"That's the pitch. But the rest of the documents tell a very different story. In fact, the firm is running a series of sales contests with all the 'professionalism' of a used car lot . . .

"These salespeople were paid on commission. The higher the sales the higher the percentage of the customer's fee they got to keep.

"There are sales contests. The winner receives a handsome green Master's jacket. Each monthly winner qualifies for a Grand Master's Tournament, with large prizes . . .

"So take this one piece of advice . . . If someone offers to help you find a great job as long as you'll pay several thousand dollars in advance, do as follows:

"A. Find door

"B. Walk out same

"C. Do not return."

Over the last twenty years, I have had to listen to grown men and women cry over the telephone, all because they signed a contract. Most often they were executives, or senior managers, who never had to go job-hunting before, and unknowingly signed up with some executive counseling firm that was fraudulent, or at least on the edge of legality.

If you want to avoid their tears in your own job-search, don't sign any-thing -- ever.[2]

My advice -- for what it's worth: don't sign up with *anyone* who offers you a contract, or charges other than by the hour.

---

2. If you are **dying** to know more, and your local library has back files of magazines and newspapers (on microfiche, or otherwise) there was a period when bad firms and counselors came under heavy fire (1978-1982) and you can look up some of the articles of that period, as well as those articles which have appeared more recently, to wit:

"A Consumer's Guide to Retail Job-Hunting Services," Special Report, reprinted from the *National Business Employment Weekly*; available from National Business Employment Weekly Reprint Service, P.O. Box 300, Princeton, NJ 08543-0300. 1-800-730-1111. $8 by mail; $12.95 by fax. A *very* thorough series of articles on the industry, and its frauds, which names *names,* and gives the addresses of Consumer protection agencies in each state, to whom you may complain. **Required reading** for anyone who wants to avoid getting 'burned.'

" 'Employment counselors' costly, target of gripes," *The Arizona Republic*, 10/8/89.

"Career-Counseling Industry Accused of Misrepresentation," *New York Times*, 9/30/82.

"Consumer Law: Career Counselors and Employment Agencies" by Reed Brody, *New York Law Journal*, Feb. 26, 1982, p. 1. Reed was Assistant Attorney General of the State of New York, and more recently Deputy Chief of the Labor Bureau within that State's Department of Law; in this capacity he became the leading legal expert in the country, on career counseling malpractices, though unfortunately (for us) he now works overseas in Europe, in another profession.

"Career Counselors: Will They Lead You Down the Primrose Path?" by Lee Guthrie, *Savvy Magazine*, 12/81, p. 60ff.

"Franklin Career Search Is Accused of Fraud In New York State Suit," *Wall Street Journal*, 1/29/81, p. 50.

"Job Counseling Firms Under Fire For Promising Much, Giving Little," *Wall Street Journal*, 1/27/81, p. 33.

GOOD ANSWERS

Well, those are the bad answers. How about the good ones? Yes, there are such things: career counselors who charge by the hour. With them, there is no written contract. You sign nothing. You pay only for each hour as you use it, according to their set rate. Each time you keep an appointment, you pay them at the end of that hour for their help, according to that rate. Period. Finis. You never owe them any money. You can stop seeing them at any time, if you feel you are not getting the help you wish.

What will they charge? You will find, these days, that the best career counselors (and some of the worst, too) will charge you whatever a really good therapist or marriage counselor charges per hour, in your geographical area. Currently, in large metropolitan areas, that runs around $100 an hour, sometimes more. In suburbia or rural areas, it may be much less - - $40 an hour, or so.

That fee is for individual time with the career counselor. If you can't afford that fee, ask whether they also run groups. If they do, the fee will be much less. And, in one of those delightful ironies of life, since you get a chance to listen to problems which other job-hunters in your group are having, the group will often give you more help than an individual session would. Not always; but often. It's always ironic when *cheaper* and *more helpful* go hand in hand.

If the career counselor in question does offer groups, there should (again) never be a contract. The charge should be payable at the end of each session, and you should be able to drop out at any time, without further cost, if you decide you are not getting the help you want.

There are, incidentally, some career counselors who run free (or almost free) job-hunting workshops through local churches, synagogues, chambers of commerce, community colleges, adult education programs, and the like, as their community service, or pro bonum work (as it is technically called). I have had reports of such workshops from a number of places in the U.S. and Canada. They surely exist in other parts of the world as well. If money is a big problem for you, in getting help with your job-hunt, ask around to see if such workshops as these exist in your community. Your chamber of commerce will likely know, or your church or synagogue.

A Sampler

This is not a complete directory of anything. It is exactly what its name implies: a **Sampler.** Were I to list all the career counselors *out there*, we would end up with an encyclopedia. Some states, in fact, have *encyclopedic* lists of counselors and businesses, in various books or directories, and your local bookstore or library should have these, in their *Job-Hunting Section,* under such titles as "How to Get A Job in......" or "Job-Hunting in . . ."

The places listed in this **Sampler** are listed at their own request, and I offer them to you simply as places for you to begin your investigation with -- nothing more.

Many truly *helpful* places are *not* listed here. If you discover such a place, which is very good at helping people with *Parachute* and creative job-hunting or career-change, do send us the pertinent information. We will ask them, as we do all the listings here, a few intelligent questions and if they sound okay, we will add that place to next year's edition.

We do ask a few questions because our readers want counselors and places which claim some expertise in helping them finish their job-hunt, *using this book.* So, if they've never even heard of *Parachute*, we don't list them. On the other hand, we can't measure a place's expertise at this long distance, no matter how many questions we ask.

Even if listed here, you must do your own sharp questioning before you decide to go with anyone. If you don't take time to research two or three places, before choosing a counselor, you will deserve whatever you get (or, more to the point, *don't* get). So, please, *do your research.* The purse or wallet you save, will be your own.

Yearly readers of this book will notice that we do remove people from this Sampler, without warning. Specifically, we remove (without further notice or comment): Places we didn't mean to remove, but a typographical error was made, somehow (it happens). We also remove: Places which have moved, and don't bother to send us their new address. If you are listed here, we expect you to be a professional at *communication*. When you move, your first priority should be to let us know, *immediately*. As one exemplary counselor just wrote: "You are the first person I am contacting on my updated letterhead . . . hot off the press just today!" So it should always be. A number of places get removed every year, precisely because of their poor communication skills, and their sloppiness in letting us know where they've gone to. *Other causes for removal:*

Places which have disconnected their telephone, or otherwise suggest that they have gone out of business.

Places which our readers lodge complaints against, with us, as being either unhelpful or obnoxious. The complaints may be falsified, but we can't take that chance.

Places which change their personnel, and the new person has never even heard of *Parachute*, or creative job-search techniques.

Places which misuse their listing here, claiming in their brochures, ads or interviews, that they have some kind of 'Parachute Seal of Approval,' -- that we feature them in Parachute, or recommend them or endorse them. This is a big 'no-no.' A listing here is no more of a recommendation than is a listing in the phone book.

College services that we discover (belatedly) serve only 'Their Own."

Counseling firms which employ salespeople as the initial 'in-take' person that a job-hunter meets.

If you discover that any of the places listed in this Sampler falls into any of the above categories, you would be doing a great service to our other readers by dropping us a line and telling us so. (P.O. Box 379, Walnut Creek, CA 94597.)

THE LISTINGS which follow are alphabetical within each state, except that counselors listed by their name are in alphabetical order according to their *last* name. To make this clear, only their last name is in **bold** type.

What do the letters after their name mean? Well, B.A., M.A. and Ph.D. you know. However, don't assume the degree is in career counseling. Ask. NCC means "Nationally certified counselor." There are about 20,000 such in the U.S. This can mean *general counseling expertise*, not necessarily career counseling. On the other hand, NCCC does mean "Nationally certified career counselor." There are currently about 850 in the U.S. Other initials, such as LPC -- "Licensed professional counselor" -- and the like, often refer to State licensing. There are a number of States, now, that have some sort of regulation of career counselors. In some States it is mandatory, in others it is optional. But, *mostly*, this field is unregulated.

Some offer group career counseling, some offer testing, some offer access to job-banks, etc.

One final note: generally speaking, the places counsel *anybody*. A few, however, may turn out to have restrictions unknown to us (*"we counsel only women,"* etc.). If that's the case, your time isn't wasted. They may be able to help you with a referral. So, don't be afraid to ask them *"who else in the area can you tell me about, who helps with job-searches, and are there any (among them) that you think are particularly effective?"*

Area Codes

Throughout the U.S. now, area codes are sub-dividing constantly, sometimes more than once during a short time-span. If you're calling a local counselor, you probably don't need the area code anyway. But if you call a phone number below that is any distance away from you, and they tell you "this number cannot be completed as dialed," the most likely explanation is that the area code got changed -- maybe some time ago. (We ask counselors listed here to notify us when the area code changes, but some do and some don't.) Anyway, call Information and check.

---

*Throughout this Sampler, an asterisk before their name, in red, means they offer not only regular job-search help, but also (when you wish) counseling from a spiritual point of view; i.e., they're not afraid to talk about God if you're looking for some help, in finding your mission in life.

ALABAMA

*Career Decisions, 638 Winwood Dr., Birmingham, AL 35226. phone 205-822-8662 or 205-870-2639. Carrie Pearce Hild, M.S.Ed., Career Counselor and Consultant.

Maureen J. Chemsak, NCC, NCCC, LPC, Director of Counseling and Career Services, Athens State University, 300 North Beaty St., Athens, AL 35611. phone 256-233-8285 or 256-830-4610.

Vantage Associates, 2100-A Southbridge Pkwy., Suite 480, Birmingham, AL 35209. phone 205-879-0501 or 205-631-5544. Michael A. Tate.

Work Matters, Career Coaching, 104 Peachtree Road, Birmingham, AL 35213. phone 205-879-8494. Gayle H. Lantz.

ALASKA

Career Transitions, 2600 Denali St., Suite 430, Anchorage, AK 99503. phone 907-274-4500. Deeta Lonergan, Director.

ARIZONA

The Orion Institute, Debra B. Danvenport, M.A., L.C.C., Ph.D.(c) Director, 6945 E. Cochise Road, Suite 138, Scottsdale, AZ 85253-1485. phone 480-348-1163.

Southwest Institute of Life Management, 11122 E. Gunshot Circle, Tucson, AZ 85749. phone 520-749-2290. Theodore Donald Risch, Director. M.S., CRC.

West Valley Career Services, 10720 W. Indian School, #19-141, Phoenix, AZ 85037. phone 623-872-7303. Shell Mendelson Herman, M.S., CRC.

ARKANSAS

Donald McKinney, Ed.D., Career Counselor, Rt. 1, Box 351-A, DeQueen, AR 71832. phone 870-642-5628.

CALIFORNIA

Alumnae Resources, 120 Montgomery St., Suite 600, San Francisco, CA 94104. phone 415-274-4700.

Dwayne Berrett, M.A., RPCC, Berrett & Associates, 1551 E. Shaw, Suite 103, Fresno, CA 93710. phone 559-221-6543.

Beverly Brown, M.A., NCCC, NCC 809 So. Bundy Dr., #105, Los Angeles, CA 90049. phone 310-447-7093.

California Career Services, 6024 Wilshire Blvd., Los Angeles, CA 90036-3616. phone 323-933-2900. Susan W. Miller, M.A.

Career Action Center, 10420 Bubb Rd., Suite 100, Cupertino, CA 95014-4150. phone 408-253-3200. Sharon Bray, Ph.D., Chief Executive Officer, Libby Panwitt, Career Counselor. *A tremendously impressive career center, one of the most comprehensive in the U.S., with a large number of job listings (81,000) and other resources, including individual counseling, workshops, books, videos, etc.*

Career and Personal Development Institute, 690 Market St., Suite 402, San Francisco, CA 94104. phone 415-982-2636. Bob Chope.

Career Balance, 215 Witham Road, Encinitas, CA 92024. phone 760-436-3994. Virginia Byrd, M.Ed., Work/Life Specialist, Career Management.

Career Choices, Castro Valley, CA. phone 510-733-6644. Dana E. Ogden, M.S.Ed., CCDV, Counselor and Trainer.

Career Counseling and Assessment Associates, 9229 West Sunset Blvd., Suite 502, Los Angeles, CA 90069. phone 310-274-3423. Dianne Y. Sundby, Ph.D., Director and Psychologist.

* Career Development and Vocational Testing Services, 2515 Park Marina, Suite 203-B, Redding, CA 96001. phone 916-246-2871.

Career Development Center, John F. Kennedy University, 1250 Arroyo Way, Walnut Creek, CA 94596. phone 925-295-0610. Susan Geifman, Director. *Open to the public. Membership or fee.*

Career Development Life Planning, 3585 Maple St., Suite 237, Ventura, CA 93003. phone 805-656-6220. Norma Zuber, NCCC, M.S.C., & Associates.

Career Dimensions, Box 7402, Stockton, CA 95267. phone 209-957-6465. Fran Abbott.

Career Planning Center/Business Action Center, 1623 S. La Cienega Blvd., Los Angeles, CA 90035. phone 310-273-6633.

Career Strategy Associates, 1100 Quail St., Suite 201, Newport Beach, CA 92660. phone 949-252-0515. Betty Fisher.

Center for Career Growth and Development, P.O. Box 283, Los Gatos, CA 95031. phone 408-354-7150. Steven E. Beasley.

Center for Creative Change, 3130 West Fox Run Way, San Diego, CA 92111. phone 619-268-9340. Nancy Helgeson, M.A., MFCC.

The Center for Life and Work Planning, 1133 Second St., Encinitas, CA 92024. phone 760-943-0747. Mary C. McIsaac, Executive Director.

* The Center for Ministry (An Interdenominational Church Career Development Center) 8393 Capwell Dr., Suite 220, Oakland, CA 94621-2123. phone 510-635-4246. Robert L. Charpentier, Director.

Stephen Cheney-Rice, M.S., 2113 Westboro Ave., Alhambra, CA 91803-3720. phone 818-281-6066, or 213-740-9112.

The Clarity Group Inc. 388 Market Street, Suite 500, San Francisco, CA 94111. phone 415-292-4814. George Schofield, Ph.D. (specializes in helping people who are 'stuck').

Cricket Consultants, 502 Natoma St., P.O. Box 6191, Folsom, CA 95763-6191. phone 916-985-3211. Bruce Parrish, M.S., CDMS.

Cypress College, Career Planning Center, 9200 Valley View St., Cypress, CA 90630. phone 714-484-7000.

Dream Job Coaching, 14895 E. 14th St., Suite 450, San Leandro, CA 94578. phone 510-357-2522.

Margaret L. **Eadie,** M.A., A.M.Ed. Career Consultant, 1000 Sage Pl., Pacific Grove, CA 93950. phone 831-373-7400.

Experience Unlimited Job Club. There are 35 Experience Unlimited Clubs in California, found at the Employment Development Department in the following locations: Anaheim, Corona, El Cajon, Escondido, Fremont, Fresno, Hemet, Hollywood, Lancaster, Monterey, North Hollywood, Oakland, Ontario, Pasadena, Pleasant Hill, Redlands, Ridgecrest, Riverside, Sacramento (Midtown and South), San Bernardino, San Diego (also East and South), San Francisco, San Mateo, San Rafael, Santa Ana, Santa Cruz, Santa Maria, Simi Valley, Sunnyvale, Torrance, Victorville, and West Covina. Contact the club nearest to you through your local Employment Development Department (E.D.D.).

Mary Alice **Floyd,** M.A., NCC, Career Counselor/Consultant, Career Life Transitions, 3233 Lucinda Lane, Santa Barbara, CA 93105. phone 805-687-5462.

Jan **Fritsen,** Career Counseling and Coaching, 23181 La Cadena Drive, Suite 103, Laguna Hills, CA 92653. phone 949-786-5431.

Futures . . . , 103 Calvin Place, Santa Cruz, CA 95060. phone 831-425-0332. Joseph Reimuller.

Marvin F. **Galper,** Ph.D., Third Ave., San Diego, CA 92103. phone 619-295-4450.

Deborah **Gavrin** Franquist, M.S., 1501 20th St., San Francisco, CA 94107. phone 415-642-0225.

Jack **Geary,** MA, CRC, Geary & Associates, 1100-A Coddingtown Ctr., P.O. Box 3774, Santa Rosa, CA 95402. phone 707-525-8085.

Judith **Grutter,** M.S., NCCC, G/S Consultants, P.O. Box 7855, South Lake Tahoe, CA 96158. phone 530-541-8587.

The **Guidance Center,** 1150 Yale St., Suite One, Santa Monica, CA 90403. phone 310-829-4429. Anne Salzman, Career Counselor and Psychologist.

H.R. Solutions, Human Resources Consulting, 390 South Sepulveda Blvd., Suite 104, Los Angeles, CA 90049. phone 310-471-2536. Nancy Mann, M.B.A, President/Career Consultant.

Jewish Vocational Service, 5700 Wilshire Blvd., 2nd Floor, Suite 2303, Los Angeles, CA 90036. phone 323-761-8888.

The **Job Forum,** 235 Montgomery St., 12th Floor, San Francisco, CA 94104. phone 415-392-4520.

Judy Kaplan Baron Associates, 6046 Cornerstone Ct. West, Suite 208, San Diego, CA 92121. phone 858-558-7400. Judy Kaplan Baron, Director.

Patrick **Kerwin,** MBA, NCCC, Kerwin & Associates, 926 W. Kenneth Road, Glendale, CA 91202. phone 808-246-5621.

*** Lifework Design,** 448 S. Marengo Ave., Pasadena, CA 91101. phone 626-577-2705. Kevin Brennfleck, M.A., NCCC, and Kay Marie Brennfleck, M.A., NCCC, Directors.

Lindenbaum Career and Counseling Services, 1623 Fifth Ave., Bldg. D, Suite 8, San Rafael, CA 94901-1860. phone 415-789-9113. Suzanne Lindenbaum, MSW, LCSW, BCD.

Peller **Marion,** 388 Market St., Suite 500, San Francisco, CA 94111. phone 415-296-2559.

*** Lizbeth **Miller,** M.S., 3880 S. Bascom Ave., Suite 202, San Jose, CA 95124. phone 408-559-1115. Affiliated with the Christian Counseling Center.

Montgomery & Associates, Career Development Services, 2515 Park Marina Dr., Suite 203B, Redding, CA 96001-2831. phone 530-246-2871. Gale Montgomery, Director.

Networking Grace Career Counseling, Napa, CA 94558. phone 707-226-3438. Lauralyn Bauer, M.S.

Olivia Keith **Slaughter,** LEP, Sunshine Plaza, 71 301 Highway 111, Suite 1, Rancho Mirage, CA 92270. phone 760-568-1544.

Transitions Counseling Center, 171 N. Van Ness, Fresno, CA 93701. phone 559-233-7250. Margot E. Tepperman, L.C.S.W.

Turning Point Career Center, University YWCA, 2600 Bancroft Way, Berkeley, CA 94704. phone 510-848-6370. Winnie Froehlich, M.S., Director.

Patti **Wilson,** P.O. Box 35633, Los Gatos, CA 95030. phone 408-354-1964.

COLORADO

Accelerated Job Search, 4490 Squires Circle, Boulder, CO 80303. phone 303-494-2467. Leigh Olsen, Counselor.

CRS Consulting, 425 W. Mulberry, Suite 205, Fort Collins, CO 80521. phone 970-484-9810. Marilyn Pultz.

Sherry **Helmstaedter,** 5040 South El Camino, Englewood, CO 80111-1122. phone 303-794-5122.

Life Work Planning, P.O.Box 1738, Berthoud, CO 80513. phone 970-532-5351. Lauren T. Murphy, Career Development Counselor.

Betsy C. **McGee,** The McGee Group, 2485 W. Main, Suite 202, Old Littleton, CO 80120. phone 303-794-4749.

Patricia **O'Keefe,** M.A., 1550 S. Monroe St., Denver, CO 80210. phone 303-759-9325.

Resource Center, Arapahoe Community College, 2500 West College Dr., P.O. Box 9002, Littleton, CO 80160-9002. phone 303-797-5805.

Strategic Career Moves, 2329 N. Glenisle Ave., Durango, CO 81301. phone 970-385-9597. Mary Jane Ward, M.Ed., NCC, NCCC.

Women's Resource Agency, 31 N. Farragut, Colorado Springs, CO 80909. phone 719-471-3170.

YWCA of Boulder County Career Center, 2222 14th St., Boulder, CO 80302. phone 303-443-0419. A full-service career center, fees on a sliding scale. Counseling, testing, support groups, workshops. April Peterson, NCCC, Career Services Manager.

CONNECTICUT

Accord Career Services, The Exchange, Suite 305, 270 Farmington Ave., Farmington, CT 06032. phone 800-022-1480, or 860-674-9654. Tod Gerardo, M.S., Director.

Career Choices/RFP Associates, 141 Durham Rd., Suite 24, Madison, CT 06443. phone 203-245-4123.

Career Transformations, 761 Valley Road, Fairfield, CT 06432. phone 203-374-7649. Robert N. Olsen, M.A., NCC.

James S. **Cohen,** Ph.D., Career Services, Vocational Rehabilitation Services for Injured/Disabled Workers, 205 Vernon Avenue, #211, Vernon, CT 06066. phone 860-871-7832.

Crossroads, 30 Tower Lane, Avon, CT 06001. phone 860-677-2558. Carolyn A. Stigler, Psy.D.

Fairfield Academic and Career Center, Fairfield University, Dolan House, Fairfield, CT 06430. phone 203-254-4220.

Jamieson Associates, 61 South Main St., Suite 101, West Hartford, CT 06107-2403. phone 860-521-2373. Lee Jamieson, Principal.

The **Offerjost-Westcott Group,** 263 Main St., Old Saybrook, CT 06475. phone 203-388-6094. Russ Westcott.

Bob **Pannone,** M.A., NCCC, Career Specialist, 768 Saw Mill Road, West Haven, CT 06516. phone 203-933-6383.

People Management International Ltd., 8B North Shore Rd., New Preston CT 06777. phone 203-868-0317. Arthur Miller, Founder and Principal.

Roger J. **Preis,** RPE Career Dynamics, P.O. Box 16722, Stamford, CT 06905. phone 203-322-7225.

Releasing Your Original Genius™, 998 Farmington Ave., Suite 207, West Hartford, CT 06107. phone 860-561-2142. Lorraine P. Holden, M.S.W., Career/Life Planning Consultant.

Vocational and Academic Counseling for Adults (VOCA), 115 Berrian Rd., Stamford, CT 06905. phone 203-322-8353. Ruth A. Polster.

J. Whitney Associates, 11092 Elm St., Rocky Hill, CT 06067. phone 860-721-0842. Jean Whitney, Career Manager.

The **Brandywine Center,** 2500 Grubb Road, Suite 240, Wilmington, DE 19810. phone 302-475-1880. Also at 3302 Polly Drummond Office Park, Newark, DE 19711. phone 302-454-7650. Kris Bronson, Ph.D.

YWCA of New Castle County, Women's Center for Economic Options, 233 King St., Wilmington, DE 19801. phone 302-658-7161.

DISTRICT OF COLUMBIA

Community Vocational Counseling Service, The George Washington University Counseling Center, 718 21st St. NW, Washington, DC 20052. phone 202-994-4860. Robert J. Wilson, M.S., Asst. Director for Educational Services.

George Washington University, Center for Career Education, 2020 K St., Washington, DC 20052. phone 202-994-5299. Abigail Pereira, Director.

Marilyn **Goldman,** Horizons Unlimited, Inc., 1050 17th St., N.W., Suite 600, Washington, D.C. 20036. phone 202-296-7224 and 301-258-9338.

FLORIDA

Barbara **Adler,** Ed.D., Career Consulting, 203 North Shadow Bay Dr., Orlando, FL 32825-3766. phone 407-249-2189.

Career Moves, Inc., 4331 N. Federal Highway, Suite 305, Ft. Lauderdale, FL 33308. phone 954-772-6857. Diane Alford, M.Ed., NCC, NCCC, President.

Center for Career Decisions, 6100 Glades Rd., #210, Boca Raton, FL 33434. phone 561-470-9333. Linda Friedman, M.A., NCC, NCCC, Director.

The **Centre for Women,** 305 S. Hyde Park Ave., Tampa, FL 33606. phone 813-251-8437. Dae C. Sheridan, M.A., CRC, Employment Counselor.

Chabon & Associates, 1665 Palm Beach Lakes Blvd., Suite 402, West Palm Beach, FL 33401. phone 407-640-8443. Toby G. Chabon, M.Ed., NCC, President.

The **Challenge: Program for Displaced Homemakers,** Florida Community College at Jacksonville, 101 W. State St., Jacksonville, FL 32202. phone 904-633-8316. Rita Patrick, Project Coordinator.

Crossroads, Palm Beach Community College, 4200 Congress Ave., Lake Worth, FL 33461-4796. phone 407-433-5995. Pat Jablonski, Program Manager.

Focus on the Future: Displaced Homemaker Program, Santa Fe Community College, 3000 N.W. 83rd St., Gainesville, FL 32606. phone 904-395-5047. Nancy Griffin, Program Coordinator. Classes are free.

Larry **Harmon,** Ph.D., Career Counseling Center, Inc., 2000 South Dixie Highway, Suite 103, Miami, FL 33133. phone 305-858-8557.

Ellen O. **Jonassen,** Ph.D., 10785 Ulmerton Rd., Largo, FL 34648. phone 813-581-8526.

Life Designs, Inc., 19526 East Lake Drive, Miami, FL 33015. phone 305-829-9008 (Sept.-May). Dulce Muccio Weisenborn.

New Beginnings, Polk Community College, Station 71, 999 Avenue H, NE, Winter Haven, FL 33881-4299 (Lakeland Campus). phone 813-297-1029.

The **Women's Center,** Valencia Community College, 1010 N. Orlando Ave., Winter Park, FL 32789. phone 407-628-1976.

WINGS Program, Broward Community College, 1000 Coconut Creek Blvd., Coconut Creek, FL 33066. phone 305-973-2398.

GEORGIA

Emmette H. **Albea,** Jr., M.S., LPC, NCCC, 2706 Melrose Dr., Valdosta, GA 31602. phone 912-241-0908.

Janis **Ashkin,** M.Ed., NCC, NCCC, 219 Quail Run, Roswell, GA 30076. phone 770-642-0875.

* **Career Development Center of the Southeast** (An Interdenominational Church Career Development Center), 531 Kirk Rd., Decatur, GA 30030. phone 404-371-0336. Earl B. Stewart, D.Min., Director.

* **Career Pathways,** 601 Broad St., Gainesville, GA 30501. phone 800-722-1976. Lee Ellis, Director. *Offers career-guidance from a Christian point of view, through the mails -- based on questionnaires and various instruments or inventories which they send you.*

Career Quest/Job Search Workshop, St. Ann, 4905 Roswell Rd., N.E., Marietta, GA 30062-6240. phone 770-552-6402. Tom Chernetsky. *Features instruction on Internet job-hunting.*

* **Center for Growth & Change, Inc.,** 6991 Peachtree Ind. Blvd., Suite 310, Norcross, GA 30092. phone 404-441-9580. James P. Hicks, Ph.D., LPC, Director.

D & B Consulting, 3390 Peachtree Road N.E., Suite 900, Atlanta, GA 30326. phone 404-240-8063. Deborah R. Brown, MSM, MSW, Career Consultant.

Jewish Vocational Service, Inc., 4549 Chamblee Dunwoody Road, Dunwoody, GA 30338-6120. phone 770-677-9440.

St. Jude's Job Network, St. Jude's Catholic Church, 7171 Glenridge Dr., Sandy Springs, GA 30328. phone 404-393-4578.

Mark **Satterfield,** 720 Rio Grand Dr., Alpharetta, GA 30202. phone 770-640-8393.

IDAHO

* The **Job Search Advisor,** 915 W. Iowa Ave., Boise, ID 83686. phone 208-463-2375. Christopher G. Gilliam, PHR, Job Search Advisor.

Transitions, 1970 Parkside Dr., Boise, ID 83712. phone 208-368-0499. Elaine Simmons, M.Ed.

ILLINOIS

Alumni Career Center, University of Illinois Alumni Association, 200 South Wacker Dr., Chicago, IL 60606. phone 312-996-6350. Barbara S. Hundley, Director; Claudia M. Delestowicz, Associate Director, Julie L. Hays, Staff. Full Service Career Center open to the community.

Career Path, 1240 Iroquois Ave., Suite 510, Naperville, IL 60563. phone 630-369-3390. Donna Sandberg, M.S., NCC, Owner/Counselor.

Career Workshops, 5431 W. Roscoe St., Chicago, IL 60641. phone 312-282-6859. Patricia Dietze.

Jean **Davis,** Adult Career Transitions, 1405 Elmwood Ave., Evanston, IL 60201. phone 847-492-1002.

The **Dolan Agency,** 2745 East Broadway, Suite 102, Alton, IL 62002. phone 618-474-5328. J. Stephen Dolan, M.A., C.R.C., Rehabilitation and Career Consultant.

Barbara Kabcenell **Grauer,** M.A., NCC, 1370 Sheridan Road, Highland Park, IL 60035. phone 708-432-4479.

Grimard Wilson Consulting, 111 N. Wabash Ave., Suite 2005, Chicago, IL 60602. phone 312-201-1142. Diane Grimard Wilson, M.A.

Harper College Career Transition Center, Building A, Room 124, Palatine, IL 60067. phone 708-459-8233. Mary Ann Jirak, Coordinator.

David P. **Helfand,** Ed.D., NCCC, 250 Ridge, Evanston, IL 60202. phone 847-328-2787.

Barbara **Hill,** Career Management Consultant, 427 Greenwood St., Suite 3W, Evanston, IL 60201. phone 847-733-1805.

Lansky Career Consultants, 330 N. Wabash #2905, Chicago, IL 60611. phone 312-494-0022. Judith Lansky, President. Julie Benesh, Adjunct Consultant.

* **Life/Career Planning Center for Religious,** 10526 W. Cermak Rd., Suite 111, Westchester, IL 60153. phone 708-531-9228. Dolores Linhart, Director. *Doing work with Roman Catholics.*

Living by Design, 106 S. Oak Park Ave., Suite 203, Oak Park, IL 60302. phone 708-386-2505. Barbara Upton, LCSW.

* **Midwest Career Development Service** (An Interdenominational Church Career Development Center), 1840 Westchester Blvd., Westchester, IL 60154. phone 708-343-6268.

Midwest Women's Center, 828 S. Wabash, Suite 200, Chicago, IL 60605. phone 312-922-8530.

Moraine Valley Community College, Job Placement Center, 10900 S. 88th Ave., Palos Hills, IL 60465. phone 708-974-5737.

Right Livelihood$, 23 W. 402 Green Briar Dr., Naperville, IL 60540. phone 708-369-9066. Marti Beddoe, Career/Life Counselor; or 312-281-7274, Peter LeBrun.

Jessica **Skorupa,** Ph.D., NCCC, 16750 S. 80th Ave., Tinley Park, IL 60477. phone 708-614-7664.

The **Summit Group,** P.O. Box 3794, Peoria, IL 61612-3794. phone 309-681-1118. John R. Throop, D. Min., President.

Widmer & Associates, 1510 W. Sunnyview Dr., Peoria, IL 61614. phone 309-691-3312. Mary F. Widmer, President.

INDIANA

Career Consultants, 107 N. Pennsylvania St., Suite 400, Indianapolis, IN 46204. phone 317-639-5601. Al Milburn, Career Management Consultant.

Sally **Jones,** Program Coordinator/Developer, Indiana University, School of Continuing Studies, Owen Hall, Room 202, Bloomington, IN 47405. phone 812-855-4991.

KCDM Associates, 10401 N. Meridian St., Suite 300, Indianapolis, IN 46290. phone 317-581-6230. Mike Kenney.

Performance Development Systems, Inc., 312 Iroquois Trail, Burns Harbor, IN 46304. phone 219-787-9216. William P. Henning, Counselor.

IOWA

Rosanne **Beers,** Beers Consulting, 5505 Boulder Dr., West Des Moines, IA 50266. phone 515-225-1245.

Jill **Sudak-Allison,** 3219 SE 19th Court, Des Moines, IA 50320. phone 515-282-5040.

University of Iowa, Center for Career Development and Cooperative Education, 315 Calvin Hall, Iowa City, IA 52242. phone 319-335-3201.

Gloria **Wendroff,** Secrets to Successful Job Search, 703 E. Burlington Ave., Fairfield, IA 52556. phone 515-472-4529.

Suzanne **Zilber,** 801 Crystal St., Ames, IA 50010. phone 515-232-9379.

KANSAS

*Midwest Career Development Service (An Interdenominational Church Career Development Center), 754 N. 31st St., Kansas City, KS 66110-0816. Ronald Brushwyler, Director.

KENTUCKY

The **Epoch Group,** 6500 Glenridge Park Place, Suite 12, Louisville, KY 40222. phone 502-326-9122. Phillip A. Ronniger.

LOUISIANA

Career Planning and Assessment Center, Metropolitan College, University of New Orleans, New Orleans, LA 70148. phone 504-286-7100.

MAINE

Susan L. **Arledge,** Life-Planning /Career Consultant, 50 Exeter St., Portland, ME 04102. phone 207-761-7755.

Career Perspectives, 75 Pearl St., Suite 204, Portland, ME 04101. phone 207-775-4487. Deborah L. Gallant.

Heart at Work, 261 Main St., Yarmouth, ME 04096. phone 207-846-0644. Barbara Sirois Babkirk, M.Ed., NCC, L.C.P.C., Licensed Counselor and Consultant.

Johnson Career Services, 34 Congress St., Portland ME 04101. phone 207-773-3921. R. Ernest Johnson.

Suit Yourself International, Inc., 120 Pendleton Point, Islesboro, ME 04848. phone 207-734-8206. Debra Spencer, President.

Women's Worth Career Counseling, 18 Woodland Rd., Gorham, ME 04038. phone 207-892-0000. Jacqueline Murphy, Counselor.

MARYLAND

*Call to Career, 8720 Georgia Ave., Suite 802, Silver Spring, MD 20910. phone 301-961-1017. Cheryl Palmer, M.Ed., NCC, NCCC, President.

Career Perspectives, 510 Sixth St., Annapolis, MD 21403. phone 410-280-2299. Jeanne H. Slawson, Career Consultant.

Careerscope, Inc., One Mall North, Suite 216, 1025 Governor Warfield Pkwy., Columbia, MD 21044. phone 410-992-5042 or 301-596-1866. Constantine Bitsas, Executive Director.

Career Transition Services, 3126 Berkshire Rd., Baltimore, MD 21214-3404. phone 410-444-5857. Michael Bryant.

College of Notre Dame of Maryland, Continuing Education Center, 4701 N. Charles St., Baltimore, MD 21210. phone 410-532-5303.

Goucher College, Goucher Center for Continuing Studies, 1021 Dulaney Valley Rd., Baltimore, MD 21204. phone 410-337-6200. Carole B. Ellin, Career/Job-Search Counselor.

Anne S. **Headley,** M.A., 7100 Baltimore Ave., Suite 208, College Park, MD 20740. phone 301-779-1917.

Kensington Consulting, 8701 Georgia Ave., Suite 406, Silver Spring, MD 20910. phone 301-587-1234. David M. Reile, Ph.D., NCCC, Barbara H. Suddarth, Ph.D., NCCC.

Maryland New Directions, Inc., 2220 N. Charles St., Baltimore, MD 21218. phone 410-235-8800. Rose Marie Coughlin, Director.

Irene N. **Mendelson,** NCCC, BEMW, Inc., Counseling and Training for the Workplace, 7984 D Old Georgetown Rd., Bethesda, MD 20814-2440. phone 301-657-8922.

Prince George's Community College, Career Assessment and Planning Center, 301 Largo Rd., Largo, MD 20772. phone 301-322-0886. Margaret Taibi, Ph.D., Director.

TransitionWorks, 10964 Bloomingdale Dr., Rockville, MD 20852-5550. phone 301-770-4277. Stephanie Kay, M.A., A.G.S., Principal. Nancy K. Schlossberg, Ed.D., Principal.

MASSACHUSETTS

Boston Career Link, 281 Huntington Ave., Boston, MA 02115. phone 617-536-1888.

Changes, 29 Leicester St., P.O. Box 35697, Brighton, MA 02135. phone 617-783-1717. Carl Schneider. Career counseling and job-hunt training. Individual or group therapy for job-hunters. Carl is one of the most giving-service-to-people counselors that we have in this Sampler. He's been listed here for 21 years (and counting).

Career Link, Career Information Center, Kingston Public Library, 6 Green St., Kingston, MA 02364. phone 781-585-0517. Free videos, audiocassettes, and books on job-search, plus computerized career guidance (SIGI), public access computer, and workshops. Sia Stewart, Director of the Library.

*****Career Management Consultants,** Thirty Park Ave., Worcester, MA 01605. phone 508-853-8669. Patricia Stepanski Plouffe, President.

Career Resource Center, Worcester YWCA, 1 Salem Square, Worcester, MA 01608. phone 508-791-3181.

Career Source, 185 Alewife Brook Pkwy., Cambridge, MA 02138. phone 617-661-7867. This place inherited the Radcliffe Career Services Office's library, after that Office closed permanently. Also offers career counseling.

*****Center for Career Development & Ministry,** 70 Chase St., Newton Center, MA 02159. phone 617-969-7750. Stephen Ott, Director.

Center for Careers, Jewish Vocational Service, 105 Chauncy St., 6th Fl., Boston, MA 02111. phone 617-451-8147. Lee Ann Bennett, Coordinator, Core Services.

Jewish Vocational Service, Mature Worker Programs, 333 Nahanton St., Newton, MA 02159. phone 617-965-7940.

Linkage, Inc., 110 Hartwell Ave., Lexington, MA 02173. phone 781-862-4030. David J. Giber, Ph.D.

Wynne W. **Miller,** Coaching & Career Development, 15 Cypress St., Suite 200, Newton Center, MA 02459-2242. phone 617-527-4848. Practical career counseling oriented toward finding meaning and mission.

Murray Associates, P.O. Box 312, Westwood, MA 02090. phone 617-329-1287. Robert Murray, Ed.D., Licensed Psychologist.

Neville Associates, Inc., 10 Tower Office Park, Suite 416, Woburn, MA 01801. phone 781-938-7870. Dr. Joseph Neville, Career Development Consultant.

Smith College Career Development Office, Drew Hall, 84 Elm St., Northampton, MA 01063. phone 413-585-2570. Career counseling services to the community. Jane Sommer, Associate Director.

Phyllis R. **Stein,** 59 Parker St., Cambridge, MA 02138. phone 617-354-7948. *Phyllis was the Director of Radcliffe Career Services for two decades, until its close. She is now doing private career counseling and workshops at the address above.*

Wellness Center, 51 Mill St., Unit 8, Hanover, MA 02339. phone 781-829-4300. Janet Barr.

MICHIGAN

Careerdesigns, 22 Cherry St., Holland, MI 49423. phone 616-396-1517. Mark de Roo.

Jewish Vocational Service, 29699 Southfield Road, Southfield, MI 48076-2063. phone 248-559-5000.

Lansing Community College, 2020 Career and Employment Development Services, PO Box 40010, Lansing, MI 48901-7210. phone 517-483-1221 or 483-1172. James C. Osborn, Ph.D., LPC, Director, Career and Employment Services.

*****Life Stewardship Associates,** 6918 Glen Creek Dr., SE, Dutton, MI 49316. phone 616-698-3125. Ken Soper, M.Div., M.A., Director.

New Options: Counseling for Women in Transition, 2311 E. Stadium, Suite B-2, Ann Arbor, MI 48104. phone 313-973-0003. Phyllis Perry, M.S.W.

Oakland University, Continuum Center for Adult Counseling and Leadership Training, Rochester, MI 48309. phone 313-370-3033.

University of Michigan, Center for the Education of Women, 330 East Liberty, Ann Arbor, MI 48104. phone 313-998-7080.

Women's Resource Center, 252 State St. SE, Grand Rapids, MI 49503. phone 616-458-5443.

MINNESOTA

Richard E. **Andrea,** Ph.D., 1014 Bartelmy Lane, Maplewood, MN 55119-3637. phone 612-730-9892.

Associated Career Services, 3550 Lexington Ave. N., Suite 120, Shoreview, MN 55126. phone 612-787-0501.

Career Dynamics, Inc., 8400 Normandale Lake Blvd., Suite 1220, Bloomington, MN 55437. phone 612-921-2378. Joan Strewler, Psychologist.

Human Dynamics, 3036 Ontario Rd., Little Canada, MN 55117. phone 612-484-8299. Greg J. Cylkowski, M.A., founder.

*****North Central Career Development Center** (An Interdenominational Church Career Development Center), 516 Mission House Lane, New Brighton, MN 55112. phone 612-636-5120. Kenneth J. McFayden, Ph.D., Director.

Prototype Career Services, 626 Armstrong Ave., St. Paul, MN 55102. phone 800-368-3197. Amy Lindgren, and Julie Remington, Counseling Psychologists.

Stanley J. **Sizen,** Vocational Services, P.O.Box 363, Anoka, MN 55303. phone 612-441-8053.

Southwest Family Services, 10267 University Ave. North, Blaine, MN 55434. phone 612-825-4407. Kathy Bergman, M.A., LP. Career planning services.

Working Opportunities for Women, 2700 University Ave., #120, St. Paul, MN 55114. phone 612-647-9961.

MISSISSIPPI

Mississippi Gulf Coast Community College, Jackson County Campus, Career Development Center, P.O. Box 100, Gautier, MS 39553. phone 601-497-9602. Rebecca Williams, Manager.

Mississippi State University, Career Services Center, P.O. Box P, Colvard Union, Suite 316, Mississippi State, MS 39762-5515. phone 601-325-3344.

MISSOURI

Rod C. **Cannedy,** Ph.D., Forest Institute of Professional Psychology, 2885 West Battlefield Rd., Springfield, MO 65807. phone 417-823-3477.

Career Center, Community Career Services, 110 Noyes Hall, University of Missouri, Columbia, MO 65211. phone 573-882-6803.

Career Management Center, 8301 State Line Rd., Suite 202, Kansas City, MO 64114. phone 816-363-1500. Janice Y. Benjamin, President.

* **Midwest Career Development Service** (An Interdenominational Church Career Development Center), 754 N. 31st St., Kansas City, KS 66110-0816. Ronald Brushwyler, Director.

M. Rose **Jonas,** Ph.D., The Job Doctor, 505 S. Ewing, St. Louis, MO 63103. phone 314-863-1166.

Women's Center, University of Missouri-Kansas City, 5100 Rockhill Rd., 104 Scofield Hall, Kansas City, MO 64110. phone 816-235-1638.

MONTANA

Career Transitions, 321 E. Main, Suite 215, Bozeman, MT 59715. phone 406-587-1721. Estella Villasenor, Executive Director. Darla Joyner, Assistant Director.

NEBRASKA

Career Management Services, 5000 Central Park Dr., Suite 204, Lincoln, NE 68504. phone 402-466-8427. Vaughn L. Carter, President.

CMS: Career Management Services, 5000 Central Park Dr., Suite 204, Lincoln, NE 68504. phone 402-466-8427. Vaughn L. Carter, President.

* **Olson Counseling Services,** 8720 Frederick, Suite 105, Omaha, NE 68128. phone 402-390-2342. Gail A. Olson, P.A.C.

Student Success Center, Central Community College, Hastings Campus, Hastings, NE 68902. phone 402-461-2424.

NEVADA

Career/Lifestyles, Alamo Plaza, 4550 W. Oakey Blvd., Suite #111, Las Vegas, NV 89102. phone 702-258-3353. Carol J. Cravens, M.A., NCC.

Greener Pastures Institute, 6301 S. Squaw Valley Rd., Suite 1383, Pahrump, NV 89048-7949. phone 800-688-6352. Bill Seavey.

NEW HAMPSHIRE

Individual Employment Services, 90-A Sixth St., P.O. 917, Dover, NH 03820. phone 603-742-5616. James Otis, Employment Counselor.

NEW JERSEY

Adult Advisory Service, Kean College of New Jersey. Administration Bldg., Union, NJ 07083. phone 908-527-2210.

Adult Resource Center, 100 Horseneck Road, Montville, NJ 07045. phone 201-335-6910.

Arista Concepts Career Development Service, P.O. Box 2436, Princeton, NJ 08540. phone 609-921-0308. Kera Greene, M.Ed.

Beverly **Baskin,** M.A., LPC, NCCC, CPRW, Baskin Business & Career Services, 6 Alberta Dr., Marlboro, NJ 07746-1202. phone 800-300-4079. Offices also in Woodbridge, and Princeton.

Behavior Dynamics Associates, Inc., 34 Cambridge Terrace, Springfield, NJ 07081. phone 201-912-0136. Roy Hirschfeld.

Career Options Center, YWCA Tribute to Women and Industry (TWIN) Program, 232 E. Front St., Plainfield, NJ 07060. phone 908-756-3836, or 908-273-4242. Janet M. Korba, Program Director.

Center for Life Enhancement, 1156 E. Ridgewood Ave., Ridgewood, NJ 07450. phone 201-670-8443. David R. Johnson, Director of Career Programs.

Jerry **Cohen,** M.A., NCC, NCCC, Chester Professional Bldg., P.O. Box 235, Chester, NJ 07930. phone 908-789-4404.

Loree **Collins,** 3 Beechwood Rd., Summit, NJ 07901. phone 908-273-9219.

Douglass College, Douglass Advisory Services for Women, Rutgers Women's Center, 132 George St., New Brunswick, NJ 08903. phone 908-932-9603.

Juditha **Dowd,** 440 Rosemont Ringoes Road., Stockton, NJ 08559. phone 609-397-9375.

Sandra **Grundfest,** Ed.D., Princeton Professional Park, 601 Ewing St., Suite C-1, Princeton, NJ 08540. phone 609-921-8401. Also at 11 Clyde Rd., Suite 103, Somerset, NJ 08873. phone 908-873-1212.

Susan **Guarneri** Associates, 1101 Lawrence Rd., Lawrenceville, NJ 08648. phone 609-771-1669. Susan Guarneri, M.S., NCC, NCCC, and Jack Guarneri, M.S., NCC, NCCC. Career and job-search counseling.

The **Job Club,** Princeton Unitarian Church, Cherry Hill Rd., Princeton, NJ 08540. phone 609-924-1604. Free service, open to the community.

JobSeekers in Princeton NJ. Trinity Church, 33 Mercer Street, Princeton, NJ 08542. phone 609-924-2277. Meets Tuesdays, 7:30–9:30 p.m. *The oldest continuing job club, run by volunteers, in the country.*

Job Seekers of Montclair, St. Luke's Episcopal Church, 73 S. Fullerton Ave, Montclair, NJ 07042. phone 201-783-3442. Meets Thursdays 7:30-9:30 p.m.

Mercer County Community College, Career Services, 1200 Old Trenton Rd., Trenton, NJ 08690. phone 609-586-4800, ext. 304. Career and job-search counseling. Open to non-students (though with a fee).

Metro Career Services, 784 Morris Turnpike, Suite 203, Short Hills, NJ 07078. phone 973-912-0106. Judy Scherer, M.A.

Lester **Minsuk** & Associates, 29 Exeter Rd., East Windsor, NJ 08520. phone 609-448-4600.

* **Northeast Career Center** (An Interdenominational Church Career Development Center), 407 Nassau Street, Princeton, NJ 08540. phone 609-924-9408. Roy Lewis, Director.

Princeton Management Consultants, Inc., 99 Moore St., Princeton, NJ 08540. phone 609-924-2411. Niels H. Nielsen, M.A., Job and Career Counselor.

Resource Center for Women, 31 Woodland Ave., Summit, NJ 07901. phone 908-273-7253.

Scott B. **Sigmon,** Ed.D., 1945 Morris Ave., Union, NJ 07083. phone 908-686-7555.

NEW MEXICO

Young Women's Christian Association, YWCA Career Services Center, 7201 Paseo Del Norte NE, Albuquerque, NM 87113. phone 505-822-9922.

NEW YORK

Carol **Allen,** Consultant, 560 West 43rd St., Suite 5G, New York, NY 10036. phone 212-268-5182. Career Management/Spirited Worker Seminars.

Alan B. **Bernstein** CSW, PC, 122 East 82nd St., New York, NY 10028. phone 212-288-4881.

Career Development Center, Long Island University, C.W. Post Campus, Brookville, NY 11548. phone 516-299-2251. Pamela Lennox, Ph.D., Director.

Career Resource Center, Bethlehem Public Library, 451 Delaware Ave., Delmar, NY 12054. phone 518-439-9314. Denise L. Coblish, Career Resources Librarian.

Careers by Choice, Inc., 205 E. Main St., Huntington, NY 11743. phone 631-673-5432. Marjorie ("MJ") Feld.

Career Strategies, Inc., 350 West 24th St., New York, NY 10011. phone 212-807-1340. "CB" Bowman, President.

Career 101 Associates, 230 West 55th St., Suite 17F, New York, NY 10019. phone 212-333-4013. L. Michelle Tullier, Ph.D., Director.

Center for Creativity and Work. Offices in Manhattan and Woodstock. P.O. Box 9158, Woodstock, NY 12498. phone 212-490-9158 or 914-336-8318. Allie Roth, President.

The **John C. Crystal Center,** 152 Madison Ave., 23rd fl., New York, NY 10016. phone 212-889-8500, or 1-800-333-9003. Nella G. Barkley, President. *John, the original founder of this center, died ten years ago; Nella, his business partner for many years, now directs the center's work.*

* Judith **Gerberg** Associates, 250 West 57th St., New York, NY 10107. phone 212-315-2322.

Hofstra University, Career Counseling Center, Room 120, Saltzman Community Center, 131 Hofstra, Hempstead, NY 11550. phone 516-463-6788.

Kingsborough Community College, Office of Career Counseling and Placement, 2001 Oriental Blvd., Rm. C102, Brooklyn, NY 11235. phone 718-368-5115.

Janice **La Rouche** Associates, 333 Central Park W., New York, NY 10025. phone 212-663-0970.

Livelyhood Job Search Center, 301 Madison Ave., 3rd Floor, New York, NY 10017. phone 212-687-2411. John Aigner, Director.

James E. **McPherson,** 101 Ives Hall, Cornell University, Ithaca, NY 14853-3901.

New Options, 960 Park Ave., New York, NY 10028. phone 212-535-1444.

Onondaga County Public Library, The Galleries of Syracuse, 447 South Salina St., Syracuse, NY 13202-2494. phone 315-435-1900. Karen A. Pitoniak, Librarian, Information Services. Has InfoTrac, a computerized index and directory of over 100,000 companies, plus other job-hunting resources.

Orange County Community College, Counseling Center, 115 South St., Middletown, NY 10940. phone 914-341-4070.

Celia **Paul** Associates, 1776 Broadway, Suite 1806, New York, NY 10019. phone 212-397-1020. Celia Paul, President.

Personnel Sciences Center, Inc. 276 Fifth Ave., Suite 704, New York, NY 10001. phone 212-683-3008. Dr. Jeffrey A. Goldberg.

Leslie B. **Prager,** M.A., The Prager-Bernstein Group, 441 Lexington Ave., Suite 1404, New York, NY 10017. phone 212-697-0645.

Psychological Services Center, Career Services Unit, University at Albany, SUNY, Husted 167, 135 Western Ave., Albany, NY 12222. phone 518-442-4900. George B. Litchford, Ph.D., Director. Individual and group career counseling.

RLS Career Center, 3049 East Genesee St., Suite 211, Syracuse, NY 13224. phone 315-446-0500. Rebecca A. Livengood, Executive Director.

Schenectady Public Library, Job Information Center, 99 Clinton St., Schenectady, NY. Has weekly listings, including job-search listings of companies nationwide.

Scientific Career Transitions, Stephen Rosen, Ph.D., Science & Technology Advisory Board, 1776 Broadway, Suite 1806, New York, NY 10019. phone 212-397-1021. Specializes in scientists and engineers.

VEHICLES, INC., Life Skills and Career Training, 1832 Madison Ave., Room 202, New York, NY 10035-2707. phone 212-722-1111. Janet Avery.

Volunteer Consulting Group, Inc., 6 East 39th St., 6th Floor, New York, NY 10016. phone 212-447-1236.

WIN Workshops (Women in Networking), Emily Koltnow, 1120 Avenue of the Americas, Fourth Floor, New York, NY 10036. phone 212-333-8788.

NORTH CAROLINA

*The Career and Personal Counseling Service (An Official Inter-denominational Church Career Development Center) St. Andrew's Presbyterian College, Laurinburg, NC 28352. phone 919-276-3162 Also at: 4108 Park Rd., Suite 200, Charlotte, NC 28209. phone 704-523-7751 Elbert R. Patton, Director.

Career Consulting Associates of Raleigh, P.O. Box 17653, Raleigh, NC 27619. phone 919-782-3252. Susan W. Simonds, President.

Career, Educational, Psychological Evaluations, 2915 Providence Rd., Suite 300, Charlotte, NC 28211. phone 704-362-1942.

Career Focus Workshops, P.O. Box 35424, Greensboro, NC 27425. phone 336-643-1025. Glenn Wise, President.

Career Management Center, 3203 Woman's Club Dr., Suite 100, Raleigh, NC 27612. phone 919-787-1222, ext. 109. Temple G. Porter, Director.

Sally Kochendofer, Ph.D., Charlotte, NC 28211. phone 704-362-1514. E-mail drsallyk@mindspring.com.

Diane E. Lambeth, M.S.W., Career Consultant. P.O. Box 18945, Raleigh, NC 27619. phone 919-571-7423.

Life Management Services, LC, 301 Gregson Dr., Cary, NC 27511. phone 919-481-4707. Marilyn and Hal Shook. *The Shooks originally trained with John Crystal, though they have evolved their own program since then.*

Joyce Richman & Associates, Ltd., 2911 Shady Lawn Dr., Greensboro, NC 27408. phone 910-288-1799.

Bonnie M. Truax, Ed.D., NCCC, Career/Life Planning and Relocation Services, 2102 N. Elm St., Suite K1, Greensboro, NC 27408. phone 910-271-2050. Free support group.

Women's Center of Raleigh, 128 E. Hargett St., Suite 10, Raleigh, NC 27601. phone 919-829-3711.

NORTH DAKOTA

Business & Life Resources Career Development Center, 112 North University Dr., Suite 3300, Fargo, N.D. 58103. phone 800-950-0848. Gail Reierson.

OHIO

Adult Resource Center, The University of Akron, Buckingham Center for Continuing Education, Room 55, Akron, OH 44325-3102. phone 216-972-7448. Sandra B. Edwards, Director.

Career Initiatives Center, 1557 E. 27th St., Cleveland, OH 44114. phone 216-574-8998. Richard Hanscom, Director.

Career Point, Belden-Whipple Building, 4150 Belden Village St., N.W., Suite 101, Canton, OH 44718. phone 216-492-1920. Victor W. Valli, Career Consultant.

Cuyahoga County Public Library InfoPLACE Service, Career, Education & Community Information Service, 5225 Library Lane, Maple Heights, OH 44137-1291. phone 216-475-2225.

*Diversified Career Services, Inc., 2490 Edington Rd., Columbus, OH 43221. phone 614-481-0508. Laura Armstrong, LPC, NBCC, Owner/President. Bob Armstrong, M.Div., Ph.D., LPC.

The Human Touch, 260 Northland Blvd., Suite 234, Cincinnati, OH 45246. phone 513-772-5839. Judy R. Kroger, LPC, Career and Human Resources Counselor.

J&K Associates and Success Skills Seminars, Inc., 607 Otterbein Ave., Dayton, OH 45406-4507. phone 937-274-3630, or 937-274-4375. Pat Kenney, Ph.D., President.

*KSM Careers & Consulting, 1655 W. Market St., Suite 506, Akron, OH 44313. phone 330-867-0242. Kathryn Musholt, President.

*Midwest Career Development Service (An Interdenominational Church Career Development Center), 1520 Old Henderson Rd., Suite 102B, Columbus, OH 43221-3616. phone 614-442-8822.

New Career, 328 Race St., Dover, OH 44622. phone 216-364-5557. Marshall Karp, M.A., NCC, LPC, Owner.

*Professional Pastoral Counseling Institute, Inc., 8035 Hosbrook Rd., Suite 300, Cincinnati, OH 45236. phone 513-771-5990. Judy Kroger, Counselor.

Pyramid Career Services, Inc., 2400 Cleveland Ave., NW, Canton, OH 44709. phone 330-453-3767. Maryellen R. Hess, Executive Director.

Anne **Woods,** 8225 Markhaven Ct., W. Worthington, OH 43235. phone 614-888-7941.

OKLAHOMA

Martha **Stoodley,** Rt. #1, Box 575, Checotah, OK 74426-9742.

Transitions Counseling Center, 6216 S. Lewis Ave., Suite 148 Tulsa, OK 74136. phone 918-742-4877. Michelle Jones, M.S., Owner/Career Counselor.

OREGON

Career Development, P.O. Box 850, Forest Grove, OR 97116. phone 503-357-9233. Edward H. Hosley, Ph.D., Director.

Career Pathways, P.O. Box 271, Corvallis, OR 97339-0271. phone 541-754-1958, Peggy Carrick, M.A.,LPC,NCC, Founder.

Joseph A. **Dubay,** 425 NW 18th Ave., Portland, OR 97209. phone 503-226-2656.

Lansky Career Consultants, 9335 S.W. Capitol Highway, Portland, OR 97219. phone 503-293-0245. Judith Lansky, M.A., President.

Verk Consultants, Inc., 1190 Olive St., P.O. Box 11277, Eugene, OR 97440. phone 541-687-9170. Larry H. Malmgren, M.S., President.

PENNSYLVANIA

Career by Design, 1011 Cathill Rd., Sellersville, PA 18960. phone 215-723-8413. Henry D. Landes, Career Consultant.

Career Development Center, Jewish Family & Children's Center, 5737 Darlington Road, Pittsburgh, PA 15217. phone 412-422-5627. Linda Ehrenreich, Director.

Career Strategies, 1845 Walnut St., 7th Floor, Philadelphia, PA 19103-4707. phone 215-854-1824.

Center for Adults in Transition, Bucks County Community College, Newtown, PA 18940. phone 215-968-8188.

Center for Career Services (CCS), 1845 Walnut St., 7th floor, Philadelphia, PA 19103-4707. phone 215-854-1800. William A. Hyman, Director. Lucy Borosh, Aviva Gal, Tracey Tanenbaum, Career Counselors.

Carol **Eikleberry,** Ph.D., 1376 Freeport Rd., Suite 3A, Pittsburgh, PA 15238. phone 412-963-9008.

Forty Plus of Philadelphia, Inc., 1218 Chestnut St., Philadelphia, PA 19107-4810. phone 215-923-2074.

Lathe **Haynes,** Ph.D., 401 Shady Ave., Suite C107, Pittsburgh, PA 15238. phone 412-361-6336.

Jack **Kelly,** Career Counselor. Career Pro Resume Services, 251 DeKalb Pike, Suite E608, King of Prussia, PA 19406. phone 610-337-7187.

Jane E. **Kessler,** M.A., Licensed Psychologist, 252 W. Swamp Rd., Suite 56, Doylestown, PA 18901. phone 215-348-8212.

*Lancaster Career Development Center (An Interdenominational Church Career Development Center), 561 College Ave., Lancaster, PA 17603. phone 717-397-7451. L. Guy Mehl, Director.

Options, Inc., 225 S. 15th St., Philadelphia, PA 19102. phone 215-735-2202. Marcia P. Kleiman, Director.

Priority Two, P.O. Box 343, Sewickley, PA 15143. phone 412-935-0252. *Five locations in the Pittsburgh area; call for addresses.* Pat Gottschalk, Administrative Assistant. No one is turned away for lack of funds.

RHODE ISLAND

Career Designs, 104 Rankin Ave., Providence, RI 02908-4216. phone 401-521-2323. Terence Duniho, Career Consultant.

SOUTH CAROLINA

Career Counselor Services, Inc., 138 Ingleoak Lane, Greenville, SC 29615. phone 864-242-4474. Al A. Hafer, Ed.D., NCCC, NCC, LPC.

Greenville Technical College, Career Advancement Center, P.O. Box 5616, Greenville, SC 29606. phone 864-250-8281. F.M. Rogers, Director.

SOUTH DAKOTA

Career Concepts Planning Center, Inc., 1602 Mountain View Rd., Suite 102, Rapid City, SD 57702. phone 605-342-5177, toll free phone 800-456-0832. Melvin M. Tuggle, Jr., President.

*Barb **Coleman,** Bethesda Christian Counseling Midwest, Inc., 231 S. Phillips Ave., Suite 350, Sioux Falls, SD 57104-6326. phone 605-334-3739.

University of Sioux Falls, The Center for Women, 1101 W. 22nd St., Sioux Falls, SD 57105. phone 605-331-6697. Tami Haug-Davis, Director.

TENNESSEE

****Career Achievement,** NiS International Services, 1321 Murfreesboro Road., Suite 610, Nashville, TN 37217. phone 615-367-5000. William L. (Bill) Karlson, Harry McClure, Manager.

****Career Resources,** 2323 Hillsboro Rd., Suite 508, Nashville, TN 37212. phone 615-297-0404. Jane C. Hardy, Principal.

****Dan Miller,** The Business Source, 7100 Executive Center Dr., Suite 110, Brentwood, TN 37027. phone 615-373-7771.

****RHM Group,** P.O. Box 271135, Nashville, TN 37227. phone 615-391-5000. Robert H. McKown.

World Career Transition, P.O. Box 1423, Brentwood, TN 37027-1423. phone 800-366-0945. Bill Karlson, Executive Vice-President.

YWCA of Nashville and Middle Tennessee, Career/Life Planning Program, 1608 Woodmont Blvd., Nashville, TN 37215. phone 615-269-9922.

TEXAS

Austin Career Associates, 901 Rio Grande, Austin, TX 78701. phone 512-474-1185, Maydelle Fason, Licensed Career Counselor.

Career Action Associates, 8350 Meadow Rd., Suite 272, Dallas, TX 75231. phone 214-378-8350. Joyce Shoop, LPC. Office also at 1325 8th Ave., Ft. Worth, TX 76112. phone 817-926-9941. Rebecca Hayes, LPC.

Career and Recovery Resources, Inc., 2525 San Jacinto, Houston, TX 77002. phone 713-754-7000. Beverley Marks, Director.

Career Management Resources, 1425 Greenway, Suite 203, Irving, TX 75038. phone 972-518-0101. Mary Holdcroft, M.Ed., LPC, NCC, NCCC.

Richard S. **Citrin**, Ph.D., Psychologist, Iatreia Institute, 1152 Country Club Ln., Ft. Worth, TX 76112. phone 817-654-9600.

Counseling Services of Houston, 1964 W. Gray, Suite 204, Houston, TX 77019. phone 713-521-9391. Rosemary C. Vienot, M.S., Licensed Professional Counselor, Director.

Employment/Career Information Resource Center, Corpus Christi Public Library, 805 Comanche, Corpus Christi, TX 78401. phone 512-880-7004. Lynda F. Whitton-Henley, Career Information Specialist.

Maydelle **Fason,** Employment Consultant, 1607 Poquonock Road, Austin, TX 78703. phone 512-474-1185.

New Directions Counseling Center, 8140 North Mopac, Bldg. II, Suite 230, Austin, TX 78759. phone 512-343-9496. Jeanne Quereau, M.A., LPC.

* **New Life Institute,** 1203 Lavaca St., Austin, TX 78701-1831. phone 512-469-9447. Bob Breihan, Director.

Chuck **Ragland,** Transformational Consultancy, 2504 Briargrove Dr., Austin, TX 78704-2704. phone 512-440-1200.

San Antonio Psychological Services, 6800 Park Ten Blvd., Suite 208 North, San Antonio, TX 78213. phone 210-737-2039.

***Southwest Career Development Center** (An Interdenominational Church Career Development Center), Box 5923, Arlington, TX 76005. phone 817-640-5181. Jerry D. Overton, Director-Counselor .

*Mary **Stedham,** Counseling/Consulting Services, 2434 S. 10th, Abilene, TX 79605. phone 915-672-4044.

VGS, Inc. (Vocational Guidance Service), 2600 S.W. Freeway, Suite 800, Houston, TX 77098. phone 713-535-7104. Beverley K. Finn, Director.

***Worklife Institute Consulting,** 7100 Regency Square, Suite 210, Houston, TX 77036. phone 713-266-2456. Diana C. Dale, Director.

UTAH

University of Utah, Center for Adult Development, 1195 Annex Bldg., Salt Lake City, UT 84112. phone 801-581-3228.

VERMONT

Career Networks and ProSearch, 1372 Old Stage Rd., Williston, VT 05495. phone 800-918-WORK, or 802-872-1533.

VIRGINIA

The **BrownMiller Group,** 312 Granite Ave., Richmond, VA 23226. phone 804-288-2157. Sally Brown, Bonnie Miller.

***Career and Personal Counseling Center,** 1904 Mt. Vernon St., Waynesboro, VA 22980. phone 703-943-9997. Lillian Pennell, Director.

Change & Growth Consulting, 1334 G St., Woodbridge, VA 22191. phone 703-494-8271. also: 2136-A Gallows Road, Dunn Loring (Tyson's Corner area), VA 22027. phone 703-569-2029. Barbara S. Woods, M.Ed., NCC, LPC, Counselor.

Educational Opportunity Center, 7010-M Auburn Ave., Norfolk, VA 23513. phone 804-855-7468. Agatha A. Peterson, Director.

Fairfax County Office for Women, The Government Center, 12000 Government Center Pkwy., Suite 38, Fairfax, VA 22035. phone 703-324-5735. Elizabeth Lee McManus, Program Manager.

Hollins College, Women's Center, P.O. Box 9628, Roanoke, VA 24020. phone 703-362-6269. Tina Rolen, Career Counselor.

Mary Baldwin College, Rosemarie Sena Center for Career and Life Planning, Kable House, Staunton, VA 24401. phone 703-887-7221.

McCarthy & Company, Career Transition Management, 4201 South 32nd Rd., Arlington, VA 22206. phone 703-761-4300. Peter McCarthy, President.

Office for Women, The Government Center, 12000 Government Center Parkway, Suite 318, Fairfax, VA 22035. phone 703-324-5730. Betty McManus, Director.

Psychological Consultants, Inc., 6724 Patterson Ave., Richmond, VA 23226. phone 804-288-4125.

Virginia Commonwealth University, University Career Center, 907 Floyd Ave., Room 2007, Richmond, VA 23284-2007. phone 804-367-1645.

The **Women's Center,** 133 Park St., NE, Vienna, VA 22180. phone 703-281-2657. Conda Blackmon.

Working From The Heart, 1309 Merchant Lane, McLean, VA 22101. Jacqueline McMakin and Susan Gardiner, Co-Directors.

WASHINGTON

Bridgeway Career Development, 1800 Westlake Avenue N., Suite 110, Seattle, WA. phone 206-789-5222. Janet Scarborough, M.Ed., C.M.H.C., President.

Career Management Institute, 8404 27th St. West, Tacoma, WA 98466. phone 253-565-8818. Ruthann Reim, M.A., NCC, CMHC, President.

*Center for Career Decisions, 3121 East Madison St., Suite 209, Seattle, WA 98112. phone 206-325-9093. Larry Gaffin, Career counseling and consulting.

Centerpoint Institute for Life and Career Renewal, Career Consultants, 624 Skinner Bldg., 1326 Fifth Ave., Seattle, WA 98101. phone 206-622-8070. Carol Vecchio, Career Counselor. *A multifaceted center, with various workshops, lectures, retreats, as well as individual counseling.*

Diane **Churchill,** 508 W. Sixth, Suite 202, Spokane, WA 99204. phone 509-458-0962.

*Bernard **Haldane,** 900 University Street, #17-E, Seattle, WA 98101. phone 206-382-3658. A pioneer in the clergy career management and assessment field, Bernard teaches seminars and trains volunteers to do job-search counseling. *This individual service is not to be confused with the agency that bears his name, of which he gave up ownership long ago.*

The **Individual Development Center, Inc.** (I.D. Center), 1020 E. John, Seattle, WA 98102. phone 206-329-0600. Mary Lou Hunt, NCC, M.A., President.

*People Management Group International, 924 First St., Suite A, Snohomish, WA 98290. phone 206-563-0105. Arthur F. Miller, Jr., Chairman.

WEST VIRGINIA

Ed **Jepson,** 2 Hazlett Court, Wheeling, WV 26003. phone 304-232-2375.

Frank **Ticich,** MS, LPC, Career Consultant, 153 Tartan Drive, Follansbee, WV 26037. phone 304-748-1772.

WISCONSIN

Making Alternative Plans, Career Development Center, Alverno College, 3401 S. 39th St., P.O. Box 343922, Milwaukee, WI 53234-3922. phone 414-382-6010.

David **Swanson,** Career Seminars and Workshops, 7235 West Wells St., Wauwatosa, WI 53213-3607. phone 414-774-4755. *David was on staff at my two-week workshop twenty times.*

WYOMING

Barbara W. **Gray,** Career Consultant, P.O. Box 9490, Jackson, WY 83002. phone 307-733-6544.

University of Wyoming, Career Planning and Placement Center, P.O. Box 3195/Knight Hall 228, Laramie, WY 82071-3195. phone 307-766-2398.

U.S.A. -- NATIONWIDE

Forty Plus Clubs. A nationwide network of voluntary, autonomous nonprofit clubs, manned by its unemployed members (who must give a certain number of hours of service per week on assigned committees), paying no salaries, supported by initiation fees *(often around $500)* and monthly dues *(often around $60 per month).* Varying reports, as to their helpfulness. However, one reader gave a very good report on them recently: *"I would just like to let you know that 40+, for me, has been a really big help. They provide good job search training. . . But even more importantly, for me, is the professional office environment they provide to work out of, and the fellowship of others who are also looking for work . . . As they say at 40+, 'It's hell to job search alone.'"*

If you have Internet access, a list of the North American 40+ chapters is to be found at:

http://www.fp.org/chapters/htm

Eleven of these chapters have their own Web site; in my opinion the best and most up-to-date one belongs to the Greater Washington chapter:

http://www.fp.org/

For those who lack Web access, at this writing there are clubs in the following cities (listed alphabetically by States): California: San Diego, Orange, Los Angeles, Oakland; Colorado: Lakewood, Ft. Collins, Colorado Springs; District of Columbia: Greater Washington; Hawaii: Honolulu; Illinois: Chicago; Minnesota: St. Paul; New York: New York, Buffalo; Ohio: Columbus; Oregon: Beaverton; Pennsylvania: Philadelphia; Texas: Houston, Dallas; Utah: Salt Lake City; Washington: Bellevue; Wisconsin: Brookfield; and in Canada: Toronto.

If you live in or near any of these cities, you can check the *white* pages of your phone book (under "Forty Plus") for their address and phone number.

CANADA

(These are listed by Provinces, from East Coast to West Coast, rather than in alphabetical order)

Sue **Landry,** Enhancing Your Horizons Consulting, 25 Birchwood Terr., Dartmouth, Nova Scotia B3A 3W2. phone 902-464-9110.

People Plus, PLA Centre, 7001 Mumford Rd., Halifax Shopping Centre, Tower 1, Suite 101, Halifax, Nova Scotia B3L 4N9. phone 902-454-2809.

careerguide, Ryan Bldg., 3rd Floor, 57 Carleton St., Fredericton, New Brunswick. phone 506-459-4185. Elspeth (Beth) Leroux, B.A., B.Ed., M.Ed.

Jewish Vocational Service, Centre Juif D'Orientation et de L'Emploi, 5151, ch. de la Côte Ste-Catherine, Montréal, Québec, H3W 1M6. phone 514-345-2625. Alta Abramowitz, Director, Employment Development Services. *Uses both French and English versions of* Parachute.

Kenneth **Des Roches,** André Filion & Associates, Inc., 151 Slater Street, Suite 500, Ottawa, Ontario K1P 5H3. phone 613-230-7023.

After Graduation Career Counseling, 73 Rox-borough St. West, Toronto, Ontario M5R 1T9. phone 416-923-8319. Teresa Snelgrove, Ph.D., Director.

Donner & Wheeler and Associates, Career Development Consultants, Health and Social Services Sector, 1055 Bloor St. East, Mississauga, Ontario L4Y 2N5. phone 905-949-5954. Offers workshops particularly for those in the health and social services sector. Mary M. Wheeler.

Hazell & Associates, 60 St. Clair Avenue East, Seventh Floor, Toronto, Ontario M4T 1N5. phone 416-961-3700.

Mid-Life Transitions, 2 Slade Ave., Toronto M6G 3A1. phone 416-653-0563. Marilyn Melville.

YMCA Career Planning & Development, 42 Charles Street East, Toronto M4Y 1T4. phone 416-928-9622.

Changes by Choice, 190 Burndale Ave., North York, Ontario M2N 1T2. phone 416-590-9939. Patti Davie.

Susan Steinberg, M.Ed., 74 Denlow Blvd., Don Mills, Ontario M3B 1P9. phone 416-449-6936.

Judith Puttock, B.B.A., C.H.R.P., Career Management Consultant, Strategic Career Options, Planning & Education (SCOPE), 913 Southwind Court, Newmarket, Ontario. phone 905-898-0180.

Harold Harder, B.Sc.,B.Admin.St. The Precision Group, 400 Matheson Blvd. East, Unit 18, Mississauga, Ontario L4Z 1N8. phone 905-507-8696.

Human Achievement Associates, 22 Cottonwood Crescent, London, Ontario N6G 2Y8. phone 519-657-3000. Mr. Kerry A. Hill.

David H. Wenn, B.A., M.Ed. Career Counseling. 9 Lindbrook Court, London, Ontario N5X 2L4. phone 519-660-0622.

Job-Finding Club, 516-294 Portage Ave., Winnipeg, Manitoba R3C 0B9. phone 204-947-1948.

People Focus, 712 10th St. East, Saskatoon, Saskatchewan S7H OH1. phone 306-933-4956. Carol Stevenson Seller.

Work from the Heart, 8708 136 St., Edmonton, Alberta T5R 0B9. phone 403-484-8387. Marguerite Todd.

CBD Network Inc., #201-2033 Gordon Dr., Kelowna, B.C. V1Y 3J2. phone 250-717-1821.

Susan Curtis, M.Ed., 4513 West 13th Ave., Vancouver, B.C. V6R 2V5. phone 604-228-9618.

Alice Caldwell, P.B. #19009, 4th Avenue Postal Outlet, Vancouver, B.C. V6K 4R8. phone 604-737-7842.

Conscious Career Choices, 2678 W. Broadway, Suite 203B, Vancouver, B.C. V6K 2G3. phone 604-737-3955. Marlene Haley, B.A., M.Ed., Career Counselor.

Rita Morin, R. Morin & Co., Ltd., 1503 – 1625 Hornby St., Vancouver B.C. V6Z 2M2. phone 604-688-7212.

OVERSEAS

(Listed by country and city, which are in bold type.)

Cabinet Daniel Porot, 1, rue Verdaine, CH-1204 **Geneve, Switzerland.** phone 41 22 311 04 38. Daniel Porot, Founder. *Daniel was co-leader with me each summer at my international Two-Week Workshop for twenty years.*

Kessler-Laufbahnberatung, Alpenblickstr. 33, CH-8645, **Jona b. Rapperswil, Switzerland.** phone 055 211 0977. Peter Kessler, Counselor.

•Lernen•Beraten•Begleiten•, Maria Bamert-Widmer, Churerstrasse 26, CH-8852, **Altendorf, Switzerland.** phone 055 442 55 76.

Hans-U. Sauser, Beratung und Ausbildung, Rosenauweg 27, CH-5430 **Wettingen, Switzerland.** phone 056 426 64 09.

Peter Baumgartner, Lowen Pfaffikon, Postfach 10, 8808 **Pfaffikon, Switzerland.** phone 055 415 66 22.

Madeleine Leitner, Dipl. Psych. Ohmstrasse 8, 80802 **Munchen, Germany.** phone 089 33 04 02 03.

Career Development Seminars, offered at Westfalische Wilhelms-Universitat Muenster, Dez. 1.4 Wissenschafliche Weiterbildung, Schlossplatz 2, 48149 **Munster, Germany.** phone 0251 832 4762; and at Universitat Bremen, Zentrum fur Weiterbildung, 28359 **Bremen, Germany.** phone 0421 218 3409. Both taught by John Carl Webb, Brunnenweg 10, 48153 **Muenster, Germany.**

Bridgeway Associates Ltd., Career Consultants, P.O. Box 16, Chipping Campden GL55 6ZB **London and Midlands.** phone 01386 841840. Jane Bartlett.

The Chaney Partnership, Hillier House, 509 Upper Richmond Rd. West, SW14 7EE **London, England.** phone 081 878 3227. Isabel Chaney, B.A.

Anne Radford, 303 Bankside Lofts, 65 Hopton Street, SE1 9JL **London, England.** phone 0171 633-9630.

PASSPORT, 8 Ashness Road, SW11 6RY **London, England.** phone 0171 288 1982. Janie Wilson.

Career Development. 10 York Pl., Brandon Hill, BS1 5UT **Bristol, England.** phone 0117 9254363. Philip Houghton.

Executive Partnership, Ltd., Henry James Leeke House, 3 Links Court, Links Business Park, St. Mellons, Cardiff CF3 0LT **South Wales, UK.** phone 44 (0) 29 20839500. Philip Houghton.

John Lees Associates, The Ruskin Rooms, Drury Lane, Knutsford, Cheshire WA16 6HA, **England.** phone 01565 631625. John Lees, Director.

Castle Consultants International, 9 Drummond Park, Crook of Devon, Kinross, KY13 7UX, **Scotland**. phone 0171 798 8804. Also at: 140 Battersea Park Road, SW11 4NB **London, England**. phone 44 171 798 5688. Walt Hopkins, Founder and Director.

Brian McIvor & Associates, Newgrange Mall, Slane, **County Mead, Ireland.** phone 00 353 41 988 4035. *Brian has been on staff at my international two-week workshop for four years.*

Adigo Consultores, Av. Doria 164, **Sao Paulo** SP 04635-070 **Brazil**. phone 55 11 530 0330. Alberto M. Barros, Director.

Worklife, Suite 2, 4 Bond St., Mosman, P.O. Box 407, Spit Junction NSW 2088 **Australia**. phone 612 9968 1588. Paul Stevens, Director. *Paul has been the dean of career counseling in Australia for many years.*

The Growth Connection, Suite 402, 4th Floor, 56 Berry St., North Sydney, NSW 2060 **Australia.** phone 61 2 9954 3322. Imogen Wareing, Director.

Life by Design, Suite 19, 88 Helen St., Lane Cove 2066 NSW, **Australia**. phone 61 2 9420 8280. Ian Hutchinson.

Narelle Milligan, Career Consultant, 4 McLeod Place, Kambah ACT 2902, **Australia**. phone 61 2 6296 4398.

Designing Your Life, 10 Nepean Pl., **Macquarie, Australia,** ACT 2614. phone 61 6 253 2231. Judith Bailey.

New Zealand Creative Career Centre, Ltd., 4th Floor, Braemar House, 32 The Terrace, P.O. Box 3058, **Wellington, New Zealand**. phone 64 4 499 8414. Felicity McLennan.

Life Work Career Counselling, P.O. Box 2223, **Christchurch, New Zealand**. phone 64 03 379 2781. Max Palmer.

Career Makers, P.O. Box 277-95, Mt. Roskill, **Auckland, New Zealand**. phone 649 817 5189. Liz Constable.

Find A Job You Can Love, 2/8 Hatton St., Karori, **Wellington, New Zealand**. phone 64 4 476 2554. Tim Martin.

Transformation Technologies Pte Ltd. 122 Thomson Green, 574986 **Singapore**. phone 65 456 6358. Anthony Tan, Director.

Byung Ju Cho, Seocho-Ku Banpo-dong 104-16 Banpo Hyundai Villa A-402, **Seoul,** 137-040, **South Korea.** phone 011-9084-6236.

*Readers often write to ask us which of these overseas counselors are familiar with my approach to job-hunting and career-changing. The answer is: **every one of the counselors listed above**, have attended my two-week workshop, and therefore know my approach well.*

Other overseas counselors not trained by me, but who may still be quite helpful to you, since they are experienced counselors, and are familiar with Parachute, *are:*

Judy Feierstein, M.A., 46/2 Derech Bet Lechem, 93504 **Jerusalem, Israel.** phone 02 71 06 73.

Lori Mendel, 19/6 Emanuel Haromi, 62645 **Tel-Aviv, Israel.** phone 972-3-524-1068.

Johan Veeninga, Careers by Design, Business Park "De Molenzoom," P.O. Box 143, NL-3990 DC, **Houten/Utrecht, The Netherlands.** phone 31 (0) 3403 75153.

Employment agencies for Overseas jobs:

Safe Jobs in Japan, 56 Northwood Ave., Bridgewater, NJ 08807. (**http://www. safejobsinjapan.com**). phone 908-231-0994. Located in Japan, they place college graduates who wish to teach conversational English in Japan. Above is their U.S. administrative support office.

Richard Bolles, What Color Is Your Parachute?
International Workshop held in the U.S.A.

When the subject of counseling comes up, I am asked endlessly
whether or not I do any counseling or teaching.

The answer is: I do group teaching once a year, in the summer, in
Bend, Oregon, at an International Workshop I put on, there.

We receive many letters and phone calls inquiring about this, so I
hope you won't mind if I give you the details right here, in order to
cut down on our mail and phone calls.

It is called:

The International Two-Week Workshop
on LIFE/Work Planning
at Mount Bachelor Village, Bend, Oregon

This workshop (*as its name indicates*) is international in scope. Past
participants have come from all parts of the world -- in addition to
the U.S., we have had participants from Canada, England, Wales, The
Netherlands, France, Switzerland, Italy, Germany, Scandinavia, Gabon,
Zimbabwe, South Africa, Panama, Costa Rica, Venezuela, Brazil, New
Zealand, Australia, Singapore, Korea, Hong Kong, China, and Japan.
As to vocational background, half of those attending are usually career-
counselors or those who want to be; the other half are: job-hunters of
all ages, career-changers, homemakers, union organizers, CEOs, teachers, people facing a move, people facing retirement, the recently

divorced, college students, clergy and those who are currently unemployed. They have ranged from 16–74, in age.

The workshop is held in late July or early August. The dates in 2001 are scheduled to be: **August 3rd – August 17th 2001 A.D.**

Mount Bachelor Village is a beautiful and popular resort on the outskirts of **Bend, Oregon,** *which -- as everyone knows -- is the center of the United States (Honolulu is 3,000 miles to the West, New York City is 3,000 to the East).*

It is warm and sunny there and many of our meetings are outdoors. Most of our meals are outdoors as well.

I lead the workshop the entire two weeks. The exercises are done in various ways: in the large group, in groups of sixes, in groups of three, and individually.

The total teaching time at this workshop exceeds 100 hours.

The cost for the 100 hours is $2000 (i.e. $20/hr.) -- which we believe to be a very reasonable tuition, these days.

For those who get their registration in prior to midnight on December 31, 2000, there is a special "Early Bird Registration" price of $1,000 tuition, instead of the $2,000. As this is the last Two-Week Workshop I will ever conduct, you will want to pay attention to this deadline!

At any time of the year, if you live outside the U.S., and your exchange rates are unfavorable or the cost of airfare high, you can inquire about 'our International Rate.'

Room and board *is in addition to the tuition.* For double occupancy (we pair you with a roommate of the same sex), the cost is approximately $145/day for your room, lunch and dinner; or approximately $2000 for the two weeks. For single occupancy (a room to yourself) the cost is approximately $179/day for your room, lunch and dinner; or approximately $2500 for the two weeks. You're on your own for

breakfast, though we do have a Continental breakfast - - coffee/tea and pastries - - available without charge, at the beginning of each morning's first session.

The workshop is filled on a strictly first come, first served, basis, and is limited to the first 48 people who apply. However, there are usually some last-minute cancellations, so always phone or fax us to inquire, rather than simply concluding that it is already filled.

If you wish additional information, or wish to request a brochure and registration blank, contact:

> Norma Wong, Workshop Registrar
> What Color Is Your Parachute?
> P.O. Box 379
> Walnut Creek, CA 94597-0379

Fax No.: 1-925-837-5120 (twenty-four hours a day)
Phone No.: 1-925-837-3002 (9 a.m.–5 p.m. Monday thru Friday, Pacific Coast Time)

Index

Update 2002

TO: PARACHUTE
P.O. Box 379
Walnut Creek, CA 94597

I think that the information in the 2001 edition needs to be changed, in your next revision, regarding (or, the following resource should be added):

_____

_____

_____

_____

_____

I cannot find the following resource, listed on page _____:

_____

_____

_____

_____

_____

Name _____

Address _____

Please make a copy.

Submit this so as to reach us by February 1, 2001. Thank you.

Other Resources

Additional materials by Richard N. Bolles
to help you with your job-hunt:

The What Color Is Your Parachute? Workbook
This handy workbook leads the job-seeker
through the process of determining exactly
what sort of job or career they are most
suited for, easily streamlining this poten-
tially stressful and confusing task. $9.95

Job-Hunting on the Internet,
1999 Edition, revised and expanded.
This handy guide has quickly established
itself as the ideal resource for anyone who's
taking the logical step of job-hunting on
the Internet. $12.95

The Three Boxes of Life,
And How to Get Out of Them
An introduction to life/work planning. $18.95

How to Find Your Mission in Life
Originally created as an appendix to *What
Color Is Your Parachute?*, this book was written
to answer one of the questions most often
asked by job-hunters. $14.95

Job-Hunting Tips for the So-Called Handicapped
A unique perspective on job-hunting and career-
changing, addressing the experiences of the
disabled in performing these tasks. $12.95

The Career Counselor's Handbook
(with Howard Figler)
A complete guide for practicing or aspiring
career counselors. $17.95

For additional copies of *What Color Is Your Parachute?*
or other fine books and posters from Ten Speed Press,
please visit our Web site at www.tenspeed.com,
or call us at 1-800-841-2665.

For additional insight and advice from Richard N. Bolles,
please visit the companion site to *What Color Is Your
Parachute?* at www.JobHuntersBible.com.